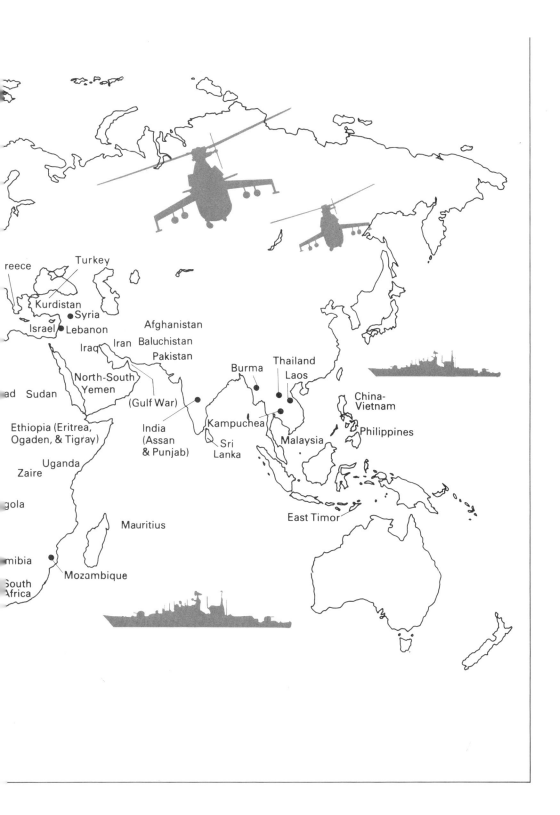

THE WORLD IN CONFLICT 1990

War Annual 4

Brassey's titles of related interest

JOHN LAFFIN
Brassey's Battles: 3,500 Years of Conflict, Campaigns and Wars from A-Z
JOHN LAFFIN
War Annual 1
War Annual 2
War Annual 3

Also by John Laffin

Military
Middle East Journey
Return to Glory
One Man's War
The Walking Wounded
Digger (The Story of the Australian Soldier)
Scotland the Brave (The Story of the Scottish Soldier)
Jackboot (The Story of the German Soldier)
Tommy Atkins (The Story of the English Soldier)
Jack Tar (The Story of the English Seaman)
Swifter than Eagles (Biography of Marshal of the R.A.F. Sir John Salmond)
The Face of War
British Campaign Medals
Codes and Ciphers
Boys in Battle
Women in Battle
Anzacs at War
Links of Leadership (Thirty Centuries of Command)
Surgeons in the Field
Americans in Battle
Letters from the Front 1914–18
The French Foreign Legion
Damn the Dardanelles! (The Agony of Gallipoli)
The Australian Army at War 1899–1975
The Israeli Army in the Middle East Wars 1948–1973
The Arab Armies in the Middle East Wars 1948–1973
Fight for the Falklands!
On the Western Front: Soldiers' Stories 1914–18
The Man the Nazis Couldn't Catch
The War of Desperation: Lebanon 1982–85
Battlefield Archaeology
The Western Front 1916–17: The Price of Honour ⎫
The Western Front 1917–18: The Cost of Victory ⎬ Australians at War
Greece, Crete & Syria 1941 ⎭
Secret and Special
Holy War: Islam Fights
World War 1 in Postcards
Soldiers of Scotland (with John Baynes)
British Butchers and Buglers of WW1

General
The Hunger to Come (Food and Population Crises)
New Geography 1966–67
New Geography 1968–69
New Geography 1970–71
Anatomy of Captivity (Political Prisoners)
Devil's Goad
Fedayeen (The Arab-Israeli Dilemma)
The Arab Mind
The Israeli Mind
The Dagger of Islam
The PLO Connections
The Arabs as Master Slavers
Know the Middle East

And other titles

THE WORLD IN CONFLICT
1990

War Annual 4

Contemporary warfare described and analysed

JOHN LAFFIN

BRASSEY'S (UK)

(a member of the Maxwell Pergamon Publishing Corporation plc)

LONDON · OXFORD · WASHINGTON · NEW YORK

BEIJING · FRANKFURT · SÃO PAULO · SYDNEY · TOKYO · TORONTO

UK (Editorial)	Brassey's (UK) Ltd., 24 Gray's Inn Road, London WC1X 8HR, England
(Orders, all except North America)	Brassey's (UK) Ltd., Headington Hill Hall, Oxford OX3 0BW, England
USA (Editorial)	Brassey's (US) Inc., 8000 Westpark Drive, Fourth Floor, McLean, Virginia 22102, U.S.A.
(Orders, North America)	Brassey's (US) Inc., Front and Brown Streets, Riverside, New Jersey 08075, USA Tel (toll free): 800 257 5755
PEOPLE'S REPUBLIC OF CHINA	Pergamon Press, Room 4037, Qianmen Hotel, Beijing, People's Republic of China
FEDERAL REPUBLIC OF GERMANY	Pergamon Press GmbH, Hammerweg 6, D–6242 Kronberg, Federal Republic of Germany
BRAZIL	Pergamon Editora Ltda, Rua Eça de Queiros, 346, CEP04011, Paraiso, São Paulo, Brazil
AUSTRALIA	Brassey's Australia Pty Ltd., PO Box 544, Potts Point, NSW 2011, Australia
JAPAN	Pergamon Press, 5th Floor, Matsuoka Central Building, 1–7–1 Nishishinjuku, Shinjuku-ku, Tokyo 160, Japan
CANADA	Pergamon Press Canada Ltd., Suite No. 271, 253 College Street, Toronto, Ontario, Canada M5T 1R5

Copyright © 1990 John Laffin

First edition 1990

Library of Congress Cataloging in Publication Data
A CIP catalogue record for this book is available from the Library of Congress and the British Library.

British Library Cataloguing in Publication Data
Laffin, John *1922–*
The world in conflict 1990: contemporary warfare described and analysed. – (War annual; v. 4)
1. War, 1900—
I. Title   II. Series
909.82

ISBN 0–08–037334–8

Printed in Great Britain by BPCC Wheatons Ltd

Contents

Introduction

In Imperial days—roughly up to 1950—when a war came to an end it was over, a clean cut. Fighting was going on throughout Monday, an armistice was signed on Tuesday and that was that. The cause of the original dispute might still fester, to erupt in another war 20 years later, but the end of combat was understood and accepted. This no longer seems to apply. During 1989 the war between the Soviets and the Afghan Mujahideen officially came to an end but without a pause the Afghan civil war—the real war—continued. The Gulf War (Iran–Iraq) ended but much fighting went on after the truce, including an Iraqi chemical war against the Kurds. It might, however, be said that this was a war within a war.

In the Introduction to *The World in Conflict 1989* **WAR ANNUAL 3**, I noted that the Soviet withdrawal from Afghanistan and the Vietnamese withdrawal from Cambodia (Kampuchea) did not mean the end of fighting in these countries. I also pointed out that in other arenas, such as Angola and Sri Lanka, hopes concerning peace were at that time unrealistic. *Talk of* negotiation and peace—rather than *talks about* peace—falsely raised people's hopes. Since then, some progress has been made over Angola but the conflict in Sri Lanka can readily be described as the world's dirtiest war.

The people of East Beirut might dispute that unenviable ranking for Sri Lanka. During 1989 the Syrians shelled them for 179 consecutive nights. The gunners also fired on small boats carrying frantic refugees to ferries waiting offshore to take them to safety in Cyprus.

For those people caught up in a war, that war is the worst and the dirtiest. It is only an observer who can afford the luxury of making comparisons. The ethnic minorities of East Timor, Bangladesh and Burma, fighting for survival in genocidal wars, know nothing of any other war.

During 1988 and the first part of 1989 the phrase 'global trends' was much used in discussion about a move towards peace through conciliation and negotiation. The superpowers were so conciliatory and co-operative that they brought the Cold War virtually to an end. Astonishingly, a Soviet general visited British defence establishments and the KGB opened its doors to foreign television cameras. The KGB wanted to show that it was just another intelligence agency, not a blunt instrument for state oppression.

However, the urge to use such an instrument disfigured China's emerging image of tolerance. The army's massacre of students and the subsequent hunting down and execution of 'trouble-makers' was a shocking reminder that governments which come to power by force try to stay there by force. The trouble in Peking and other cities was in no sense a war, hence it is not included in this volume but it was alarming enough to remind the world that deeply-held resentments can lead to war.

It has been suggested by people who should know their history better, that the tremendous cost of fighting a war may reduce the risk and incidence of war. No nation ever refused to involve itself in a war on the grounds of expense. The truth is that, while no nation can afford a war, every nation is prepared to go into debt for generations to pay for one. The fact that, in 1989–90, the Soviet Union's economy was in a parlous state is not even a minor factor in its leaders' readiness, 'if need be', to wage a war. The United States cannot afford its Strategic Defence Initiative (Star Wars) but it is finding the money for it. Vietnam cannot afford to possess the world's fifth largest army but, by ruining its economy and keeping millions of people in poverty, it maintains that army.

Not surprisingly, during 1988–90, the arms trade was the world's biggest industry in terms of money changing hands. It is not surprising either that some leaders, with an eye to cost effectiveness, are increasingly attracted to chemical weapons.

London   JOHN LAFFIN

Afghanistan War

Background Summary

In December 1979 the Soviet Union invaded Afghanistan for the stated reason of helping the Afghan government 'to maintain control over rebellious elements'. President Hafisullah Amin was killed in the fighting and Babrak Karmal succeeded him. Groups of Mujahideen or holy war warriors, mostly tribesmen from the mountains, opposed the Afghan regular army and the allied Soviet forces. These large combined armies controlled parts of Afghanistan and caused a large-scale flow of refugees to Pakistan. They were unable to subdue the Mujahideen and at the end of 1985 the armies dominated only 35 per cent of the country. By this time the Soviet High Command had built up a vast military infrastructure to help the 'Democratic Republic of Afghanistan' (DRA). With Babrak Karmal unable to make progress against the Resistance, the Soviet commanders replaced him with Dr. Muhammad Najibullah—'Comrade Najib'—former head of KHAD, the secret police. By mid-1987 more than 400,000 Soviet personnel had served in Afghanistan.

Summary of the War in 1988–89

Heavily backed by the US, the Mujahideen Resistance not only held out against the Soviet-DRA army but went on the attack. Most aid reached the Mujahideen through Pakistan, which also provided asylum for the millions of refugees. The main difficulty confronting the Resistance was the lack of co-ordination among its various groups. Split along tribal and ideological lines, they could achieve no unified command, except in the north where Ahmed Shah Massood founded the Supervisory Council of the North. This council exercised considerable control over the *Jamiat-i-Islami* groups in the rural areas of Parwan, Kapisa, Baghlan, Kunduz and Badakhshan provinces.

Another important leader, Abdul Haq, leader of the *Hezb-i-Islami* group, built a military school where leaders of all ranks were taught the skills of a type of warfare which incorporates both conventional and guerrilla activity.

It was discovered during May 1988 that Iran's Revolutionary Guards were also training Mujahideen commanders, and in particular the Shia Muslims among them. Nasr, a Shia fighting group in the central Hazarat highlands, has received weapons and specialist advice from Iran since 1980. Massood was one of the Resistance leaders to benefit from Iranian help.

However, the course of the war was changed, during 1987–88, by the increased supply of the American anti-aircraft missile, the Stinger. Using Stingers, guerrillas trained in Pakistan were bringing down Soviet aircraft at the rate of one a

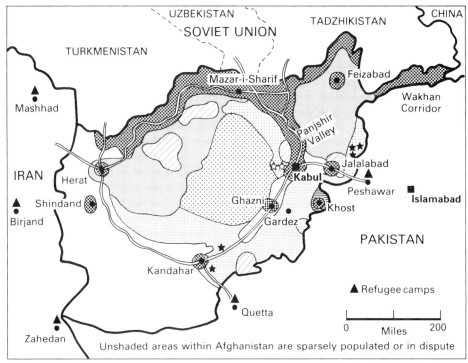

Unshaded areas within Afghanistan are sparsely populated or in dispute

The Afghanistan Resistance

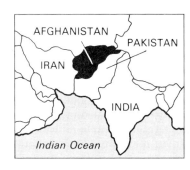

Fundamentalists

Jamiat-i-Islami; led by Barhannudin Rabbani.
Regarded as the best fighters.

Hezb-i-Islami; led by Younis Khalis.
Second only to Jamiat in quality.

Hezb-i-Islami breakaway faction; led by
Gulbuddin Heckmatyar.
Receives the most arms but has third best
fighting strength.

☆　Ittehad-i-Islami; led by Rasul Sayyaf;
backed by Saudis.

Traditionalists

Harakat-i-Inqilib; led by Nabi Mohammedi.　An inefficient group.

National Islamic Front of Afghanistan; led by Pir Sayyed Ahmed Gailani;
many religious followers.

★　National Front for the Rescue of Afghanistan; led by Sigbatullah Mojadedi, a monarchist.

Minor Resistance Groups

Shia Muslims. Much talk but little action.

Other groups, either non-aligned or with mixed loyalties.

The Communists

The People's Democratic Party of Afghanistan, with Soviet support. The PDA is an amalgam
of the Parcham and Khalq factions. President Najibullah (Comrade Najib) is a Parchamite.
The second most important figure is Muhammad Gulabzoi, a Khalqi and the Interior Minister.
Parcham-Khalq enmity is notoriously bitter.

day. Such losses—and, even more, the fear of greater loss—radically reduced the level of air support for ground operations.

The Soviet High Command conducted slow-moving advances backed by long-range artillery and multiple rocket bombardments. More high-altitude bombing and night air raids were carried out to reduce losses by Stinger attack. Realisation of the potency of the Stinger, backed by the British-made Blowpipe missile, influenced the Russians in considering a withdrawal from Afghanistan. They had become aware of a parallel with Vietnam and they did not want to suffer the humiliation of the Americans.

In South Logar, in October 1987, the Mujahideen were victorious in a 12-day operation against Soviet and DRA forces. At the end of the year, Ahmed Shah Massood captured the garrison town of Koran in a brilliant surprise attack. During the same period the Soviet-DRA force relieved besieged Khost, but at great cost and after a six-week battle. The morale of the besieging guerrillas was not damaged and their ability to operate was not impaired. Khost was no more than a Pyrrhic victory for the Soviet army.

The Mujahideen were becoming increasingly successful in co-ordinating their military efforts and the Soviet leaders in Moscow determined on total withdrawal from Afghanistan, while still supporting Najibullah with money and weapons. The Geneva agreement on Soviet withdrawal was signed on 14 April 1988. The main provision was that between 15 May 1988 and 15 February 1989 the 115,000-strong Soviet army would leave Afghanistan, half of them before 15 August. The agreement was an implicit Soviet admission that the Soviet army had lost the war. It remained to be seen whether the DRA could win it without Soviet help. In the West, it was generally believed that the government and its army would collapse. The US and most Western countries closed their embassies and predicted that the guerrillas would overthrow Najibullah within days.

The last of the Soviet troops, who had occupied Afghanistan for over nine years, withdrew on 15 February 1989, as laid down in the 1988 Geneva Accords. They left behind them a decimated population in a country devastated by bombing and scattered with landmines. Over one million Afghans, mostly civilians, were killed in the course of the occupation; over five million more are refugees in Pakistan, Iran and the West.

The War in 1989–90

While some men of the DRA army feared a Resistance victory and quickly deserted to the guerrillas, most stayed loyal. Neither the government nor the military chiefs showed any panic but announced their resolve to win the war against the rebels. Those foreign diplomats who remained in Kabul reported that at every level army and air force officers seemed confident that they could check any guerrilla offensive without direct Soviet help, provided that the Kremlin kept its promise of a plentiful supply of arms, weapons, trucks and tanks.

Without exception, the guerrilla leaders expected to be able to occupy the more remote positions which had been jointly held by Soviet and DRA soldiers. This rarely happened. Army units, even at platoon level, held their ground. On analysis, their stubbornness and confidence owed much to their Soviet training.

The Battle for Jalalabad

The rebels' first serious attempt to seize a city was the battle for Jalalabad, Afghanistan's third largest city. The seven-group Mujahideen Alliance, from its HQ in Peshawar, Pakistan, planned to use Jalalabad as an interim capital for their opposition government. The Alliance leaders believed that international recognition would follow once the government was established on Afghan territory.

The long-awaited offensive began on 6 March 1989, with an estimated 14,000 Mujahideen virtually surrounding the city with its 254,000 population. Holding it were 10,000 troops of the 9th and 11th Divisions, supported by militia units and secret police fighting as auxiliaries. On several nights the government flew in reinforcements by helicopters. Kabul claimed that Pakistan army advisers and troops were assisting the rebels, though Islamabad denied this.

In Kabul, Soviet Ambassador Yuli Vorontsov, who is also a first deputy Foreign Minister, alleged that Pakistani soldiers disguised as Mujahideen were actually directing the fighting from within Afghanistan. Abdur Sayyaf, the Prime Minister in the rebels interim government, denied this. In fact, it was a joint effort; the Pakistanis' Inter-Services Intelligence was directing tactics, while the guerrillas did the fighting.

The attack proceeded slowly. The rebels advanced to the airport, occupied it and then retreated as the army strength increased. There followed a succession of small-arms fights, with bands of guerrillas walking or cycling to the front in the morning and returning at dusk to sleep in deserted villages. Many rebels moved into the bungalows of former Soviet advisers near Samarkhel. These buildings then became a main target for government artillery and air raids.

During the first few weeks, according to government spokesmen, the guerrillas fired 12,000 shells and rockets into the city. They captured the 11th Division's base at Samarkel, six miles south-east, and some minor posts. However, this left the guerrilla commanders having to mount costly frontal assaults against the town's formidable inner defences. The garrison was supported by Scud-B missiles fired from the east of Jalalabad. Fighter aircraft from Bagram air base strafed guerrillas in the open.

Aircraft kept up a steady attack, flying up to 20 sorties a day and dropping cluster bombs. One of their victims was a guerrilla on a roof, who, in a typical act of bravado, was photographing the raiding aircraft.

By April there was little sign of the co-ordinated assault which was much talked about in the Alliance offices in Peshawar. The guerrillas were unable to organise a full-scale assault because of the differences and friction which had handicapped them during the Soviet occupation. While all seven groups were fighting around Jalalabad, there was no overall commander. The rivalry between them led to bizarre situations. For instance, when the rebels seized the vital highway to Kabul, the only land route along which Jalalabad could be supplied, instead of closing the road permanently they rotated the units supposed to be blocking it. Each time the guard was changed the government slipped convoys through.

Part of the blame for the slow assault lay with the Pakistani military command. It was they who exerted pressure for a rapid attack on Jalalabad and they also attempted to dictate the tactics. Pakistan's Inter-Services Intelligence, which acts as the guerrillas' arms supplier, was the main instigator of the assault.

In May 1989 government troops broke out of the besieged city and recaptured several key positions. An armoured column, moving east, cleared the road to Torkhum on the Pakistan border, the main supply route for the guerrillas. The tanks and armoured personnel carriers (APCs) also recaptured outposts which had been in guerrilla hands for two months. Two large ammunition convoys reached Jalalabad from Kabul, allowing government artillery to resume bombardment of rebel positions in the surrounding hills. The guerrillas became increasingly disillusioned with the offensive.

In the middle of July 1989, government troops dealt a crushing blow to Mujahideen morale when they recaptured the important army base of Samarkhel. In a night attack from three sides, the DRA troops overwhelmed the guerrillas. The Afghan News Agency, the official mouthpiece of the so-called interim government, was quick to say that the reverse was due to the guerrillas' lack of arms and ammunition. This was, in fact, true. There had been a serious hitch in the flow of supplies to the rebels and DRA Intelligence officers were aware of it.

The aerial bombardment accompanying the government's attack on Samarkhel was one of the heaviest of the war. Nevertheless, during the attack three DRA pilots defected, with their aircraft (two helicopters and one SU-22), to Pakistan. The guerrillas lost at least 500 men killed and 1,500 wounded in the fighting for Jalalabad, a great number for any guerrilla force.

The Jalalabad battle was a severe setback for the Pakistani military. Former Pakistan ministers confirm that after signing the Geneva Accord in April 1988 the late President Zia had drawn up a plan, involving Pakistani armoured columns and the air force, to back a guerrilla assault on Kabul at the moment when Soviet troops left Afghanistan. His death and the new political situation in Pakistan, with the election of Benazir Bhutto as president, pushed these plans into abeyance. But the military cannot afford to see the guerrillas fail.

The Pakistani army leaders have long maintained that only with a pro-Pakistan government in Kabul can Pakistan secure the Afghan border and the volatile tribal belt between the two countries, hold off India's ambitions in the region and bring about the return of the five million refugees. 'Pakistan's future depends on the Mujahideen winning the war and destroying Najibullah', a leading official has said. Pakistan's covert assistance to the guerrillas is no longer so covert. In the Jalalabad offensive, small numbers of intelligence officers and personnel from the army's artillery, communications and engineering branches helped the guerrillas to plan the siege and use the new heavy weapons supplied by the US. This was not enough. The failure of the siege of Khost in 1987 and of Jalalabad demonstrated that artillery barrages and mass assaults are not enough to dislodge a well-entrenched enemy.

Najibullah's Performance

Western and Soviet leaders have been surprised by Najibullah's political mettle. By imposing a state of emergency early in 1989 he consolidated his power, broadened the role of his People's Democratic Party of Afghanistan (PDPA) and contained the in-fighting among rival factions. He has appealed to Afghan xenophobia by linking the Mujahideen with involvement of Pakistanis and Muslim fundamentalists from Saudi Arabia. Najibullah also exploited the widespread relief at the Soviet departure.

In a series of carefully-arranged interviews, he called on US and Pakistani leaders 'to revise their approach to the political situation in Afghanistan'. In June 1989 he said: 'I think the developments since the completion of the withdrawal of Soviet troops provide good grounds for rethinking by those hostile to us.'

Soviet arms pouring in since the final Soviet troop withdrawal in February 1989 have enabled the army to hold the major cities. Sometimes up to 600 tanks, ammunition trucks and APVs rumble through Kabul in demonstrations designed to show not only the Mujahideen but their Pakistani and American backers that the regime is still powerful.

Despite the government's efforts to portray itself as non-Communist and Islamic, to many Afghans Najibullah is closely linked with the 1978 coup that prompted the Muslim uprising and brought about the Soviet intervention. He was the Russians' main adviser in preparations for the invasion.

'It is unlikely that Najibullah can stay in power', a foreign official said. 'Afghans have good memories. They know that Comrade Najib was head of the KHAD secret police, that he was placed in power by the Soviets and that he has presided over the ruin of the country.' Many Afghans hold him responsible for more than one million lives lost.

Unable to exert control outside the large cities, Najibullah has been striking deals with individual rebel leaders in exchange for autonomy in their own region. In a speech in July 1989, the President called for individual commanders to negotiate and said he was ready to consider 'any new proposal to end the fighting'. His schemes to deepen the divisions already existing between rebel factions have been his most interesting and effective achievements.

In another speech, this time to provincial military commanders, Najibullah said: 'People are gradually realising the national character of this regime and now want national peace on the basis of the objective realities and national tradition of our country. We want peace. The people of Washington and Islamabad are war-mongers.'

Government Forces' Strength

Late in 1989 President Najibullah had armed forces of considerable strength, totalling probably 150,000. About 55,000 serve in the army and air force, 10,000 in the border command, 35,000 in KHAD, 25,000 in the Sarandoy and another 25,000 in various irregular mercenary militias. A further 20,000 serve in part-time militia groups.

In the run-up to the Soviet withdrawal, Najibullah raised a new force, the Guard Corps comprising three brigades, to take over the defence of Kabul from Soviet units. The Guard Corps has since been absorbed into the larger Special Guard, which also consists of the 37th Commando Brigade, some Sarandoy mobile units and artillery battalions. The Special Guard, about 10,000-strong, provides the government with a limited capability for mobile warfare. The President also recalled several thousand Afghans who were studying at Soviet schools and military academies. The arrival of 300 of these officers in Kandahar in March 1989 caused dismay among the guerrillas, who regard them as ruthless.

Najibullah accelerated the re-equipment of the air force and it is probably larger than most Western estimates. Current air strength is: 90 Sukhoi bombers, many of the SU-22 Frogfoots; 20 MiG-27 Floggers; 50 MiG-21 Fishbeds; 20 MiG-17 Frescos; 60 Mil-8/17 Haze and 30 Mil-24 Hind helicopters. In addition, there are 40 An-26/36 Curl/Cline and 12 An-12 Cub transports.

In January and February departing Soviet units turned over much weaponry to the Afghan army. Among this bounty were BM-27 multiple rocket launchers, 15 122-mm self-propelled guns, BMP-2 infantry fighting vehicles, BTR-70 APCs and AGS-17 automatic grenade launchers. The Russians also gave the Afghans large numbers of Kamaz trucks and additional improved T-62 tanks.

Islamabad—Spy Capital

For almost a decade the American CIA, Britain's MI6, Pakistan's ISI and other agencies fought a covert war against Kabul. Once the intelligence war ceased to be covert, the number of foreign spies multiplied. Islamabad has the largest CIA station in the world. Between 1980 and 1990 the CIA channelled $2 bn in arms and another $1 bn in supplies to the Mujahideen. Having staked so much on the war, the CIA became desperate for Mujahideen success.

European agencies are a little less obvious then the CIA. In 1986, MI6 ran a covert operation to supply Abdul Haq, of the fundamentalist *Hezb-i-Islami*, with Blowpipe missiles. The CIA and ISI were irritated with MI6 for trying to promote the claims of ex-King Zahir Shah. The French nominee was Ahmad Shah Massood of the *Jamiet-i-Islami*, the guerrilla commander in the Panjshir Valley. Massood has limitations because he does not belong to the majority Pathan ethnic group.

West Germans and Swedes also have strong intelligence groups in Islamabad. Newcomers include the Saudis, whose intelligence chief in Islamabad is Prince Turki al Faisal. Numerous Egyptian intelligence agents are present to keep track of fundamentalist Egyptians who have joined the Saudi-backed guerrillas and could return home fully trained to sow fundamentalist unrest. The Iranians are promoting the Shia factions.

General Grekov's Analysis

Following the Soviet disengagement from war in Afghanistan, Western analysts were eager to know what effects the long conflict would have on Soviet military thinking and practice. Major General Yuriy Pavlovich Grekov, Chief of Staff of 40th Army between February 1986 and August 1988, brought the important lessons to light in a restricted report.

The most important lesson, he said, was in the handling of heliborne troops. 'In Afghanistan I really understood what it means to land a force from helicopters', he wrote. The landing of thousands of soldiers in mountainous terrain, often under Mujahideen fire, was a serious challenge to the Soviet leaders on the spot. While relieving Khost, they sent in 44 heliborne soldiers to force guerrillas from key positions. The guerrillas held their fire until the helicopters were lifting off, then opened up with machine-guns and rifles. The Russians were killed to a man and the helicopters were damaged. Despite this and other disasters, General Grekov believes that heliborne operations will be a major factor in any future war involving the Soviet Union.

Maintaining communications, logistic support and co-ordinated delivery of fire support by helicopters, aircraft and artillery was also a challenge, Grekov reported. He also mentioned co-ordination of fire support with small sub-units deep in the rear of enemy positions.

Grekov criticised the narrow specialisation of the Soviet officer. Graduates of military schools, even though they might think in combined-arms terms, actually expected artillery and air force officers to direct and co-ordinate fire for them. Since, in Afghanistan, this was often not possible, Grekov urged better training of army officers. His report was largely taken up with improvements in training. In Afghanistan, he said, it was important for every soldier to be proficient in the use of assault rifle, machine-gun, sniper rifle, grenade launcher and radio set. It was not enough for élite units to be given wide training; the men of all frontline units had to become multi-proficient.

In some cases, Grekov criticised failures of equipment. He did not specify which items but it is known that other officers demanded better infantry radio equipment and high-altitude uniforms. Grekov concluded that the war had been an impressive laboratory and training ground. 'There was not one general or officer in the headquarters of our army who did not participate personally in battles', he said. 'This is priceless experience.'

A former Chief of General Staff, Marshal Sergei Akhromyev, took up this point when he described the officers who served in Afghanistan as 'the golden fund of the army'. He said: 'We must treat them with care, train them solicitously and promote them'. Certainly, hundreds of officers with Afghanistan service have been promoted by three or four grades.

Aspects of the Grekov report were discussed in certain journals, notably *Voyenni Vestnik*. For instance, Colonel P. Popovskikh wrote at length about the differences between the conventional chain of command and variations found to be preferable in Afghanistan. He urged that decision-making should, in various circumstances, be left to brigade or even battalion commanders and not referred to superior headquarters. Several actions in Afghanistan had been 'indecisive', he commented, because of the delay in the communication-command structure.

Resistance Political Moves

A *shura* or consultative council of Afghans opposed to the Najibullah regime took place in Rawalpindi, Pakistan. After two weeks of negotiations and disagreements over its composition, the *shura* elected an 'interim government' on 23 February 1989. It comprised members of the Pakistan-based seven-party Resistance alliance.

Party and leader	Votes	Position/portfolios
Professor Sibghatullah Mujaddedi	174	President/Minister of Health

Jabhyar-i-Milli-Niyat (Afghan National Liberation Front)		
Professor Abdur Rasul Sayyaf *Ittehad-i-Islami* (Islamic Unity)	173	Prime Minister/Minister of Communications
Maulavi Mohammed Nabi Muhammadi *Harakat-i-Inqilab-i-Islami* (Islamic Revolution Movement)	139	Minister of Defence/ Agriculture/Scientific Affairs
Engineer Gulbuddin Hekmatyar *Hezb-i-Islami* (Islamic Party (Hekmatyar))	126	Minister of Foreign Affairs/Tribal Affairs/Justice
Maulavi Mohammad Yunis Khales *Hezb-i-Islami* (Islamic Party (Khales))	102	Minister of Interior/National Security
Professor Burhanuddin Rabbani *Jamiat-i-Islami* (Islamic Society)	99	Minister of Reconstruction/Islamic Guidance/Mines and Industry
Pir Sayed Ahmed Gailani *Mahaz-i-Milli-yi-Islami* (National Islamic Front of Afghanistan)	86	Minister of Supreme Court/Education/Finance

The parties headed by Mujaddedi, Muhammadi and Gailani are 'moderate' or traditionalist in character, the latter being strongly in favour of the restoration of the former King Zahir Shah, now in exile in Italy. The other four are fundamentalist, the most extreme being those of Sayyaf and Hekmatyar.

On 10 March, a symbolic first Cabinet meeting was held a few kilometres inside Afghanistan, followed by a second in early April. The interim government stated its intention of holding elections within about six months. However, if it is to form the basis of a viable administration it must first broaden its composition to include under-represented elements. For instance, the Tajiks have disproportionately little involvement in the interim government. They form the second largest ethnic group after the Pashtuns, and together with the Uzbeks make up the bulk of Rabbani's *Jamiat-i-Islami*, which has played an important part in the fighting against the Soviet and Afghan government troops.

Members of the Iran-based eight-party Resistance alliance, mainly comprising Shia Muslims from the Hazarajat in central Afghanistan, did not take part in the *shura*, when disagreements over the size of their contingent could not be resolved. The Peshawar alliance parties were prepared to allow only 60 out of the total 519 *shura* seats to the Shias, who demanded 100. Before the Soviet invasion in 1979, Shias had made up about 10 per cent of the population, the vast majority of the rest being Sunni Muslims. But as relatively few Shias fled from Afghanistan in the intervening years, they claimed that they comprised a higher percentage of the now reduced population and thus deserved a larger proportion of the seats. Nevertheless, three or four Cabinet posts were designated to be held open for Shia representatives.

Commanders from inside Afghanistan were not fully represented, neither were 'good Muslims', that is, non-Communists and low ranking PDPA members from Kabul, whom the alliance was in principle prepared to accept. The interim government says it is still negotiating with the Shia groups and others, with the aim of broadening participation. But agreement on the composition of future administrations will not be easy to achieve, as nearly a decade of Soviet occupation and war has wrought fundamental changes in the structure and distribution of the various ethnic, tribal and religious groups and destroyed traditional negotiating mechanisms.

The formation of the interim government is seen as a positive step by many countries outside the Communist bloc. Saudi Arabia, Bahrain, Sudan and Malaysia have officially recognised it. At a meeting of the Islamic Conference Organisation on 16 March 1989 the interim government was invited to occupy the Afghan seat, which had been vacant since the regime was expelled from the organisation in 1980. The question of recognition does not arise for Britain as, in common with many other Western countries, it maintains diplomatic relations with States, not governments. Nevertheless, the British Foreign Secretary, Sir Geoffrey Howe, met members of the interim government when he visited Pakistan in March 1989 and encouraged them to continue their efforts to broaden participation to include other groups in the government.

Regime Manoeuvring

Prospects for a peaceful solution are poor as long as Najibullah refuses to step down and allow a new government to be elected. He is conscious of the continuing weakness of the PDPA, and of his own failure to reconcile the rival Parchami and hard-line Khalqi wings of the party. The Parchami faction comprises mainly the urbanised intelligentsia who take a more gradualist approach to building Communism, while the predominantly rural-based Khalqis have favoured a violent overthrow of the traditional system with a swift imposition of Marxism-Leninism on the country. Najibullah admitted in an interview with the Soviet government newspaper *Izvestiya* on 18 April 1989 that factionalism was 'exerting a negative influence on the party ranks'.

On 19 February, only four days after the last Soviet troops left, Najibullah declared a state of emergency and set up a Supreme Council for the Defence of the Homeland, replacing the Cabinet, with himself at its head. Many Articles of the Constitution were suspended, allowing confiscation and search of property, interception of mail and telephone conversations and limiting freedom of expression and assembly. The majority of former Cabinet ministers who did not belong to the PDPA were replaced by party members. Most notable was the removal of Dr. Mohamad Hasan Sharq who, as a non-PDPA member, had been presented as an example of Najibullah's willingness to share power. These moves were probably made to placate the Khalqis who had never agreed with Najibullah's much publicised policy of 'national reconciliation', introduced in January 1987, which was intended to win over those not implacably opposed to his rule.

Najibullah has probably now given up hope that this policy will ever succeed, but still maintains his public stance in favour of power-sharing.

The regime is making strenuous efforts to drive wedges between various opposition groups and to this end is renewing its old tactics of wooing minority sections of the population, and emphasising the cultural and linguistic differences of each group. The Shia Hazaras are a priority target. On 23 February the formation of a 'centre to mobilise Hazara nationality affairs' was announced. And there are reports that the regime has offered to give semi-autonomous status to the Hazara-jat region—probably recognising it own inability to maintain control over this remote area. Najibullah is also trying to alienate the Resistance military commanders inside Afghanistan from their political leaders in Pakistan. In a radio speech on 27 March he addressed the internal commanders of the Mujahideen as 'compatriot brothers', offering them local autonomy in return for a cease-fire, while condemning the alliance leaders as 'extremist warmongers'.

The PDPA leaders are still attempting to change their political image. In an interview with a Western news agency on 2 April, Foreign Minister Abdul Wakil declared: 'We are never going to construct Socialism or Communism in this land'. Attempts to put all the blame for past mistakes on to the Khalqis, as well as denials that the PDPA is a Communist party, began under Karmal's leadership, but the Afghan people will find it hard to believe that such sentiments stem from a genuine change of heart and not from a desperate attempt to retain some power in the face of overwhelming opposition from the Resistance. Similarly, the regime's alleged support for Islam and Najibullah's attempts to present himself as a devout Muslim are unlikely to impress the bulk of the people, who will not have forgotten past repression by the regime, and in particular Najibullah's former position as head of KHAD from 1980 to 1986.

Soviet Role

Najibullah's regime is making great efforts to discredit the resistance and its supporters, especially Pakistan. As well as trying to weaken the people's confidence in the resistance, by emphasising differences between various groups, the regime has made numerous allegations of large numbers of Pakistani troops taking part in the fighting. But neither Afghanistan nor the Soviet Union, which has made similar claims, have been able to produce any evidence to support this. A show-trial of two young men alleged to be Pakistani military intelligence agents captured in Afghanistan and who made confused and conflicting statements, won the regime little credibility. In response to a proposal by the UN Secretary General, Pakistan agreed in April to the establishment of three UN Good Offices Mission for Afghanistan and Pakistan (UNGOMAP) bases on the Afghan–Pakistani border at Tarkham, Chaman and Parachinar, to facilitate monitoring of cross-border activity.

The Soviet Union is also supporting the regime with military supplies, including SCUD missiles. Its forces left behind many millions of dollars worth of equipment when they withdrew. The regime's dependence on the Soviet Union and its intention to maintain close ties, if it were to stay in power, are clear. In an interview published in the Soviet party newspaper *Pravda* on 29 March, Prime Minister Keshtmand said: 'Without Soviet help Afghanistan will be unable to remain a progressive, independent and non-aligned State'. An even clearer indication of the regime's intentions was given by Defence Minister Tanay of the Khalqi faction of the PDPA, when he said on 21 April that there was a possibility of 'turning to our great friend, the Soviet Union, for support and for any type of assistance based on the friendship and co-operation treaty'.

Before the completion of the withdrawal, the Soviet Deputy Foreign Minister and Ambassador to Afghanistan, Yuli Vorontsov, had a number of meetings with the resistance groups based in Pakistan and Iran in an attempt to persuade them to allow the PDPA a substantial role in a coalition government. The Soviet Union was keen to enhance its international reputation by establishing some sort of political settlement before it withdrew, instead of leaving behind a state of continued fighting with an uncertain future for its protege.

Civilian Suffering

According to a report issued in February 1989 by the UN Human Rights Special Rapporteur, Dr. Felix Ermacora, the regime admits that it continues to hold some 3,500 political prisoners. Dr. Ermacora notes that prisoners still appear to be ill-treated and tortured during interrogation by police and KHAD agents, adding that the conditions in which prisoners are kept while awaiting trial are deplorable.

Dr. Ermacora's report also refers to the suffering of the general population, caused by the continued fighting, largely as a result of regime bombing of civilian areas and of the 'presence of mines scattered all over the country'. A striking incident of civilian casualties took place in late January during the Soviet withdrawal, when an estimated 600 civilians died in Soviet and regime artillery attacks near the Salang pass, the main route from Kabul to the Soviet border. The use of Soviet-supplied SCUD missiles, which are of little military use as they are inaccurate at relatively short range, has had a devastating effect on areas around Jalalabad and towards the Pakistani border. On three occasions, SCUD missiles have landed inside Pakistan. There have also been unconfirmed reports of regime forces using chemical weapons.

The danger from the fighting and the further destruction of agriculture—including cultivated areas, livestock, and irrigation networks—have led to an increase in the number of refugees leaving the country. There is still a net outflow. Official Afghan figures give the number of refugees who returned between the start of the 'national reconciliation' policy in January 1987 and January 1989 as 185,945 (101,814 from Pakistan and 84,131 from Iran)—a tiny proportion of the more than five million refugees in the two countries.

Even after the fighting has ended few Afghans will be able to return until some progress has been made on mine clearance. Dr. Ermacora found that casualties from anti-personnel and booby-trap mines had 'increased drastically' over the previous few months. His report states: 'Information tends to confirm the allegation that Soviet troops laid new mines during their withdrawal from various areas'. Estimates of the number of mines are as high as 30 million and the UN Co-ordinator for Relief to Afghanistan, Prince Sadruddin Aga Khan, has given a high priority to resolving the mine problem. In October 1988, a group of British army engineers visited Pakistan at Prince Sadruddin's request and produced a survey detailing the scale of the problem. In mid-February a 'mine awareness and clearance' training programme started in Pakistan. The Soviet Union has made some contribution to the operation by agreeing to provide dummy mines for training purposes. However, it did not make available maps of the minefields.

UN and other international relief agencies are providing food and medical supplies to refugees and to civilians throughout Afghanistan. In Kabul the food shortage became severe during and after the Soviet withdrawal, both because of the difficulty of transporting supplies though areas of heavy fighting in harsh weather conditions and because of inefficiency—and probably also corrupt practices—on the part of the regime. In January, there were Soviet accusations of 'criminal neglect—maybe with malicious intent—of a number of senior Afghan bureaucrats', responsible for planning the organisation of food supplies.

New Hardships for Women

The conflict in Afghanistan has heightened life's contradictions for Afghan women, caught between traditional Islamic conservatism and the modern demands of war. Scores of thousands are widows, putting new strains on an Islamic society already split by competing ideologies.

Masuma Esmati Wardak, a veteran campaigner for women's rights and president of the All-Afghanistan Women's Council, said: 'The war is bringing more women into work, taking over duties in factories, as police officers and in hospitals'. The Women's Council, which is linked with the ruling Communist Party, also trains women to find jobs in light industry and offices.

Wardak, one of seven women members in the Afghan lower house of Parliament, says that her organisation tries to help the growing number of widows with accommodation and to ensure that they get the full salary of their dead husband or son. Wardak argues that Islam gives women specific rights and that in Afghanistan's villages women work unveiled alongside men. 'It is only in the refugee camps in Pakistan that they have gone back to the *chador*'.

Whoever wins the war, Afghanistan's women will remain oppressed and disadvantaged. One in every 10 women dies in childbirth, according to the World Health Organisation. While 39 per cent of men are considered literate, only 8 per cent of women can read or write.

The Arab-Islamic Factor

Islamic militants from Saudi Arabia, Egypt and other Arab nations began to join the Mujahideen soon after the war began in December 1979. Most of these foreign Muslims travelled to Afghanistan on their own initiative, not as part of organised political or religious groups. This changed in the mid-1980s, with a marked increase in the involvement of militant Arab Muslims, most of them followers of Wahhabism, a strict puritan sect of Islam. According to their spokesman, the foreigners were in Afghanistan to fight 'all Islam's enemies, Americans and Russians'.

According to some guerrilla and other sources, Arab determination to create a 'new Islamic man' among the Afghans was causing serious division within the Resistance in 1989. The rift was expected to provoke violent confrontations between the Arab-backed extremists and other Afghan groups, including some of the fundamentalist groups.

Some Afghan fundamentalists, notably members of Hekmatyar Gulbuddin's *Hezb-i-Islami*, have long received Arab support but are at loggerheads with the Wahhabi for political reasons. Other Afghans, because of their traditional independent nature, simply resent being told what to do by outsiders, whether Muslims or not.

According to Western diplomats, the Arab Wahhabi are seeking to dominate the holy war *Jihad* and impose their will on the Afghans through intense missionary work and by wooing the Mujahideen with money, guns, uniforms and other support. Wahhabi-allied Mujahideen, who are paid the equivalent of $50 a month, are usually recognisable by their lavish equipment and camouflage fatigues.

'It is very clear what the Arabs are doing', Abdul Haq said. 'They give you everything you need and when you don't do what they want, they cut off the aid.'

Those Western diplomats prepared to talk about the matter say that many Afghans join the Wahhabi for cash rather than ideological reasons. This appears to be the case in Nangrahar, Kunar, Paktia and other provinces. Among the pro-Wahhabi groups, the largest is *Ittihad-i-Islami*, led by Abdul Rasul Sayyaf. It would retain little Afghan support without its Arab backing. This also applies to *Jamaat Ulduwaat*, a local Wahhabi party.

Arab extremists in Afghanistan are trying to turn the Afghans against non-Muslim foreigners, whom they see as a threat to their proselytising. Some Arabs threaten to kill visiting Westerners and several attacks have been made. Such behaviour has aroused concern and anger among Afghans. The Arabs treat their customs, hospitality and Islamic practices with arrogance and disdain, some Afghans say.

Western diplomats who have served in Afghanistan say that Afghans can only be 'rented', never completely 'bought'. Therefore, the influence of Arab extremists will wane once their support is no longer needed. Diplomats currently serving in Kabul question why Pakistan and moderate Arab governments allow Muslim extremists to cross into Afghanistan for what amounts to practical terrorist training.

One Arab 'volunteer', identified as Abu al-Kakar, told Edward Girardeti: 'Afghanistan does not matter. It is Islam. We are here to release all our brothers from East and West. We have to show them the true Islam. Many are uneducated and do not know the true path. This is our duty in the service of Allah, the all-merciful'.

Prognosis

The Afghan conflict is no longer a simple issue of poor guerrilla against Soviet aggressor. It has become a regional tug-of-war involving the Soviet Union, the USA, Pakistan, Iran, India, China, Saudi Arabia, Arab religious zealots, drug traffickers and international aid organisations—of which there are 130.

While both sides to the central dispute retain foreign backers prepared to arm them the war could continue for years. Territorially, neither the army nor the guerrillas can expect to make significant gains. The guerrillas control the countryside, the army holds the centres of population. Without a unified command—in the Western sense of the term—the Resistance cannot hope to win the war.

The Turning Point

By July 1989 open warfare had broken out among the groups of the divided Afghan Resistance and about 90 per cent of the guerrilla commanders had ceased fighting the Kabul government. Thirty guerrillas, including seven commanders belonging to the fundamentalist *Jamiat-i-Islami* Party, were massacred on 9 July by the rival *Hezb-i-Islami* Party of Gulbuddin Hekmatyar. The massacre took place as the *Jamiat* group was passing through the Farkhar district of Takhar province in northern Pakistan. This was merely one incident of many as the various groups consolidated the areas they held.

Senior Western diplomats associated with UN and US policy on Afghanistan conceded that the powerful field commanders had ceased all operations against the Kabul regime except the indiscriminate firing of rockets into the residential suburbs of Kabul. Ahmed Shah Massood in the Panjahir Valley and Ismael Khan in western Pakistan even refused to attack convoys of weapons and supplies being sent from the Soviet Union to Kabul. Hekmatyar, who has no commanders of any real ability in Afghanistan but has received the bulk of US-supplied weapons, accused Massood, Khan and others of doing a deal with the Kabul government.

One Western diplomat said: 'There is an unwritten ceasefire between the field commanders and the Kabul regime. As never before there is a need for a peace initiative or the Mujahideen may just crumble from within, making any negotiations with the Najibullah regime pointless. The regime does not even mind that civilians are killed or maimed by rocket fire. It only turns the people against the Mujahideen'.

Abdul Haq told a Mujahideen news agency in Islamabad that his fighters were ordered to attack only military targets. 'However', he said, 'since we do not have advanced and sophisticated weapons, the target may be missed occasionally. We are unhappy about this but there is no other way. As long as the Communist puppet regime is in Kabul we cannot lay down arms and destroy the sacrifices of 11 years of *Jihad*'.

Meanwhile, with heavy Soviet supply, the army was able to fire more SCUD missiles. Five hundred—at a cost of $1 million each—were fired between March and July 1989.

Western Re-assessment of the War

During the winter of 1989–90, with fighting at a low ebb, Western strategists were forced to consider whether the Mujahideen could ever take Kabul. These strategists especially the American ones—had underestimated the strength and resolve of the government forces while overestimating the ability of the Mujahideen to develop from guerrilla fighters into conventional soldiers.

Observers for foreign governments had also overestimated the effectiveness of Abdul Haq. Army officers sent in by the Pentagon in November and December 1989 reported that despite Abdul Haq's claims to have 4,000 men under his command, the true figure could be as low as 500. He was forced into the desperate and dangerous expedient of trying to buy commanders in the Kabul area.

At the end of 1989 the Mujahideen were still receiving large quantities of military supplies but the inability of the leaders to co-ordinate their military activities meant that the equipment was not being used to best advantage.

Even with his 'Islamic Army' of about 9,000 fighters, Ahmed Shah Massoud was in no position to threaten Kabul seriously. Despite his own confidence, his plans can only be fulfilled after years of conflict.

In a change of practice, at the end of 1989, the US government decided to deliver aid direct to the senior commanders, rather than channel it through Pakistan's Inter-Services Intelligence (ISI). The discord between many Mujahideen commanders and the ISI was intense early in 1990. The ISI officer wanted to tell the Mujahideen how to conduct their operations but the Mujahideen, triumphantly believing that they had defeated a superpower, were not prepared to listen to the ISI officers.

Lieutenant-General Abdul Haq Ulomi, the most powerful soldier in the government, said in December that 100,000 former guerrillas were operating as pro-government militias, helping the defence forces. The general and his brother, Colonel General Nurul Haq Ulomi, and the senior strategists advising President Najibullah.

Soviet Casualties

The Soviet Army General Staff issued, in December 1989, 'final figures' for casualties in Afghanistan. The death toll between 1979–89 was put at 13,833, of which 11,381 were combat casualties. The remainder died of wounds or illness or through 'careless handling of their weapons'. Deaths of officers amounted to 1,979 or 14 per cent of the total losses. The new figures indicate that Soviet losses peaked in 1984 when total deaths were 2,343, including 305 officers. Previous Western estimates had suggested that up to 50,000 Soviet soldiers may have been killed in Afghanistan. This estimate is in line with the tendency to exaggerate casualties of a belligerent country considered to be unfriendly.

References

I am indebted to several foreign diplomats in Afghanistan, not all of them Western, for information in this account of the war.

The report made by the Russian General Grekov about the 'lessons' of Afghanistan came from a Soviet source. However, Grekov's report was then discussed in the journal *Voyenni Vestnik*, March 1989.

Edward Girardet of *The Christian Science Monitor* during April 1989 is my main source for information about the growing influence of the Arab Islamic extremists in Afghanistan. Girardet is a veteran of the Afghanistan war and has probably spent more time there than any other Western correspondent.

Aspects of the war discussed in War Annual 3:
Apart from a short summary of the war in general and a longer one of the years 1987–88, there were sections on:
The Soviet Union and Pakistan
As Russians see the war
Rebuilding guerrilla bases
The Abdul Huq interview

Mujahideen commanders trained in Iran
Role of the Stinger
Islamic International Brigade
Western victims of the war
The Southern Logar offensive
Capture of Koran
Relief of Khost
Massacre at Kolalgu
Soviet withdrawal
Mujahideen transitional government plans
Women in the war
Return of the monarchy?
Human rights in Afghanistan

Guerrilla-Civil War in Angola

GROPING TOWARDS PEACE

Background Summary

The civil war began before Angola's independence from Portugal in 1975 and became more widespread and violent after it. The Popular Liberation Front of Angola (MPLA) formed the government while the National Union for the Total Liberation of Angola (UNITA) was in opposition. Angola is strategically important because it lies close to the oil tanker routes which, in the event of a major war, would link the Middle East to Europe and the US. This attracted superpower interest.

At the request of the Soviet Union, Cuba sent 13,000 troops to Angola to help the MPLA. South Africa helped UNITA. South African involvement was the consequence of fighters from the South-West African People's Organisation (SWAPO) using Angola as a base for war against South Africa. Dr. Jonas Savimbi, dynamic leader of UNITA, controlled a third of Angola in the east and engaged in conventional as well as guerrilla warfare. He had some major successes, such as his victory at Mavinga, 1985, and the holding of Jamba, his main base, against Cuban-MPLA attack.

As Savimbi widened his sphere of operations, the Pentagon and CIA increased the flow of American arms. Enlisting the aid of neighbouring Zaire, Savimbi began operations in the north. By the end of 1986 UNITA was issuing daily communiqués in the manner of a regular army at war. Nevertheless, by 1987 the war had reached stalemate. The Marxist government of President Eduardo Dos Santos promised to 'reduce UNITA to impotency'.

Summary of the War in 1988

The South African Defence Forces (SADF) intervened in Angola to block a major MPLA offensive against UNITA bases. With Soviet assistance, the Cuban-MPLA army planned a two-prong attack against UNITA with the ultimate objective of taking Jamba. After considerable fighting, the MPLA was badly mauled in two SADF offensives, *Operation Hooper* and *Operation Modular*, in January and February respectively.

The operations brought to an end the South African pretence that aid for UNITA was 'marginal and merely supportive'. In mid-1988 the SADF had 9,000 soldiers, 600 guns and 500 tanks and armoured cars in Angola. In the major battle for Cuito Cuanavale, 8,000 South Africans and UNITA troops confronted 10,000 Cubans and MPLA troops. The action was not decisive but the balance of casualties and material losses favoured South Africa.

UNITA controlled a much greater area than it actually occupied but it was

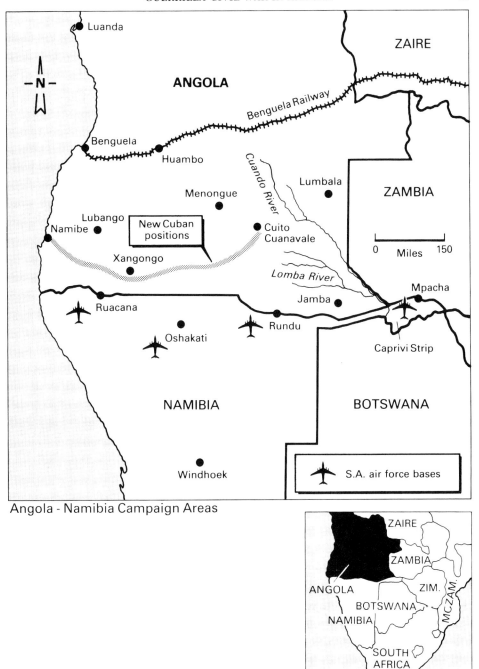

Angola - Namibia Campaign Areas

incapable of an assault on Luanda, the capital, and other major centres. Similarly, the MPLA, even with massive field support from the Cubans and Soviet logistical support, had little prospect of defeating UNITA. This realisation by both principals to the war led to exploratory peace talks in London in May 1988. In August, Angola and South Africa reached a cease-fire agreement but since UNITA took no part in this arrangement it was tactically insignificant.

In November 1988, UNITA—or more probably its Right-wing backers in the West—flew a group of Press correspondents to Jamba to meet Savimbi. The purpose was for Savimbi to stress that his war was far from over.

'Maybe in Pretoria, maybe in Luanda and Havana, the mood is rejoicing', he said. 'And maybe some of you expected to find here a mood of depression. But here the mood is very good.'

Dr. Savimbi insisted that, far from being a setback to his forces, any peace settlement represented his long-awaited opportunity to force the MPLA to the negotiating table. He welcomed the prospect of removing the international dimension from the conflict.

'But it does not solve the war', he said. 'The Cubans came to Angola because of the civil war between the MPLA and UNITA. It was not to build bridges. The South Africans intervened because of the civil war between UNITA and MPLA. So you cannot solve the problem of the South Africans and the Cubans and say we have peace, without solving the problem between UNITA and MPLA. That is why we are not afraid of an agreement.'

He predicted that the signing of the peace treaty would be followed immediately by an MPLA offensive against UNITA and another attempt to take Jamba. But the offensive could not succeed as long as the Cubans stayed out of it.

'What makes a conventional force formidable is air and armour', he said. 'I am in possession of the best missiles as far as the air is concerned and as far as armour is concerned. What do I have to fear?'

He was dismissive of any loss of Western support. He conceded that Namibian independence would present logistical problems as far as South Africa was concerned but insisted that he had built up adequate weapons reserves. 'If the Cubans really go, if it is not a trick, I think it will take less than one year to force the MPLA to talk to us.'[1]

The War in 1989

A major factor beyond the control of the direct belligerents influenced the war in 1989: the Soviet Union took a more pragmatic view of its role in Africa and of the racial conflict in southern Africa. Under President Gorbachev's realistic direction, the Russians abandoned their assumption that a classic socialist revolution would overthrow the white minority in South Africa. Instead, the Soviet planners concluded that a destructive and endless race war would take place, not necessarily only between blacks and whites.

Gorbachev suggested that the Soviet Union should withdraw from its costly involvement in Angola. His Cuban allies were strongly opposed to this idea. The Cuban President, Fidel Castro, and his generals consider that Cuban prestige is high because of the army's creditable performance in Angola and Namibia. Anything other than a long, slow gradual withdrawal would damage this reputation. Cuba offered to reduce its forces; in fact, the number was increased to 50,000. South Africa insisted that all Cubans should leave by the end of 1989. The Cubans said they would settle for a four-year withdrawal while the Angolan government offered to 'induce' its Cuban allies to leave within three years.

After eight years of mediation, the United States achieved a set of international accords to give Namibia its independence and to remove all foreign troops from Angola.

This was the timetable for the Angola-Namibia Accord:

1989

January 22: Joint appeals commission, including the US and USSR, established to arbitrate disputes over verification of troop withdrawals. Token UN force would monitor withdrawals in Angola.

April 1: UN Resolution 435 to take effect. This calls for withdrawal of South Africa from Namibia and independence of Namibia under UN-supervised elections. Cuba withdraws 3,000 of its 50,000 troops from Angola.

July: South African military forces in Namibia to be reduced to 1,500.

August 1: All Cuban troops in southern Angola must be stationed north of the 15th parallel.

November 1: 25,000 Cuban troops must have left Angola. Remaining Cuban troops must be stationed north of 13th parallel. Elections to be held in Namibia and remaining South African troops leave that country.

1990

April 1: 8,000 Cuban troops to leave Angola.

October 1: 5,000 Cuban troops to leave Angola.

1991

July 1: All Cuban troops are out of Angola.

None of the conditions reassured UNITA. In February 1989, Savimbi sent a senior official to Washington. He told the Americans that UNITA had reason to distrust the Cubans over their promises to withdraw. It also had information that MPLA forces would make a major offensive during 1989. With the cutting off of $80 million in aid from South Africa and the sealing of the Namibian border, UNITA is largely dependent on the US covert supply line. The UNITA official pleaded for increased covert US aid.

UNITA also wanted more sophisticated weapons, such as the Stinger missile, which it said were necessary to face more advanced aircraft recently provided to Angola by the Soviet Union. Officials of the new Bush administration said that the US would not establish diplomatic relations with Angola or give away other 'carrots' until national reconciliation was under way. They said that US support for UNITA would continue undiminished.[2]

In the last week of June 1989 the 'impossible' happened. Savimbi and Dos Santos met in Zaire, at a summit arranged by President Mobutu and 16 other African leaders. After day-long talks, Savimbi and Dos Santos announced that they had agreed to a cease-fire and to open direct peace talks. 'We have taken the first step', Santos said.

The two sides agreed to the establishment of a mediation commission under Mobutu's chairmanship to deal with 'technical issues' and to meet again in Zimbabwe in August. President Kenneth Kaunda of Zambia, who was present, said that Savimbi would leave Angola for voluntary exile. Other participants doubted this, assuming that Savimbi would want to stay on the scene to keep UNITA alive as a political party. The biggest obstacle to a final settlement may arise if Dos Santos remains determined to preserve Angola's one-party system and his control of that system.

Peace-feelers have not stopped the fighting. Angolan forces pushed into the heartland of Savimbi's Ovimbundu tribesmen. During March and April the troops captured three towns in central Angola, including Savimbi's birthplace of Munhango.

Savimbi's 60,000 men seem as determined as ever. They roam freely in 16 of Angola's 19 provinces and constantly attack government posts and patrols. UNITA has enough arms and money to go on fighting for two more years even without further help.

When the Cuban troops withdraw, Dos Santos' position will hardly be stronger. He is so dependent on the Cubans that he has them guarding his presidential palace as well as the important American-operated oil installations in the Cabinda enclave. The Angolan army, one of the best equipped in black Africa, is not well trained in counter-insurgency tactics. Dos Santos lacks the solid base of a tribal chief, so his survival may ultimately depend on whether he can revive Angola's sickly economy. But while oil production brings in about $2 bn annually, Luanda spends half of it on Soviet weapons. In fact, Angola is the world's tenth largest importer of weapons.

The conflict has left scars on Angolan society. It has displaced 500,000 people inside the country and another 400,000 in neighbouring States. Between 1980–85, 100,000 adults and 150,000 infants died as a result of famine and food disruption. Since 1985, children have continued to die at a US-estimated rate of 55,000 a year. The country is eager for peace but it will be a dismal peace for many Angolans. The struggle against hunger will go on for years and uncleared mines are likely to be a continuing danger.

New Report on Battle of Cuito Cuanavale

During 1989 the South African commander of operations *Modular, Hooper and Packer* in South-East Angola, Colonel Deon Ferreira, spoke for the first time about his operations. His statements are interesting because of a barrage of claims by anti-South African groups that South Africa was defeated at Cuito Cuanavale. As a political result, the critics said, South Africa was forced into the agreement over Namibia.

Ferreira said: 'If defeat for South Africa meant the loss of 31 men, three tanks, five armoured vehicles and three aircraft, then we lost. If victory for the Cubans and Angolans meant the loss of 4,600 men, 94 tanks, 100 armoured vehicles, 9 aircraft and other Soviet equipment valued at more than one billion rand, then they won.'

For the first time, Colonel Ferreira divulged that his three sets of orders at the time had been:

● To halt and reverse the MPLA/Cuban advance on the UNITA strong-holds of Mavinga and Jamba. (*Operation Modular*)
● To inflict maximum casualties on the retreating enemy. (*Operation Hooper*)
● To attempt to force the enemy to retreat west of the Cuito River. (*Operation Packer*)

Ferreira said that it 'would not have been impossible' for his force to take Cuito Cuanavale, but he had no orders to do so. In any case, he said, intelligent military strategy did not allow for the placing of a two-mile-wide river between his forces and his target. 'We were east of the river, and the town was on the west bank.'

During the press conference attended only by South African journalists, Ferreira was asked why this information had not been made public to counter Angolan claims of a MPLA victory. He replied that because the Namibian settlement negotiations had reached such a critical stage South Africa's involvement in South-East Angola was played down. For political reasons, it had been decided to admit only to limited assistance to UNITA.

Ferreira stressed that UNITA was indirectly instrumental in the South African success, as their forces had cleared the entire south of Angola of MPLA and SWAPO presence. This laid the basis for the 'super functional' South African logistical supply lines.

'The enemy's Soviet MiG 23s were the single most serious threat to our operations', the Colonel said. 'We were constantly harassed by them but UNITA had Stingers, which kept the planes at high altitudes.'

The direct key to the South African success in the three operations, Ferreira said, was the troops' training and discipline, as well as the massive advantages of the South African G5 and G6 155-mm long range guns.[3]

The MPLA and Cubans do not see the battle of Cuito Cuanavale in the same light as Colonel Ferreira and they have convinced some Western observers that Cuanavale was a South African defeat. One of them was Jeremy Harding, who reported:

'The MPLA have reversed South Africa's fourth military push of the 1980s at the obscure little town of Cuito Cuanavale. They did so over a gruelling six-month period, at a high cost, with assistance from the Cubans and the decisive benefits of Soviet air power, for which the South African air force was no match. Nonetheless the failure of the SADF to take the town, and the number of white losses incurred in the process, have called the war into question among South Africa's whites and led Pretoria to reconsider its military commitments in Angola.'[4]

Information from the region suggests that there was not much left of Cuito Cuanavale after four weeks of siege by 4,000 UNITA troops and heavy bombardment by the South African artillery. The guns lobbed up to 200 shells a day into the MPLA-held town. These guns are probably the most accurate in the world for the 35-40km range of which they are capable. They fire 155-mm shells and are highly mobile. The G5 can be towed around at high speed while the G6 is self-propelled.

The removal of Cuito Cuanavale from the Angolan radar network grid created a serious gap in the air defences of Angola, a crisis which the Soviet Union had spent enormous sums of money trying to prevent. South African forces hastened to Savimbi's aid to prevent a breakthough to UNITA HQ. During this operation the South Africans captured several sophisticated Soviet missile and radar systems, between 60 and 80 new and undamaged Soviet T54/55 tanks and large numbers of other vehicles. With all this booty, South Africa has replaced Israel as the main source of captured, new generation Soviet military weapons systems. Brought back behind South African lines were more than 10 complete SAM 8 installations. These were the first examples of the SAM 8 systems to fall into Western hands.[5]

Fighting Resumes

Three months after Angola's president Dos Santos and Jonas Savimbi agreed to a ceasefire their forces were again fighting. In September 1989 fighting was widespread and Savimbi claimed to have killed 1,000 government troops for a loss of 300 of his own. At the same time, Savimbi repudiated the agreement and made a counter-proposal which Dos Santos described as 'a return to square one'.

President Mobutu of Zaire, the broker of the peace talks, has been blamed for their collapse. According to African political sources, he was so anxious to achieve agreement and the consequent praise that he distorted the peace-making process. During the talks, in Gbadolite, Zaire, as Mobutu shuttled between the two sides, he led each one to believe that the other had made greater concessions than was in fact the case.

A more sinister interpretation can be put on Savimbi's repudiation of the agreement. It is that the Americans had come to believe that with the Cubans out of Angola, Savimbi could fight on and win. In London, in October 1989, Savimbi announced that he was happy with the level of American support. He said, 'Militarily we have what we need to counter any offensive from the MPLA. That is why during the September offensive they lost almost 100 tanks and why they lost MiGs. UNITA, at this moment, is well-equipped to meet any threat from the MPLA.'

According to Savimbi, the Cuban withdrawal had not weakened the MPLA. 'The Soviet advisers are still active with the MPLA in planning. During the September offensive they were at command posts at tactical level. They were in small numbers of twenty to thirty but at advanced lines.'

Savimbi repeated UNITA's claims that chemical weapons have been used against his forces since 1985 and including the September battles. He produced documentation that at least 450 UNITA troops and civilians had been affected by chemical weapons. Independent evidence—from foreign doctors and UN officials—supports Savimbi's allegations.

In January 1990 the war had been in progress for 30 years. Eighty per cent of Angola's population was born after the conflict began and they have known nothing but violence and instability.

References

1. Savimbi's comments, as presented here, are a summary from several Press sources. David Beresford of the *Guardian*, London, wrote the most comprehensive report of the one-day meeting.
2. A UNITA report available to the author.
3. Colonel Ferreira's report was published in *Paratua*, the South African Defence Forces journal, in March 1989. Allowing for a degree of propaganda, I have found *Paratua* reports to be accurate.

4. In *London Review of Books*. 1 September 1988. Assessment of the battle hinges on whether or not the SADF was trying to capture and occupy Cuito Cuanavale. Despite Colonel Ferreira's emphatic statement that this was not the intention, a number of well-informed South African journalists believe that it was.
5. Western intelligence sources.

Aspects of the War discussed in War Annual 3:
 South Africa's campaign plans
 Angola's air defence systems
 The air war
 Testing of equipment
 Cubans in Angola: the Aids factor
 Cuban/Angolan use of nerve gas
 Soviet interest in South Africa
 The peace talks
 Organisation and equipment
 Soviet change of policy

Bangladesh Guerrilla War

CREEPING GENOCIDE

Background Summary

This war has been in progress in the Chittagong Hill Tracts since 1971. The Hill Tracts area is a sparsely inhabited region of a densely populated country— at least 110 million people in an area of 55,598 square miles. Of this, the Hill Tracts cover 10,000 square miles of valleys and forested hills. Its indigenous population, mainly tribal and Buddhist, is divided into 32 tribes with a total of 600,000 people. The Chakma tribe is the largest, numbering 300,000.

When India and Pakistan became independent in 1947 the Hill Tracts chiefs sought recognition of the area as a native State or as part of a confederation with tribal areas of north-east India. Instead, the Hill Tracts were incorporated into East Pakistan, a Muslim State.

After nine months of bloody civil war, East Pakistan became Bangladesh in 1971. The new government at once embarked on a campaign to drive out the tribal peoples and give their land to Muslim Bengali settlers. The Buddhists formed a self-defence association, the *Jana Sanghati Samity* (JSS). The Chakmas created a JSS military wing, the *Shanti Bahini*. Since the Buddhists had no martial tradition this was a remarkable achievement.

Armed by India and, at that time, by the Soviet Union, the *Shanti Bahini* startled the Bangladeshi government by their military prowess. In 1984 the government sent the 24th Division, the 'Bengal Tigers', into the Hill Tracts. The commander, Major General Noor Uddin Khan, had orders to find a 'permanent solution to the Hill Tracts problem'.

The *Shanti Bahini* guerrillas raided army outposts and ambushed patrols and the army resorted to terror tactics against non-combatant villagers. Many fleeing Chakmas sought refuge in India, which did not want them.

Unable to trap the guerrillas, General Uddin Khan sent messages to their leaders that Buddhists could stay in the Hill Tracts if they converted to Islam. To the Buddhists this forced conversion to a hated religion was intolerable and thousands more fled the country. Uddin Khan built on this success by ordering his troops to begin a campaign of rape to drive out still more Buddhists.

Political opposition in Bangladesh to President Muhammad Ershad indirectly helped the guerrillas, since the greater part of the army was engaged in putting down urban riots.

The War in 1988–89

The government again made a drive to get rid of the tribal peoples. The *Shanti Bahini* fighters, numbering no more than an estimated 5,000, faced an occupation

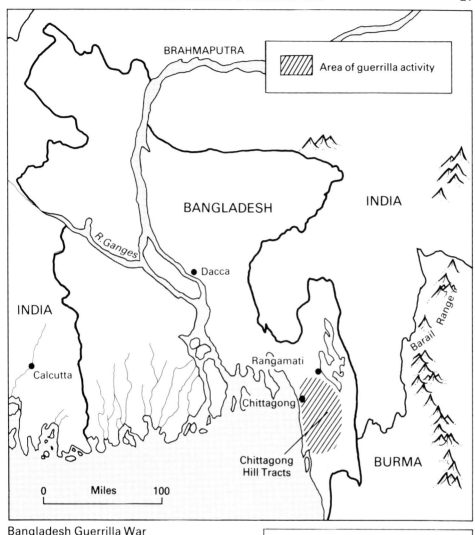

Bangladesh Guerrilla War

army of 40,000 as well as paramilitary forces of 85,000. General Uddin Khan employed a new and terrifying tactic in 1988. One by one, he selected villages from which the guerrillas were known to have come and subjected them to planned atrocity. By systematic torture, rape and execution he hoped to bring the guerrillas out of the jungle, as worried men sought news of their families.

The army trapped only a few guerrillas in this way because the regular troops have been no match for the guerrillas in night movement. They are able to infiltrate the most tightly drawn nets of soldiers. Even so, the army's tactics made it difficult for the villagers to supply the fighting men with food and shelter. Meanwhile, Muslims are being settled in those areas pronounced 'clean'—that is, free of Buddhist peasants.

The government promotes Islam as a tactic against the tribes. The President calls for action in the form of *jihad* or holy war against 'infidels and unbelievers', an incitement for aggression against the Buddhists. Gangs of civilian Muslims seeking land in the region have been permitted to hunt down guerrillas. The government has also tried to keep all foreigners out of the Hill Tracts so that information about its campaign of creeping genocide cannot reach the outside world.

Despite all the Bangladeshi efforts, the *Shanti Bahini* continues to operate. In May 1989 the army command issued an order-of-the-day about guerrilla thefts from army camps and dumps. Sentries must be more vigilant, the order stated. Sentries are, in fact, a principal guerrilla target and many are silently killed. Occasionally the guerrillas manage to blow up a road as an army convoy is passing and on at least two occasions during 1989 they attacked outposts and wiped out the garrisons.

With young men joining the *Shanti Bahini*, the number of guerrillas remains fairly constant but their fields of operation are steadily decreasing in area. The Bangladeshi government is proceeding with its policy of deforestation and as the jungle area shrinks so does the *Shanti Bahini*'s cover.

The desperate Chakmas and other tribes can only hope for a change of government and a more humane and liberal government. Coups and counter-coups are a feature of Bangladeshi politics and the Hill Tract peoples hope one of them will stop the war against them.

This seems unlikely. With its Muslim population rapidly increasing, Bangladesh remains poverty stricken. The plight of half a million Buddhists is a minor matter for all the many opposition parties in Bangladesh.

The only support for the Chakmas and the other tribes comes from Amnesty International and the Anti-Slavery Association. Neither is in a position to provide what the *Shanti Bahini* leaders believe is their only salvation—outside military help. India is the only realistic source and during 1989 the JSS leadership sent emissaries to President Rajiv Gandhi to appeal for his help. They pointed out that their plight is as desperate as that of any groups in Sri Lanka, where the Indian army intervened in an attempt to prevent further bloodshed. Gandhi did not personally talk to the JSS delegations but it is known that, with so many other problems concerning his own minorities, he is unlikely to take on that of the Chakmas.

Burma Guerrilla War

AND NOW—'THE WAR OF THE CITIES'

Background Summary

During the Second World War, the Karen people of Burma fought with the British army against the invading Japanese, 1941–45. They were promised an independent homeland after the war but were denied it. Since 1949 the Karen National Liberation Army (KNLA) of 4,500 has been fighting for this homeland, together with guerrillas from the Kachin, Kayan, Shan, Arakan, Mon, Naga, Kerreni and other tribes. Collectively, they make up about a quarter of the 41 million people of Burma, with the four million Karens the largest group.

Militarily, they are vastly outnumbered by the Burmese armed forces of 186,000. The army alone has a strength of 170,000. In addition, there are the People's Police Force of 38,000 and the People's Militia of 35,000. The Karens' battlefield is the hill and jungle region of eastern Burma, on the Thailand border. Other groups fight the State in the Irrawaddy delta and the mountainous north. Commander of the KNLA, as well as President of the National Democratic Front Alliance (NDFA), is General By Mya, who fought with the British in the Second World War.

The Karen men began as guerrillas but they became regular soldiers. In their capital, Marniplaw, they established an HQ with most of the branches that a European army would have. New recruits are given 16 weeks training in weapons and warfare and fitted with uniforms.

Summary of the War in 1987–88

The anti-government Burmese Communist Party People's Army (BCPPA) took advantage of the army's preoccupation with the Karens in the south to attack government posts in the north. An army counter-offensive drove off the BCPPA but the government caught few guerrillas. By Mya, by far the most experienced of the government's opponents, ambushed an army column and caused heavy casualties. The army retaliated by attacking Klerdy, a KNLA stronghold.

In a systematic attempt to deal with the many rebel groups, the army turned 25 of its 91 infantry battalians into 'independent battalions'. This was to give the commanding officers greater speed of manoeuvre.

During 1988 the Burmese army called its military operations 'The Campaign of the Four Cuts'. They proposed to cut the Karens' trade routes; to cut off outside aid; to cut off one rebel group from another; and to cut off the rebels' heads.

The Karens' resistance continued to be a slow, stubborn rearguard action against overwhelming odds. Meanwhile, the army continued its atrocities.

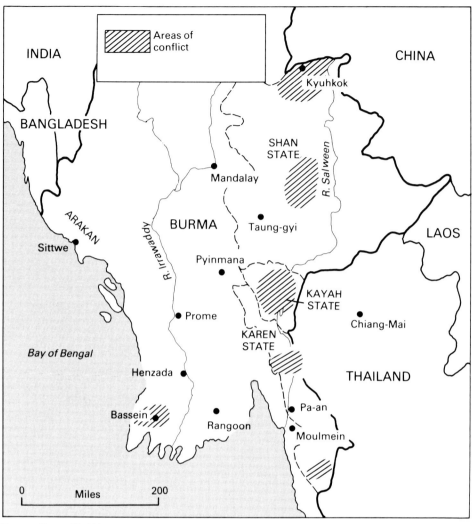

Burma Guerrilla War

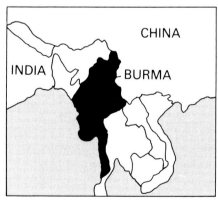

Amnesty International alleged that the security forces were killing and torturing villagers as a routine part of operations to eliminate ethnic rebels.

In the face of fierce opposition from student groups in Rangoon and other dissident organisations, President Ne Win resigned in August 1988 and was replaced by Sein Lwin, a hardliner known as 'the Butcher'. His appointment angered the public and violence engulfed Burma. Sein Lwin broadcast a command to riot police deployed in the capital—'I order you to *yike that, pyit that*'. (Beat, kill; shoot, kill.)

The Conflict in 1988–89

In August 1988 President Maung Maung took over from Sein Lwin. He promised to hold multi-party elections that would end 26 years of one-party rule, by the Burma Socialist Programme Party (BSPP). However, he failed to set a date for the balloting and the demonstrations went on. The national student movement became an uprising. Three leading dissidents—former Generals Aung Gyi and Tin Oo as well as Aung San Suu Kyi, daughter of one of Burma's great nationalist heroes—wrote to Maung Maung formally rejecting the proposed elections. They were joined by U Nu, a former Prime Minister ousted from power in 1962.

As the confrontation grew, the greater part of the military apparently remained loyal to Maung Maung and to Burma's strongman, the former BSPP chairman, despotic Ne Win. On 17 September about 6,000 soldiers, sailors, and airmen joined the revolt, briefly as it turned out. In Rangoon, graduates of the Defence Services Academy, mostly Majors and Lieutenant Colonels, issued a statement urging the formation of an interim government that would include the opposition.

General Saw Maung, Burma's Minister of Defence and chief of the armed forces, ousted Maung Maung. Proclaimed President, Saw Maung immediately pledged to restore law and order and promised to hold multi-party elections in 1990. On national television he appealed to the opposition to avoid splitting the military.

This plea was widely interpreted to mean that the government doubted the loyalty of its own troops. Its concern seemed justified. Of the nine regional commands, only about half were believed to remain loyal to Ne Win. But regional command troops were locally recruited and almost certainly would not fire on their own people if ordered. A captain of one of three élite divisions in Rangoon went over to the opposition, creating fevered speculation about the fealty of even the most trusted troops of the Tatmadaw, the army.

Various proposals were being made. One called for a non-partisan government formed from leading figures representing various 'interests' and 'forces' in Burmese society, rather than political parties. U Nu, always an independent if erratic politician, supported this idea. So did Aung San Suu Kyi, who had no political backing but immense personal appeal. 'The country accepts me because they trust me and they associate me with my father', she said. Her father was assassinated in 1947 and Suu Kyi believed that large numbers of people remembered him with affection.

Saw Maung made several speeches to the military in which he promised 'good news'. He was referring to a major worry of leading government and military officials—their personal safety. They had been horrified by public beheadings of people believed to be government agents. Many officials and their families sought refuge at Rangoon General Command, a military base 14 miles north of Rangoon, or at Tower House, a guarded multi-storey building near Ne Win's villa at Inya Lake.

In the last week of September 1988, Saw Maung announced that members of the military and civil servants could no longer belong to the BSPP. That decision effectively divorced the army from the ruling party and was an attempt to show the opposition that the BSPP did not claim 'ownership' of the armed forces.

However, the army itself—composed entirely of volunteers—was itself politicised and its leaders were jealous of their authority. It seemed unlikely that they would readily relinquish power to the 10 opposition parties or any group of them. During the fighting, which took on the dimensions of a civil war, about 4,000 people died. Most were civilians.

Renewed War Against the Karens

In November 1988, the Burmese army began one of its most intensive campaigns against the Karen forces. This was partly to focus general Burmese attention on a 'foreign' enemy and thus reduce the turmoil in the cities. The army chose its campaigning area carefully—a 75-mile crescent along the border of the Mae Sot district of Tak Province in Thailand. The Karens have five strongholds here, Wangkha being the most important. The offensive was designed to disrupt the cross-border black market trade which the Karens use to finance their insurgency.

The Karens' bases fell one by one. Wangkha was the fifth to fall, in mid-May 1989. According to government figures, 35 soldiers were killed and 95 wounded, while 43 rebels died. The casualties were rather less than those in the battle of Malela, where 177 soldiers and 'more than 600 guerrillas' were reported to have been killed.

However, the army was unable to capture Kaw Moo Ra camp, in Karen State. The garrison of about 1,200 held out against 3,000 troops when attacked in mid-May. According to the Karens, government troops crossed the Moei River border into Thailand to gain a tactical advantage. They also allege that Thailand has a secret agreement with the Burmese army, allowing them to use Thai territory to attack Karen positions from behind. The local Thai commander, Lieutenant General Siri Tiwaphan, had denied this charge but it would be difficult for Burmese army units to reach and use certain high ground without Thai connivance.[1]

In July the army again tried to capture Kaw Moo Ra. Troops began pounding the base with mortar fire on 23 July, prior to launching an infantry assault. At least 42 Burmese soldiers were killed and many more were wounded before the attack was beaten off. Thai border sources said that the Karens lost only two men killed and one wounded.

Kaw Moo Ra is situated in a curve of the Moei River that juts into Thailand. It can be attacked from Burma only with artillery or by frontal assault on a well-defended 250-yard strip of land between two bends of the river.

Thai gunners fired 15 warning rounds at a Burmese mortar base in hills to the east of the camp after about 80 mortar rounds fell inside Thai territory at the village of Ban Wang Kaew, just opposite Kaw Moo Ra.

The Karens say that the Burmese paid a heavy price for their victories in the campaign and claim to have killed 2,000 and wounded 4,000. Thai sources put the figures at 300 Burmese killed and 600 wounded. They confirm that Karen casualties were light—six killed and 17 wounded.

Influence of Aung San Suu Kyi

During the early months of 1989 Aung San Suu Kyi became the undisputed leading opposition politician. Wherever she travelled on the campaign trail peasants lined the road to catch a glimpse of the woman who dared oppose the military junta.

Supporters in her party, the National League of Democracy, handed out buttons showing a photograph of her assassinated father. As she has spent 25 years living in Britain and has an English husband, Suu Kyi has no choice but to exploit her father's reputation.

The military government banned political pamphlets for the election promised in 1990, so the most potent tactic in Suu Kyi's campaign is the distribution of video tapes. An aide recorded her public moves and words each day, the tapes were copied and re-copied to be spread throughout Burma. The régime, which bans anything but its own message on the country's television programmes, prevented video stores from selling Suu Kyi tapes. After this ban they were disseminated through the black market.

Her leadership does more than provide some unity to a fractured political opposition. She also challenges the military's major justification for staying in power so long—that the army represents the legacy of her father. Ne Win was subordinate to Aung San during the struggle for independence.

The government charged her with having active Communists on her staff. Also, they say she threatened the dominant race, the Burmese, by promising autonomy to other nationalities, such as the Karens. Even in the splintered opposition she has detractors. Some student leaders resent her taking the lead after hundreds of students were killed by the army in August 1988.[2]

In July 1989 the military junta recognised Suu Kyi's real power by putting her under house arrest for 'up to one year' and denying her contact with anyone except her immediate family. Her telephone line was cut, her personal secretary and other members of her National League for Democracy were removed. Her family was forbidden to meet foreign diplomats or any members of any political party. A government spokesman said that Suu Kyi had been spreading dissension among the military and 'sowing hatred' for the army among the people. A similar detention order was served on General Tin Oo.

Burma's 'Yellow Army'

The nation's 140,000 Buddhist monks, with their shaved heads and yellow robes draping off one shoulder, could eventually prove decisive in Burmese affairs. Known as the 'yellow army', their political leanings are watched as closely as those of the military rank-and-file which, after a lapse in 1988, remained obedient to the senior commanders in 1989.

During the violence in Rangoon and elsewhere, some young monks stood on the frontline of protests and were shot. Others, during the anarchy, directed traffic in Mandalay. In Rangoon, a few monks stopped students from beheading a group of soldiers. Some monasteries have given refuge to opposition leaders.

The monks' potential as an explosive catalyst in bringing down the government is recognised and feared by the leaders. Burma has a long history of rulers who lost power when leading monks withdrew their support. Their power comes from the ability to deny a leader the right to donate to the clergy and thereby gain heavenly merit.

The government has warned senior abbots not to mix religion and politics. Even so, the top commanders visit monasteries to explain their programme and purpose, to take part in ritual ceremonies and to 'seek advice' from the monks.

Knowing the real nature of Buddhism in Burma, the government has appealed to peasants not to follow the urban people who use 'foreign terms according to their own wishes'. The most insidious foreign term is 'democracy'.

Burma's dormant vanguard of monks is an amorphous group without organisation, making it difficult for the government to use them for political ends. Internal disputes and differing sects have prevented a strict hierarchy from forming. John Ferguson, a professor specialising in Burmese affairs, said: 'When the main body of the monkhood goes on the streets to support the students, then the revolution will be successful'. He said that soldiers will be reluctant to shoot more protesting monks because of a fear of losing spiritual credit for later lives.[3]

The End of the Rebel Communist Party

In mid-April 1989 a Communist insurrection ended after 41 years of warfare against the Burmese government. The Communist Party of Burma (CPB), founded in August 1939, played an important part in the struggle against the Japanese occupation during the Second World War. In contrast, its war against its own government ended ignominiously.

Following independence from Britain in January 1948, the CPB declared its profound dissatisfaction with the new government. 'Any independence wrested from the hands of the imperialists without a war is a sham.' With this, the CPB went underground and began an armed struggle against the democratic government of U Nu.

Well-led, the CPB's fighters overran several country towns and managed to control large areas. The desperate U Nu appealed to the Indian Prime Minister, Pandit Nehru, and was given massive aid. The CPB was forced into jungle areas, from where it waged a guerrilla campaign.

For some time the CPB, though staunchly Maoist, received no aid from China. Following the military coup against U Nu in 1962 and a massacre of students in Rangoon, the Chinese at last promised aid to the CPB. Burmese Communists who had earlier fled to China also provided large sums of money. After lengthy training in China, the CPB fighters, now numbering about 15,000, selected infiltration routes for an aggressive return to Burma. Since the border between

Burma and the Chinese province of Yunnan is 1,200 miles long there was no real problem.

The first CPB units crossed into Burma on 1 January 1968 and captured the border town of Mong Ko. Well armed, they outfought the Burmese army units and drove them from many outposts. By 1973 the CPB controlled an area of 12,000 square miles in Shan and Kachin States and brought its strength up to 25,000.

Suspicious, fanatical and irrational, the CPB leadership was profoundly influenced by the Chinese Cultural Revolution. In the early 1970s it executed idealistic young intellectuals who had joined the ranks, as well as veterans no longer considered sufficiently dedicated to Maoism.

Meanwhile, the army had found a new strategy. It attacked the weaker CPB bases in central Burma. In 1970–71 the Communists were pushed out of the Irrawaddy delta and in 1975 from the Pegu Yoma mountains. The CPB's leadership remained fanatically Maoist and when Mao died in 1976 these men fiercely criticised Deng Xiaoping, his likely successor. When Deng took power in China a year later he repaid the insults by reducing Chinese aid to the CPB to a minimum.

The leadership seemed to have no conception of changing times or of the different mentality of the non-Burmese people who now comprised the larger part of its rank-and-file. They were Shans, Was, Akhas, Kachins and others. The leaders remained wedded to nothing more intelligent than Chinese human-wave tactics—without the millions of Chinese to make the waves. Many CPB fighters were slaughtered when they attacked Burmese army positions.

Discontent among the rank-and-file simmered for years but did not erupt, apparently because of the real fear and authority wielded by the leaders. In 1988 the unrest in Rangoon and elsewhere emboldened the disaffected CPB soldiers. During the night of 16–17 April 1989 a force of mutineers stormed the CPB's general HQ at Panghsang in Shan State. The 250 ethnic Burmese CPB leaders fled to China. Within two weeks, the mutiny had spread to all CPB units.

The leaders of the mutiny tried to hold the units together as a 'New CPB', but this task was impossible. The old CPB broke into its original ethnic constituent parts. The government now faces the problem of dealing with about 16,000 men in perhaps eight different 'armies'. None of them is thought to be avowedly Communist, though all will hope for some financial and logistical support from China.

The former Burmese chief of staff, General Tin Oo, said that there was no possibility of the CPB ever being able to raise an army. 'Not one of the leaders who have fled to China is younger than 65', he has said. 'They themselves killed off the younger men who might now be new leaders.'[4]

The Army and Politics

In June 1989 the government of Burma officially changed its name to The Union of Myanma but while many ordinary Burmese objected to the new title the army quickly accepted the change. The Burmese Army's total loyalty to the military régime resembles that of the People's Liberation Army of China to its political leaders. After the revolt by some soldiers in September 1988, the army recovered its cohesion and dominance.

The State Law and Order of Restoration Council (SLORC) which assumed power after the massacre of demonstrators in September 1988 uses the army as its power base. The military has always provided the best route for upward social mobility. In addition, it is lucrative, especially for officers. They enjoy privileges such as rations of imported whisky and cigarettes and the right to acquire cheap vehicles and land after certain length of service. Another extra source of income comes from bribes in the opium growing areas of Shan State and in the jade mines of Kachin State.

Indirect encouragement of corruption provides every soldier with an interest in preserving the existing military government. The Directorate of the Defence Services Intelligence (DDSI), which is one of Asia's most efficient secret police forces, keeps all soldiers of every rank in line.

Several officers, whithout combat experience, have become influential through personal political connections. The most prominent of all is Brigadier Khin Nyunt, who spent only a year in a Light Infantry Division before Ne Win selected him as chief of the DDSI and First Secretary to SLORC. In fact, he is the virtual head of SLORC and is even more powerful then General Saw Maung. Khin Nyunt reports direct to Ne Win. To consolidate his hold on power, Khin Nyunt appointed old classmates and friends of the Officers Training School to all the key posts in the army. He is aided in all that he does by another brigadier, Tin Oo—no relation of the retired general Tin Oo who supports Aung San Suu Kyi.

The rise to power of Khin Nyunt and Tin Oo has caused resentment among more experienced officers and it is they who might turn against the régime. Diplomatic sources in Rangoon say that dissident army officers with pride in the 'old army' could well overcome their fear of DDSI, declare for the National League of Democracy and its chief, General Tin Oo (Retd), and overthrow the hardliners.

Until this happens, everything that happens in Burmese politics is subject to the control and censure of the army.

References

1. The details of the battles come from Thai sources. Thai Army intelligence officers closely monitor the fighting.
2. Diplomats in Rangoon rate Suu Kyi highly. They say that her lack of political experience and her long absence from Burma would not hamper her as a national leader. A Swedish embassy official said: 'Being back from exile gives her a certain romantic appeal and she is untarnished by scandal'.
3. In an interview with American journalist Clayton Jones.
4. In a talk with the author. Tin Oo, still only in his 50s, would be a senior figure in any democratically elected government.

Aspects of the War discussed in War Annual 3:
    The War of the Cities
    Military and civil administration in the Karen army

Cambodia's New Phase

OLD FEARS OF KHMER ROUGE

Background Summary

Cambodia became Kampuchea but during 1988 it officially reverted to the name of Cambodia which, in any case, was what much of the Western media had never ceased to call it. When the French pulled out of Indo-China in 1954, the Vietnamese community saw themselves as France's natural successor. The French had trained loyal Vietnamese to act as administrators in Vietnam, Laos and Cambodia. There followed the American attempt to keep South Vietnam, Laos and Cambodia out of the Hanoi Communists' control. Once the Americans had been defeated in 1975, Vietnam had no difficulty in securing Laos. When the Vietnamese marched into Cambodia in 1979 to remove the barbarous Khmer Rouge, which had beaten the American-supported government, their control of the region seemed complete.

The Chinese found this unacceptable. Vietnam was allied to the Soviet Union, China's enemy since the Communist alliance had collapsed a generation earlier. China's view was that Vietnam and its satellites must come under some degree of Chinese supervision. It regarded the Khmer Rouge as a useful ally. Under the infamous Pol Pot, the Khmer Rouge killed possibly two million Cambodians out of a total population of seven million. They died for no other reason than that they opposed Pol Pot or were suspected of doing so.

Vietnam invaded the country in December 1978 'to protect the south-western flank from hostile influence', code language for China. The Soviet Union backed Vietnam. The other groups, both non-Communist, were Son Sann's Khmer People's National Liberation Front (KPLNF) and Prince Sihanouk's *Armeé Nationale Sihanoukienne* (ANS). These three parties—two non-Communist and the Khmer Rouge genocidal ultra-Maoist—formed an unstable alliance.

Heng Samrin became President and put Cambodia's army under Vietnamese command. The opposition groups took to the jungle. In 1979 China mismanaged an invasion in support of the Cambodian insurgents. The conflict then became a war of resistance against foreign (Vietnamese) occupation. It was not a genuine guerrilla war, in that Cambodian fighters did not live off the land and fight as irregulars. They established bases and developed fixed lines of defence.

Under immense Vietnamese military pressure, the KPNLF and ANS lost all their bases and the Khmer Rouge lost its mountain stronghold, Phnom Malai. The resistance fighters retreated to Thailand, where they established bases as well as camps for their 250,000 refugees. The Vietnamese laid more than one million mines along the 450-mile Cambodia–Thailand border in an attempt to seal it against guerrilla incursion, and in January–May 1986 Vietnamese units moved into eastern Thailand to contain the guerrillas.

37

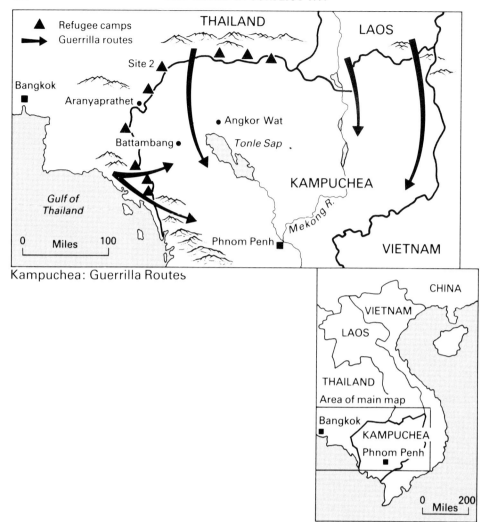

Kampuchea: Guerrilla Routes

In 1986 the Vietnamese-Cambodian army suffered 7,000 casualties and the guerrillas 5,000. In 1987 the guerrillas numbered 66,000 men in their three main groups, the Khmer Rouge with 35,000, KPNLF with 16,000 and ANS with 10,000. There are also smaller groups. In numerous raids, the guerrillas entered Cambodia along four main trails and carried out attacks behind Vietnamese-Cambodian army lines.

The war was proving costly for Vietnam. By 1988 about three million Vietnamese people were on the verge of starvation and President Gorbachev told the Vietnamese President, Nguyen Co Thach, that the Soviets could not continue to pay $3 million a day for Vietnam's campaign in Cambodia.

By 1989 more than 25,000 Vietnamese soldiers had been killed in Cambodia. The conflict had led to Vietnam's almost complete international isolation and a refusal by most Western nations to provide aid until the army was withdrawn.

The successful convening of the Jakarta Informal Meeting (JIM) on Cambodia in July 1988 and the Chinese–Soviet talks at senior level at the end of August helped bring the prospect of a political solution a little nearer. In the meantime Hun Sen had become Prime Minister of Cambodia and was more conciliatory than Heng Samrin, his President.

Khieu Samphan, head of the Khmer Rouge, condemned the meeting, agreed to none of the proposals and put forward his own proposals. Following a Vietnamese withdrawal, the armed forces of all four Cambodian factions would be confined to barracks. He also demanded the eventual establishment of a quadripartite army with each faction limited to 10,000 men. The Cambodian leaders rejected the plan.

The Chinese–Soviet talks on Cambodia focused on the danger of a takeover by the Khmer Rouge after a Vietnamese withdrawal. The Vietnamese tried to establish a linkage between withdrawal of their troops and internationally-agreed measures to prevent such a takeover. As Khmer Rouge sponsors, the Chinese objected to such linkage but said that their support of the Khmer Rouge would cease once the Vietnamese withdrawal was complete. The Russians asked China to ensure that Pol Pot would never return to power, which China said would be possible. The Vietnamese gave a clear commitment to withdraw most of their troops from Cambodia by the end of September 1989 and all of them by 1990.

The War in 1989

'The War of the Villages'

Foreign diplomats in Phnom Penh gave the name 'the war of the villages' to the low-level skirmishing, throughout 1989, between Khmer Rouge guerrillas and the village militia. This militia network forms the first line of defence against the guerrilla enemy. The area concerned covers the Abandoned Mountains and the Elephant Mountains and the valleys between.

Many farmers admit selling rice to Khmer Rouge patrols to avoid confrontation. There is little evidence of active support for the marauders but an uneasy *modus vivendi* exists between parts of the rural population and the guerrillas. However, the village militiamen make no pacts with them.

The Khmer Rouge men make many night forays in search of village officials to kidnap or kill. The main protection against these attacks is the village militia, which on occasions drives off the Khmer Rouge. Militiamen defending the village of Prey Kley defeated the raiders in a 30-minute skirmish and news of the unexpected victory spread through the countryside.

The effects of these guerrilla raids are painful. On the morning after the fight a young militiaman went to a nearby stream for water and walked on a plastic landmine. The resulting explosion mangled his left leg, which was amputated. In places where the Khmer Rouge has stepped up the action the fighting has resulted in large numbers of wounded local residents having to be taken to the inadequately-equipped hospitals.

Despite the civilian casualties, the militiamen became more emboldened during 1989. During an assault on the hamlet of Baeng Mkak, defenders killed the commander and deputy commander of the attacking Khmer Rouge force. After this setback the guerrillas left Baeng Mkak alone for three months, though the villagers knew that they would be back for revenge, sooner or later.

Highways are empty by 3pm for fear of Khmer Rouge ambushes. Memories of atrocities are still vivid. Around Chhun Kiri, people recall that the Abandoned Mountains were once the Big Mountains. The new name came into use after the Khmer Rouge forced the evacuation—or abandonment—of Kampt province in 1978. More than 20,000 people were herded along steep paths. The old people and the young children had to be abandoned. In the end, the 8,000 people who had survived the march died on the trail of starvation and malaria.

The town of Sisophon has been fortified with a large mud rampart, fox-holes and trenches. Artillery posts were set up on the surrounding hills and a large army camp was established north of the town. The Khmer Rouge and one of the non-Communist resistance groups, KPNLF, have attacked Sisophon in the past. In May 1989 KPNLF units reached within three miles of the town before the outposts drove them off.[1]

On 7 January 1989, the 10th anniversary of the founding of the Phnom Penh government, Prime Minister Hun Sen announced: 'The Khmer Rouge are beaten physically and on the battlefield. We have broken their backs.' This claim was justified in terms of raising morale but the continuing war of the villages shows that the Khmer Rouge guerrillas will persist in their efforts to take over the country.

In March 1989 the Vietnamese army began using a new anti-personnel mine and introduced it to the Cambodian army. About the size of a tennis ball in size and orange-red in colour, the mines were first used at Tonsay Tak village against the ANS guerrillas who attacked the place. Normally buried, the mine is detonated through contact or by wire. According to the ANS, the mine, which is manufactured in Vietnam, is of poor quality and easily disarmed. However, this may be an attempt to downplay its effectiveness. Used in large numbers, the tennis-ball mine could protect villages. Most mines used by the Vietnamese in Cambodia are wooden box or pressure-plate mines of Soviet manufacture.[2]

It became clear in June 1989, for the first time, that the Soviet Union had resumed deliveries of weapons and equipment to the Cambodian government. A shipment arrived on 20 March and another late in May; both came in through Cambodia's only deep-water port, Kompong Som. The shipments included 24 T-55 main battle tanks, 30 130-mm and 105-mm guns, several 76.2-mm howitzers and a number of rocket systems, as well as large supplies of small arms ammunition.

Meanwhile, the Thai army took the unprecedented step of establishing a stockpile of Chinese arms—the first known Communist stockpile in a non-Communist country. The move worried Thailand's partners in the Association of South-East Asian Nations (ASEAN). What most troubles them is the possibility of the Chinese arms reaching the Khmer Rouge.

The Thai Foreign Ministry objected to the establishment of the arms depot, since it came at a time when regional and international situations were stable. But army leaders said the munitions were for defensive purposes and would help solve logistics problems. Thai military mistakes in the skirmishes with Laos showed the need for quick supply if Vietnam, Laos or even Burma caused a border fight.[3]

Khmer Rouge Strategy

According to Khmer Rouge statements Pol Pot has retired, but Thai intelligence reports suggest that he may still actually be the leader. The nominal leader of Khmer Rouge—or Party of Democratic Kampuchea—is President Khieu Samphan but Son Sen appears to have more influence. Son Sen, an elusive figure, holds several positions. He is vice president of the Khmer Rouge, Minister of the Co-ordinating Committee on National Defence of the three-party resistance coalition, and Commander-in-Chief of the Khmer Rouge army. On top of all that, he is field commander of Battlefield Command 1001, with possibly 15,000 men under his direct orders.

During the period of Khmer Rouge rule, when the massacres occurred, Son Sen was Defence Minister. His public statements during 1989 were conciliatory but many observers doubt his sincerity. He claimed that the Khmer Rouge would not provoke civil war during the Vietnamese withdrawal and that this party supported, without conditions, the proposal for a UN peace-keeping force in Cambodia.

However, he claimed that Vietnam was deceiving the world about its intention to withdraw. In May 1989, when Vietnam stated that it had 50,000 troops in the country, Son Sen put the figure at 110,000. The Vietnamese, he said, were moving troops from urban areas to less visible positions in the countryside.

Son Sen denied that the Khmer Rouge was secretly stockpiling arms and ammunition but intelligence reports from several sources say that this has happened. One report claims that the Khmer Rouge could wage a war for two years without further supply of munitions.

The Khmer Rouge, Son Sen said, no longer has revolutionary ideals, only patriotic ideals. In any case, the war in Cambodia was not a revolutionary war but a guerrilla war waged by the population to liberate the country. The Khmer Rouge, according to Son Sen, was committed to a four-party transitional government under the leadership of Prince Sihanouk.[4]

Sinister events connected with the Khmer Rouge occurred during 1989. Probably the most disturbing was the disappearance in May of 4,000 Cambodian refugees from a UN-sponsored camp at Taluan into the jungle on the Thai–Cambodian border. The 'evacuation' of the 4,000 refugees was part of a Khmer

Rouge plan to establish 'liberated zones' inside Cambodia. Such zones would be out of reach of any international agreement on the repatriation of Cambodian refugees. Also, they could act as bases for the Khmer Rouge army.

Taluan is one of four Khmer Rouge civilian camps in Thailand, with a combined population of 55,000, receiving international assistance. The Khmer Rouge also controls a further 100,000 refugees in camps in remote areas to which international agencies have no access.

The Khmer Rouge uses civilian porters to carry supplies to their troops deep in Cambodia, hence the need for pools of labour. Also, by keeping control over guerrillas' families the Khmer Rouge leaders ensure the loyalty of their men. The civilians are, in effect, hostages. The snatching of the 4,000 refugees was yet another indication that the Khmer Rouge was preparing for a guerrilla war. Despite the horrors of the 'killing fields', China continues to support the Khmer Rouge.

The guerrillas appear able to roam freely, thereby making much of the countryside unsafe for travel. They are particularly well entrenched in the Cardomom Mountains along the south-eastern border with Thailand.

US Policy On Cambodia

The Bush administration and other legislators favoured the idea of backing the non-Communist resistance led by Prince Sihanhouk. In July 1989 the Democratic Senator, Stephen Solarz, chairman of the House Asian and Pacific committee, said: 'I think it is fair to say that the fate of an entire nation literally hangs in the balance. History will not forgive us if we stand idly by while Pol Pot once again turns Cambodia into an Asian Auschwitz'.

On the other side, a number of legislators opposed the sending of arms on the ground that arms aid could backfire and make a political settlement and a coalition among anti-Khmer Rouge forces less likely.

They were stating what the administration and Senator Solarz apparently did not understand—that the non-Communist resistance groups were allied to the barbarous Maoist Khmer Rouge. Whatever was given to Sihanouk's ANS and to Son Sann's KPNLF would, in one way or another, be used by the Khmer Rouge.

The administration argued for 'enhanced support'. In military terms this meant light arms and ammunition. Senator Solarz stated that Sihanouk's group could use about $30 million in such aid. In fact, several Asian and West European countries were already providing some arms and training so that Sihanouk could expand his forces to about 46,000 men. The immediate importance of US aid would be political, not military, according to the Bush administration.

US support would also allow the non-Communist resistance to withstand the military showdown with the Khmer Rouge which many diplomats in Cambodia believe is inevitable. But others argued that US arms could easily fall into Khmer Rouge hands. Many who opposed aid use US involvement in Vietnam as a model.

The Chinese government's bloody repression of student demonstrations in Peking and other cities deeply influenced attitudes about Cambodia. For many leading American politicians the events in China reinforced the need to strengthen Sihanouk. If the Chinese leaders could order their army to kill their own students they could also send the Khmer Rouge against the government in

Phnom Penh. But other politicians insisted that Sihanouk must break all ties with the Khmer Rouge—that is break the anti-Vietnamese alliance—before he could be given US military aid.

The sharply differing attitudes in Washington emphasised American worry over Cambodia and the fear in some quarters that it could be a repeat of the Vietnam experience. The Bush administration and Senator Solarz drew on more recent examples, such as Afghanistan. There, they argued, US military assistance made the critical difference for Afghan guerrillas resisting aggression and allowed the US to play an important part in ending the Soviet occupation without actually fighting. The proposed assistance to Sihanouk would be provided covertly to give the countries channelling it 'plausible deniability', but it would also be publicly known so that Sihanouk could benefit politically.

One of the most forthright opponents of American aid being given to the 'unholy alliance of resistance forces' is the American observer Strobe Talbott. He wrote:

> 'The Bush administration repeatedly says it does not want the Khmer Rouge to dominate a new Kampuchea. But it endorses the idea of a four-part coalition that would embrace and thereby, it is hoped, co-opt the Khmer Rouge. Speaking of the prospective coalition, Secretary of State James Baker told the Senate: "You're going to have the Khmer Rouge there, that's a fact of life".
>
> 'That is true only if the US and the Khmer Rouge's principal patrons, China and Thailand, make it so. More civil war is inevitable after the Vietnamese pull out. With their record, the Khmer Rouge can hardly be expected to participate in a peaceful democracy. If they and the non-Communists remain aligned against the Phnom Penh leaders, the three-against-one combination will probably end in the defeat of the odd faction out. That will allow Khmer Rouge to turn their guns on the other two.
>
> 'The US does have another choice. It could back a three-part coalition that includes the two non-Communist factions and the leaders in Phnom Penh but forcefully excludes the Khmer Rouge. Not unless and until the two non-Communist groups accept that alignment should Washington provide them with arms. The result would be a different three-against-one equation that might lead to the eventual disintegration of the Khmer Rouge. That would be a far happier fact of life for Kampuchea as well as a consequence for US policy of which Americans could, for a change, be proud.'[5]

The Cambodian Army

Officials in Phnom Penh claim that the armed forces total 200,000 men and women. The figure is suspect but even if it were true many of the soldiers are inadequately trained, badly equipped and poorly motivated militiamen. The regular army numbers only about 35,000, all conscripts apart from the career officers. Most troops are in not much better state of training than the militia irregulars.

The Vietnam army failed to teach their allies of the Cambodian army even the essentials of guerrilla warfare and counter-insurgency tactics. The soldiers were said to know little about camouflage and their officers little about co-ordinated unit movement in jungle.

It is possible that some Western observers have been misled into accepting Cambodia as having strong armed forces because, on paper, they seem powerful enough. The army claims to have 6 infantry divisions, 3 independent infantry regiments, 1 cavalry regiment, 4 tank battalions and 60 independent battalions, a mixture of infantry, reconnaissance, artillery, air defence and provincial militia units. In themselves these figures are reassuring but they can show nothing of the low state of morale.

The army has 80 tanks but all are old and unreliable. In any case, tanks would be useless in jungle terrain against the Khmer Rouge. The army claims to possess 'nearly 400' artillery pieces but the Vietnamese instructors gave the gunners little training in modern artillery practice. There is a shortage of qualified artificers to repair the guns. Only 12 helicopters are known to exist in the Cambodian forces yet these aircraft are essential in counter-insurgency operations.

The Vietnamese army, belatedly conscious of the Cambodian army's short-comings, agreed to leave behind a number of Vietnam advisers. They are being integrated into the Cambodian army to stiffen its morale. Helicopter landing sites and small airstrips have been established in rural areas, mostly near the Thai border, to allow a quick re-insertion of Vietnamese regulars should the military situation deteriorate.

Despite all its shortcomings, the Cambodian army defeated a Khmer Rouge force in battle in an area near Pailin. This clash, which took place late in 1988, was the first significant test for the Cambodians, without Vietnamese support.

The Vietnamese Army

Established in December 1944 with 34 guerrillas under Communist leader Ho Chi Minh and the slogan 'politics takes command', the Vietnamese army enjoys the reputation of having defeated three great powers, France, the United States and China.

In American-made films, the Vietnamese army is depicted as villainous and its troops are sometimes called the 'Prussians of Asia'. At home it is often criticised by young Vietnamese, mainly because many veterans abuse their party positions. Some prominent Vietnamese say that the next Communist Party chief must not be a military hero.

With a population of 63 million, Vietnam has a regular army of one million men and women, together with three million in the other services and paramilitary forces. *Per capita*, it is the world's largest military. Overall, it is fifth largest after those in China, the Soviet Union, the US and India.

The army faces large-scale demobilisation in 1990. By then not only will all soldiers be out of Cambodia but Hanoi hopes to have better relations with Peking. Roughly half of Vietnam's troops are stationed along the border with China.

General Tran Cong Man, editor of the army's newspaper, has conceded that demobilisation is going slowly and that all depends on how China acts towards Vietnam. The level of daily mortar shellings across the border is taken as an indicator of fluctuations in friendship. From about 900 a day in 1986, the number in 1989 was 150 a day.

The size of the army will eventually equal about one per cent of the population, roughly 630,000 soldiers. A large number of retirements and reductions are taking place in 1989–90. While the trimming goes on, paramilitary units are being improved.

The essential struggle in Hanoi over the military concerns the degree to which the party directs army affairs. Communist ideology, which demands the motivation of soldiers with the 'spirit of class hatred', has required tight control. Since 1988 the party leaders have loosened day-to-day authority in the economy and cultural fields but have changed little in military matters.

The military has begun a campaign to restore discipline and to renew goodwill with civilians. For instance, there are 'sworn brotherhood' pacts between soldiers and local youths. Soldiers have been advised to be self-critical about their behaviour.

Many articulate army men link their difficulties to the party's 'economic renovation'. They complain of poor living conditions. A senior officer, Lieutenant General Le Quang Hoa, writing in one of the army's journals, said: 'Our soldiers are not fed or clothed adequately, nor are there sufficient medicines. They live in cramped quarters which are hot in summer and chilly in winter. Their shoes, caps, blankets, sleeping mats and mosquito nets are either insufficient or in tatters'.

Lieutenant General Nguyen Quyet, the third-ranking military leader, warned in 1989 that the army had to seek ways of saving itself. Benefits provided by the party were deficient, while delays in demobilisation and poor living conditions had created unrest among younger officers who want promotions.

'The military's difficulties', he wrote, 'far exceed those of the country in general and are even more difficult for those who have left the army.'[6]

Propaganda, the British SAS and the Khmer Rouge

The KPLNF and ANS gained ground in Cambodia from September to December 1989 by making secret deals with local commanders of government forces. In addition, there was an element of psychological warfare as the ANS brought in salt, petrol and medicines to distribute to villagers and win their support. For its part, the Khmer Rouge embarked on a propaganda war against the Phnom Penh government by reporting the capture of a number of government positions. Such claims, some of them true, unsettle the government. Khmer Rouge broadcasts to the people are similar to those of the earlier bloody years. 'Parents and compatriots, please call on your children and husbands quickly to desert for home in order to stay alive.' Perhaps the most disturbing report in the late 1989 period was that the SAS had trained Cambodian guerrillas. While they were not members of Khmer Rouge, this organisation is the dominant force in the coalition and would benefit from the training given to the ANS and KPLNF.

References

1. Details of Sisiphon from Terry McCarthy, *The Independent*, London.
2. *Jane's Defence Weekly*, 24 June 1989.
3. Information from diplomats in Bangkok.
4. Son Sen was interviewed by Robert Karniol for *Jane's Defence Weekly*, 6 May 1989.
5. In *Time* Magazine, 1 May 1989.
6. Some of this information came from General Son Treng Cong Man, of the Vietnamese army.

The Central American Arena

In January 1987, when President Arias of Costa Rica put forward proposals in an effort to further the 'peace process' in Central America, it was hoped that at long last the region would move away from its crippling wars. The 'Arias Accord' became the Guatemala Peace Agreement on 7 August 1987. Signed by the Presidents of Costa Rica, El Salvador, Guatemala, Honduras and Nicaragua, it won much international support. Arias was awarded the 1987 Nobel Peace Prize.

A significant clause in the agreement reads: 'The Governments of the five Central American states request Governments of the region and Governments from outside the region, which are providing either overt or covert military, logistical, financial or propaganda support, in the form of men, weapons, munitions and equipment to irregular forces or insurrectionist movements, to terminate such aid. This is vital if a stable and lasting peace is to be attained in the region'.

The urgent request was aimed mainly at the Soviet Union, the United States, Cuba and Spain. Despite the Arias Accord, peace remained a long way off if only because of the bitter hostility between various groups in each country, especially Nicaragua, Guatemala and El Salvador.

The image of Washington's closest ally in Central America, Honduras, was tarnished in 1988 when an Amnesty International report disclosed that death squads linked to secret military groups were emerging, just as had happened in El Salvador and Guatemala. Honduras became the first country to stand trial before the Inter-American Court on Human Rights. The army was accused of harbouring death squads and 'causing the disappearance' of civilians. The most disturbing development was the murder of two prominent witnesses in the international court case.

For years Honduras was a reluctant party to President Reagan's campaign against Nicaragua's Marxist Sandinistas. While acting as host to the Contras of Nicaragua, in exchange for extensive military aid, Honduran leaders repeatedly and falsely denied that rebel bases existed within their borders. In March 1988 the Hondurans were compelled by Washington to halt a Sandinista cross-border attack aimed at Contra camps.

President Reagan's personal goals for Central America had not been fulfilled when his second term of office finished at the end of 1988. Still, the State Department professionals' more realistic long-term aim of a stable Pax America was progressing. The Sandinistas seemed more conciliatory towards opposition; the Salvadoran warlords appeared to have chosen ballots rather than bullets. The US attempt to drive the corrupt President Noriega from Panama failed initially but it showed that the Americans were determined to clean up Central America. Pan-

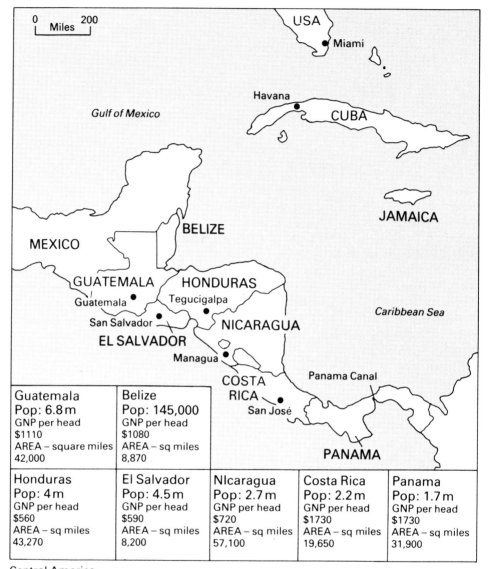

Central America

ama is not a part of Central America, as defined by the countries themselves, but it became a test case of the US's ability or inability to help the new political middle-class into power in the region.

Sometimes American intervention has seemed clumsy. For instance, in late July 1989, when the Central American Foreign Ministers held a meeting in Guatemala, Bernard Aronson, US Assistant Secretary of State for Inter-American affairs, flew to Guatemala to put pressure on them. The Foreign Ministers were preparing an agenda for a meeting of the five Central American presidents and Aronson had come to urge that they keep the Contras in being until the Nicaraguan elections in February 1990. In this way, it was hoped, the Sandinistas would be more likely to conduct fair elections.

The Aronson move angered Contra opponents in the US. Senator Christopher Dodd, chairman of the Senate Foreign Relations sub-committee, said that the administration's action, through Aronson, broke an agreement with Congress to support the peace process. If such pressure continued, Dodd warned, Congress might cut off Contra funds completely in November.

Certain misconceptions about the Central American conflict need to be identi-fied for students of this unhappy region. One of these—that economic pragma-tism has replaced Stalinist ideology—is mentioned in the analysis of the Contra war. Another is that the Soviet Union is no longer interested in giving heavy financial backing to bankrupt Marxist-Leninist regimes in the Third World. This is not so. On 14 February 1989 the Soviet Union delivered nine North Korean torpedo boats to the Sandinistas and during 1988 had provided another $515 million worth of military equipment. The truth seems to be that the Soviet govern-ment will continue to support its satellites militarily, while pressing the West to provide economic assistance.

Another misconception is that because of their own profound economic troubles, the Soviet Union, Cuba, East Germany and other Communist States have been co-operative in joining the efforts to end the ruinous wars of Angola and Afghanistan. Within this context, runs the simplistic view, the Central Amer-ican troubles can be resolved. In fact, it was effective and consistent Western aid, mostly American, to the Angolan and Afghan rebels that edged the Soviet leaders towards negotiated settlements.

An even more serious misconception is that Central American governments, whether of the Right or Left, are learning that economic solutions to problems are better than military solutions. This is not so. Whatever their precipitating causes, the conflicts in Central America are about power. Most of the belligerents would prefer to wreck their countries through war than give up power. Peaceful solutions through concession and compromise are considered weak solutions and, in any case, they are regarded as impermanent.

El Salvador Civil War

SLOW-MOTION VIETNAM

Background Summary

Commonly called a civil war, the conflict in El Salvador is more of a guerrilla conflict. Several organisations, all avowedly Communist, opposed the Right-wing government of Jose Napoleon Duarte of the Christian Democratic Party (CDP), which most foreign observers described as fascist. After three years of war, which began in 1980, Fidel Castro of Cuba induced the anti-government groups to amalgamate. The three bodies which resulted are:

1. The Democratic Revolutionary Front (FDR), an amalgam of revolutionaries and representatives of the Left-wing parties.
2. The United Revolutionary Directorate (URD), a 15-member war council of top guerrilla *commandantes*.
3. The Farabundo Marti National Liberation Front (FMLN), a co-ordinating organisational body.

Joaquin Villalobos of the People's Revolutionary Army (ERP) became the main guerrilla leader in 1983. Other important figures are: Shafik Jorge Handal, General Secretary of the Salvadoran Communist Party; Eduardo Cantaneda (alias Ferman Cienfuegos), leader of the Armed Forces of National Resistance (FARN); and Robert Roca, of the Central Americas Workers Revolutionary Party.

The Duarte regime was ruthlessly oppressive. In the period 1978-84 the murder total of his death squads was more than 50,000. Nevertheless, US financial aid enabled the army to increase its strength to 50,000. Even this was insufficient and in 1987 Duarte brought in conscription for 18-year-olds.

The army certainly transformed itself. It had been nothing more than a bunch of 12,000 brutal men. Under the influence of American army advisors, it became a professional counter-revolutionary force of 57,000 soldiers.

Some areas were declared free-fire zones. This meant that the army shot on sight anybody found there, and that they destroyed all human habitation, crops and animals. The purpose was to prevent guerrillas from finding shelter and food. By 1987 no more than 8,000 guerrillas were still fighting but, armed and supplied by Cuba and Nicaragua, they remained formidable.

Summary of the War in 1987-88

A powerful, conservative group of army officers of the Military Academy's 1966 graduating class, nicknamed the Tandona, became worried by the Arias peace plan, which they believed would enable Nicaragua to give more support to

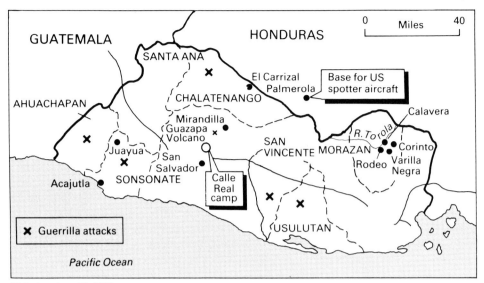

El Salvador Civil War

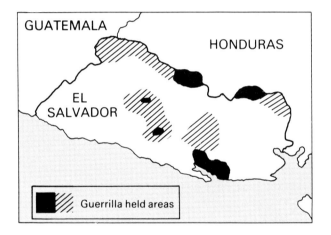

the guerrillas. They objected to the return from abroad, without arrest, of moderate rebel leaders who refused to renounce their alliance with the guerrillas.

Three international revolutionary groups were known to be operating in support of FMLN. They were *Alfaro Vive Carajo* from Ecuador, *Tupac Amaru* from Peru and *Bandera Roja* (Red Banner) from Venezuela. Elections were scheduled for 20 March and the FMLN groups worked to disrupt them. In the elections Duarte's CDP lost to the ultra-Rightist Republican Nationalist Alliance (ARENA). Under El Salvador's constitution the vote did not mean the end of CDP power but that Duarte would have to govern with a minority until the presidential elections of March 1989. A few months after the election Duarte flew to the US for treatment for liver cancer.

The War in 1989

The ARENA won a landslide victory in March but its presidential candidate, Alfredo Cristiani, could not be installed until May. In the meantime, ARENA and the dying Duarte clashed over several issues. The first came with the formation of a new paramilitary unit of 74 businessmen and middle-class professionals. This 'patriotic civil defence' unit was formed under the sponsorship of the army itself, with the aim of helping in the fight against increasing attacks by guerrilla 'urban commandos'.

The Catholic Church condemned the unit. It was, the bishops said, similar in form and function to the death squads of the early 1980s. On reflection, President Duarte agreed. He said that, as nominal commander-in-chief of the armed forces, he should have been consulted about the unit's formation. He instructed his Defence Minister to dissolve the group, on the grounds that it could 'generate a death squad structure'.

ARENA leaders argued that urban civil defence was essential. The unit was supposedly disbanded but continued to work undercover with the army. Everybody knew that within two months the new president would rescind Duarte's ban.

Duarte then made a second decision which infuriated ARENA and the Rightists. At the request of Archbishop Arturo Rivera y Damas, he informed the Defence Ministry that he was arranging for 109 wounded guerrillas in government hands to be flown to Mexico and then to Cuba and Europe for treatment. There was instant uproar. ARENA accused Duarte of freeing terrorists and the chief of police accused him of allowing 'assassins of the people' to leave the country. The Service chiefs objected because the rebel administration was under stress in protecting, moving and caring for wounded fighters and they did not want this strain to be eased.

The Attorney General, Mauricio Colorado, intervened and threatened to prosecute Duarte over the matter. Colorado is another extremist ARENA member, appointed in April after the murder of the previous Attorney General. Duarte backed down and found a formula for rescinding his humanitarian gesture, claiming that the rebels had machine-gunned the house of the head of the National Assembly, Ricardo Valdavieso.

The guerrilla leadership denied responsibility for the attack and claimed that ARENA had staged the machine-gunning, in which nobody was injured, to sabotage their arrangement with Duarte.

The rebels offered negotiations but ARENA chairman, Armando Calderon, rejected them. 'The party will never negotiate any action which is outside the law and the constitution', he said. President-elect Cristiani announced that he was prepared to negotiate only the terms of the rebels' surrender. FMLN then proposed to call off attacks on the members of the incoming cabinet and leaders of the armed forces, and to end their destruction of the electricity network and private business. All it wanted in return, it said, was for the government to put on trial ARENA's founder, Roberto D'Aubuisson, for the murder of Archbishop Oscar Romero in 1980. The ARENA leaders ignored the proposal.

The new government's chief of staff, Antonio Rodrigues Porth, and Rightist ideologue Edgar Chacon, were then assassinated. The guerrillas vehemently denied responsibility for these killings, while admitting to other murders. The two killings brought new laws. A person can now be gaoled for up to four years for passing out materials deemed 'subversive', 10–12 years for destruction of public property, and 5–10 years for providing information encouraging foreign countries to 'intervene in El Salvador's own affairs'.

President Cristiani defends the laws as providing appropriate punishment for violation of the laws of the Salvadoran democracy. Critics[1] of the new laws stress that there are already laws that punish violent acts. The danger of ARENA's reforms, they say, is that they create new categories of terrorism and subvert the public order, whose interpretation would be left to the ARENA-controlled judiciary and the military.

The 'Hearts and Minds' Campaign

In November 1988 the army began an operation to win the people over with food, medicine and promises of development projects. Command of this campaign was given to Colonel Rene Emilio Ponce, the most powerful field commander in the Salvadoran military. Ponce's theory was that the guerrillas could be hurt much more by deprivation of their base of support than by casualties in their own ranks.

The army's campaign was designed to manipulate people's behaviour. Any change to the miserable social conditions that perpetuate the war was incidental. The civic-action strategy, as Ponce calls it, continued into 1989 but without winning significant trust from the peasants. The officers and men assigned to the campaign are hindered by the army's longstanding reputation for brutality.

Ponce impressed some foreign observers with his enthusiasm for the 'hearts and minds' scheme. The army allowed journalists to accompany civic-action teams and one reported that he had seen an army officer dancing with a peasant woman, as rural farmers were handed free medicine.

The peasants present friendly smiles to the strangely unaggressive soldiers but some psychologists, monitoring the expected success of the campaign, reported that they were often afraid. The army has been known to use all kinds of dirty tricks to ferret out guerrilla sympathisers. Many peasants cannot read but they know that the affable Colonel Ponce was a member of a security unit which harboured death squads in the early 1980s. It is difficult for them to reconcile his record with his hand-shaking friendliness.

The Salvadoran Army

The military's structure makes it difficult to deal with inefficiency and corruption and virtually impossible to eradicate the human rights abuses. After graduation from the military academy, members of each class or *tanda* are promoted more on the basis of class affiliation than merit. Officers know that they will not be criticised, let alone disciplined, for their actions.

A Salvadoran journalist in exile said: 'You don't go into the army to be a hero but to get rich. Good looters are rewarded more than good fighters—and with so much US bounty there is plenty of scope for looting. The system condones corruption'.

Even blatant abuses escape punishment because no army court martial would find an officer guilty. Colonel Mauricio Staben was known to be implicated in a kidnapping ring, an attempted coup and various human rights violations but even he was not convicted. Staben is second-in-command of the 3rd Brigade at San Miguel.

As a result of American pressure, the army now has a façade of professional responsibility but dreadful atrocities still occur. A company of the Jiboa Battalion marched into the hamlet of San Francisco, rounded up 40 residents and read off a list of 11 names. These people, seven men and four women, were alleged to have 'collaborated with subversives'. One woman managed to convince the officer in charge that she was innocent but the other 10 were killed by grenade or bullet. One of the women victims of the slaughter had nine children, another had five.

The first official version was that the victims were guerrillas killed in battle. Pressed for more details, the Fifth Brigade commander, Colonel Chaves Cesares, explained that the 10 were killed in a guerrilla ambush. Colonel Ponce declared: 'It's illogical, it's inconceivable to imagine we would kill in cold blood today, that we are returning to those old times'.

However, the Supreme Court of Justice ordered the bodies to be exhumed and medically examined. The doctors found that seven of the victims had bullet holes and powder burn marks in the back of the head. Their verdict was that the peasants had been shot at very close range. A UN human rights observer who happened to be in El Salvador that week said: 'It might be inconceivable to Colonel Ponce, but these people were butchered by the army'.[3]

According to foreign diplomats, the military is split between senior officers of the rank of colonel and above, who follow American guidelines on counter-insurgency tactics, and young officers who see no solution to the problem other then slaughtering guerrillas.

Roman Catholic Church observers and aid workers in El Salvador disagree. They say that there is little to choose between senior and junior officers. A priest said: 'For all of them, this is total war. They will certainly try the hearts and minds approach but it is a cynical exercise. The officers' professional pride is hurt by their inability to wipe out the guerrillas so they kill the only targets they can find, people who are suspected of being sympathetic to the guerrillas.'[4]

The Cienfuegos Interview

It is rare for a Salvadoran guerrilla leader to give an interview, since it is only by being inaccessible that the five main rebel commanders stay alive. However, in Managua, while en route to Europe to present the rebels' cause, Ferman Cienfuegos of FARN felt safe enough on Nicaraguan territory to answer questions. His comments gave the best insight for some time into the attitudes and demands of the guerrilla opposition.

We are spreading the war from the countryside to the cities, thus we are advancing. We are conducting regional actions and even national actions. This is an integrated offensive. It's an offensive aimed at negotiation. We must gain the advantage in order to bring about negotiations.

The armed forces remain the real power in El Salvador. When they call the country a democracy and claim that problems are being resolved, this is not true. The political parties do not represent anybody. Political power is concentrated in the army. Nobody respects the government and nobody pays it any attention. Backing the military is the economic and military aid of the United States.

The FMLN is now stronger and there has to be a change from when Reagan was President in 1981. Our leadership has matured and the struggle in our country has also matured. We expect more pragmatism and more realism from the Bush administration. It has the opportunity to get to know the FMLN.

The Reagan administration approached the Central American conflict as one of ideological confrontation with the Soviet Union and from that perspective maintained that any advance of any revolutionary movement was an advance for Soviet expansionism. This made it more difficult to understand that the national security of the United States was not being put in danger. Our revolutions—the Sandinista, the Salvadoran, the Guatemalan—are not aimed against the US. They are actions of people to defend their own interests. We have never been a threat to the US, nor could we be.

None of the Central American revolutions are thinking about establishing foreign bases. Ideally, Central America would be a zone without military bases. This would include getting rid of the US bases. The problem is that the US has converted Central America into a region of US bases. For our part, we are not talking about countering this by establishing bases of another power. We have been criticised for using car bombs but you have to look at how many civilian casualties there have been. A car bomb can be exploded for propaganda and without any victims. Car bombs are not to cause victims but to gain notice. It is a way of dispersing propaganda.

An agreement can be reached. This depends mainly on the role and attitude of the US. If the US continues with military aid there can be no political situation to the conflict. But if the US moves towards aiding negotiation we believe that a political situation will be accelerated. The art of negotiating is making concessions. All sides must be willing to make concessions. The US has to be one of the sides.[5]

American Aid to El Salvador

Between 1980 and the end of the Reagan administration in 1988 the US poured nearly $43,000 an hour into El Salvador to bolster the country's fragile economy and defeat its Marxist guerrillas. For a country little bigger than the island of Fiji, the transfusion of $3bn has made El Salvador the fifth-largest recipient of US aid in the world. It has received 14 times as much as the Contras of Nicaragua.[6]

El Salvador is the US's largest counter-insurgency campaign since Vietnam. For a time it seemed that there might be gains. The guerrillas were unable to win the war but the army reduced its human rights abuses and civilian rule replaced half-a-century of military regimes.

In 1988–89 the war intensified. Death squads were again in action. The country had become hopelessly dependent on American aid and corruption and internal divisions were rife. Many educated Salvadorans were openly criticising the 'US Project'. San Salvador's mayor, Armando Calderon, a leader of ARENA, told a foreign journalist: 'The US has flattened El Salvador. It is not reactivating the economy or winning the war but maintaining a *status quo* of misery and hunger'. The significance of this assessment is that it comes from a hardline Rightist who has profited from US aid.

While Nicaragua consumed most Congressional debate, El Salvador continued to enjoy a largely unquestioned consensus. The reason was simple: it had embodied the hopes of the Reagan administration and Congress that US policy could prevent Leftist revolution by fostering a viable alternative to military rule.

For the new Reagan administration, El Salvador represented the first line of defence against Communism. This project was expected to rehabilitate the US's weak world image. In the days before President Reagan's inauguration, the FMLN launched a 'final offensive'. It failed, but US intelligence reported that Nicaragua was pushing arms to the rebels by land, sea and air.

Reagan said: 'We believe that the government of El Salvador is on the front line of a battle that is really aimed at the very heart of the Western Hemisphere and eventually us.' Within days, El Salvador, a land of only 5 million people, was a centrepiece of US foreign policy. It was the place to 'draw the line' on Communist revolution in the Third World.

'Nobody in the history of Central America had received support like Duarte to resolve his country's problems', according to a Western ambassador in the region. 'But the American administration never let him go. It was never willing to confront the army and oligarchy in the midst of what it saw as a life-or-death struggle with Communism.'

Caught in an endless cycle of war and economic crisis, Duarte could not stand up to the army, the oligarchy or the US Embassy. Gradually, he alienated the people who had elected him, so that he lost the election in March 1988.

The war had displaced 500,000 peasants and another 500,000 had fled the country. With the war consuming more than half of the national budget and its US aid, there was no money for welfare and the poor were in a desperate plight.

Despite the vast US aid, the war remained even more deadlocked in 1989 than it had been in 1980. The two sides have been brought together for discussions three times but neither side has moved an inch from their original basic negotiating position. The Marxist rebels want a share of power and a radical restructuring of a feudal society. The pathologically anti-Communist army wants the guerrillas to disappear or die.

Anarchy in San Salvador

Early in November 1989, Colonel Réné Emilio Poncé became Chief-of-Staff, a promotion that had been long expected. He announced that the High Command was willing to suspend all air force and artillery operations as part of a package of concessions in exchange for an agreement by the rebels to accept a government amnesty, to demobilise and begin the process of integration into the electoral process. 'Let us seek to suspend the violence,' he said.

Three weeks later the biggest rebel offensive of the war began. At least 3,500 guerrillas entered the expensive Escalon and San Benito districts of San Salvador. This was a deliberate attempt to discredit and humiliate the army and it worked. The army could not end the rebels' first urban offensive and the US government removed 282 dependants and other Americans from the embattled capital. The rebels announced a unilateral ceasefire to allow the evacuation of foreigners— and then continued their attacks on government installations. They burned several homes and sniped at government troops.

For the first time in the conflict, the insurgents fired a surface-to-air missile at an air force jet, an A-37 bomber. The rebels were not known to have heat-seeking SA-7s until this incident. The shoulder-held SA-7 is a Soviet-designed cousin of the more advanced US Stinger missile that greatly boosted the power of the Afghan Mujahideen. The Sandanista government of Nicaragua supplied the missiles to the FMLN, despite Daniel Ortega's personal promise to President Cristiani in August not to do so. Cristiani suspended relations with Nicaragua.

The military response to the FMLN's bold incursion was to send in tanks and helicopter gunships, which not only killed some rebels but killed or wounded many civilians. As the guerrillas took up positions in the Sheraton Tower, a detachment of US Green Berets, armed with M-16 rifles and grenade-launchers, barricaded themselves for a fight. However, the rebels appeared not to know that Green Berets were in the hotel.

The army searched Lutheran, Episcopal, Baptist and Catholic churches for arms and wounded guerrillas. Foreigners working with the churches were arrested and released only if they at once left El Salvador. Even the UN building in San Salvador was attacked, resulting in the withdrawal of UN staff to Guatemala. On 16 November a government death squad shot to death six Jesuit priests, apparently in the belief that they had rebel sympathies. Oxfam's director, Frank Judd, visited El Salvador in December 1989 and on his return said, 'All social morality and decent behaviour on the part of the authorities has collapsed.'

In the worst slaughter of the decade, the death toll at the end of November 1989 was 208 troops, 676 guerrillas and hundreds of civilians. Thousands more were wounded.

TIME Magazine's editorial comment on 4 December 1989 was outspoken. 'The causes of El Salvador's cycle of violence have not gone away. By key measurable standards, from *per capita* income to infant mortality, the country is worse off today. Insead of helping to win the peace, US money has in large part financed an unwinnable war. Washington should rethink its relationship with a democratically elected government that cannot control fanatic right-wing elements in the armed forces. El Salvador's armed forces, nourished by American dollars, bear primary responsibility for the country's scandalous human rights record. Washington should cut off military aid unless travesties like the killing of the six Jesuits are stopped.'

References

1. These critics include priests of the Roman Catholic Church. The Church's two offices, Tutela Legal and Socorro Juridico, are regarded by all UN bodies as the most reliable sources of information from El Salvador.
2. It is a measure of exiles' fear of death squads that this journalist wishes to remain anonymous. He claims that prominent Salvadorans living abroad have been murdered by death squads.
3. John Carlin of *The Independent*, London.
4. In conversation with the author, London, 30 January 1989.
5. The interview was given to Chris Norton, a specialist writer on Central America, and first published in *Christian Science Monitor*, 12 December 1988. Cienfugos' aides then reprinted the interview and widely distributed it, so there can be no doubt that they were endorsing Norton's report as correct. I have presented only a summary of what was said.
6. US State Department figures.

Major aspects of the War discussed in War Annual 3:
    The Villalobos interview
    American role in El Salvador

Guerrilla War in Guatemala

UNREST FINDS A VOICE

Background Summary

Since 1954 Guatemala has known nothing but upheaval and war. The difficulties were most acute during 1982–83 when President Rica Montt was in power. The army massacred 10,000 unarmed civilians for alleged complicity with the guerrillas, who want land reform and wealth redistribution. Amnesty International estimates that 120,000 civilians have been killed since 1960. In 1983, Mejia Victores succeeded Montt and continued the oppression. His main targets were Roman Catholic priests, journalists, academics and labour leaders. In 1985 the four hard-pressed guerrilla groups formed a coalition known as the Guatemalan National Revolutionary Unity (GNRU). While GNRU's membership was probably no more than 3,500 they were well led and well armed. The most notable leader was Rodrigo Asturias, chief of the *Organizacion del Pueblo en Armas* or Organisation of People in Arms (ORPA). Asturias made so many successful attacks on army bases and supply depots that the army, 33,000-strong in 1986, responded by increased death squad activity.

In 1986 Vinicio Cerezo became the first civilian president for 32 years but General Victores remains as chief of the armed forces. He improved Montt's 'development poles', or model villages, into which peasants were forced to move. Each village is dominated by a fortified army post to prevent guerrillas from meeting the peasants.

All males between the ages of 15 and 55 are required to take part in civil defence patrols for 24 hours each week. In Guatemala's 108,889 square miles the guerrillas are easily able to hide. In exceptional operations in 1986 they sank a Zodiac-type patrol boat at Puerto Quetzal naval base and destroyed a Bell helicopter at an air base at Coban. Army patrols crossed the Mexican border to attack Guatemalans in refugee camps.

Summary of the War in 1988

The model villages scheme was pressed still further in 1988 and the activity of peasants was increasingly restricted. An insistent indoctrination programme, which the UN Human Rights Commission calls 'vicious brainwashing', aims to eradicate support for the guerrillas. Roman Catholic priests are prevented from entering the villages since the army believes them to be in sympathy with the guerrillas.

On 11 May 1988 Cerezo acted decisively against an army coup attempt. Troops loyal to him intercepted several truckloads of rebel soldiers, many of whom were later shot. Armed forces strength reached 40,500 in 1988 and the government

Guerrilla War in Guatemala

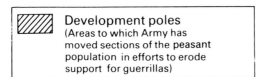
Development poles
(Areas to which Army has
moved sections of the peasant
population in efforts to erode
support for guerrillas)

claimed to possess a 'territorial militia' of 725,000 men, a vast force from a total population of 8,850,000. In contrast, the guerrillas' strength—the government claimed—was down to 2,000.

The War in 1989

Early in the year the official military spokesman, Colonel Luis Arturo Issacs Rodriguez, announced that the Leftists' rebel force had been reduced through capture, death or defection to 800 fighting men. There were many indications that this was a falsely low figure.

The army began 1989 with a systematic campaign to cripple the new civil rights organisation, the Council of Ethnic Communities, or *Runujel Junum*, headed by a rural peasant leader, Amilcar Mendez Urizar. Known by its Spanish acronym CERJ, the group has encouraged more than 10,000 peasants in 250 villages to exercise their constitutional right not to serve in the 'voluntary' civil defence patrols.[1]

With 790,000 men in the ranks, the CERJ campaign had not seriously depleted the patrols. That the CERJ exists at all, however, is viewed by General Victores as an affront. On television he produced a man of dubious reputation named Miguel Angel Reyes Melgar, who claimed to be an ex-guerrilla, to accuse Amilcar Urizar of being a rebel in disguise.

Four CERJ members, abducted by soldiers from their homes, have not been seen since April 1989. President Cerezo promised to investigate the affair but no report was made. The men are believed to have been killed. Urizar has continued his campaign against conscription and has remained relatively safe from arrest only because of his new fame.

Army officers tour the villages showing frightening videos of atrocities in Vietnam to audiences of peasants who are told: 'This could happen to you. Only the civil defence patrols protect you from horrors such as these'.[2]

Certainly the patrols play a crucial role in ensuring the army's success against the rebels. Not only do they serve as fighting troops but they help the army control the countryside and deter independent rural organisations such as CERJ.

In the highlands, where most of Guatemala's four million Indians live, the army rules with an iron fist. Peasants from the area complain to Urizar about forced conscription to the patrols. The Catholic Church says that many boys of 13 and 14 are forced to do a day's duty each week.

Colonel Rodriguez argues persuasively that the patrols are an obstacle for the guerrillas. 'By organising peasants to leave the patrols Urizar is collaborating with subversion', he has said. 'We have to increase our force not to destroy CERJ but to help people avoid going down that road.'

Urizar's argument is that the patrols are economically ruinous to the villages, which cannot afford to maintain the fortified posts thrust upon them. If peasants were not coerced or inveigled into the civil defence patrols, he said, the 800,000-strong force would dwindle to a few thousands.

It is likely that, should really large numbers of peasants withdraw from the scheme, the government would introduce a compulsory service. The army was convinced, in 1989, that it at last had the guerrillas on the run. This seemed to be the view of foreign backers of the government, notably fundamentalist

Protestant sects from the United States. One in three Guatemalans is affiliated to one of the 200 Protestant denominations, many of which encourage docility and blind obedience to government.

American Arms for Guatemala

For the first time in more than a decade American arms were sold to Guatemala. In 1977 the US Congress had forbidden the sale or donation of lethal equipment to the Guatemalan police and armed forces because of gross violation of human rights in that country.

The 1989 sale was a commercial venture, without assistance from the US Military Assistance Programme, which does provide equipment considered non-lethal such as aircraft parts, communications equipment and training in the US. The sale, by Colt Industries, was of 20,000 M16 rifles at a value of $12 million. Most of them were the standard infantry version, the M16A2. Also included were small quantities of commando models, shorter rifles with a collapsible stock.[3]

Diplomats in Guatemala City say that the M16 was modified for the Guatemalan troops. This version will not fire more than three shots in a burst, thus preventing the soldiers from firing off their full magazines. 'These troops seem constitutionally unable to fire just a few rounds', a military attaché said. 'Discipline has no effect whatever. The men are like dangerous children with weapons and spray bullets around indiscriminately.'

The Colt sale was a blow to Israeli arms suppliers who had made the Galil rifle Guatemala's standard combat weapon since the late 1970s. In 1984 the Israelis assisted the Guatemalans to establish a munitions and spare parts factory near Coban. They expected that it would service and later assemble Galils. The factory did not have the technical ability to produce parts for the Galil and the nation is in such a poor economic state that it cannot invest the necessary money in the plant. Colt already sells large quantities of the M16 to Honduras and El Salvador.

The Guatemala sale brought opposition from unexpected quarters. The dissident 'Officers of the Mountains', who had earlier staged a coup, has publicised its opposition to the sale. The Officers of the Mountains claim that $1 million was paid in illegal commissions to certain high-ranking Guatemalan army officers. Even loyalist serving officers criticise the sale on the grounds that Israel is a more reliable ally than the US, where a political row could always result in a ban on parts for the M16s.

Targeting the Indians

A cornerstone of the army's counter-insurgency programme is the campaign to induce the Indians living in the mountainous areas controlled by the 'Guerrilla Army of the Poor' to defect. The Guatemalan army has itself to blame for the Indians being hostile in the first place. In 1981 troops burned down all 49 villages in a region known as the Ixil Triangle. About 60,000 of the 82,000 Ixil Indians fled to Mexico but the others took to the mountains, where they supported the rebel guerrillas. Fear of the army kept them there, despite their hunger and miserable living conditions.

The army set up a base in the Ixil centre of Nebaj. From here it has persuaded and sometimes forced refugees to come down from the mountains. Army leaflets and loudspeakers invite the Indians to 'come down for steaming pots of good food and the welcome of your families'. Most peasants are not convinced of the army's sincerity but prefer voluntary return to being captured. 'Reorientation' as a prisoner is much harsher than as a 'repatriate'.

In Nebaj it has fed them into a 'reorientation centre', actually an anti-rebel indoctrination centre. After this, they are relocated in one of the nine new, strictly-controlled model villages. According to army figures, in 1987 1,200 refugees returned and 4,100 in 1988.

The army's theory was that guerrilla morale would fall as their pool of civilian support dwindled. In fact, the guerrillas have fought harder. In one fire-fight, the rebels sustained a five-hour clash with the army. Army casualties were still high in 1988; estimates vary from 1,200 to 3,000.

Some of the Indians have agreed to go back to the combat zone with soldiers to convince other families to come down—and to pinpoint rebel camps. Most of the men now patrol the villages to protect them from the very rebels they once helped.[4]

At one time the conflict in Guatemala was known as the 'dirtiest war'. Dirty and vicious it is, but now no more so than the wars in El Salvador and Sri Lanka.

References

1. CERJ is described by Roman Catholic Church sources as 'sincere and genuine—an honest attempt to find an opposing voice to the welter of official propaganda'.
2. The videos show mutilation of old men, women and children and the destruction of settlements. The charges against American Lieutenant William Calley, found guilty of atrocities against civilians, are stressed and illustrated. The films are horrific but not invented.
3. US Ministry of Finance information. This Ministry, rather than the Defence Ministry, handles such deals when the US government is involved.
4. Press sources in Guatemala City.

Nicaragua—The Contra War

BITTER WAR, UNEASY PEACE

Background Summary

Augusto Sandino, an army General who rebelled against the corrupt Somoza family which ruled Nicaragua for decades, is the source of the name *Sandinistas* for the people who follow his principles. Sandino was assassinated in 1933. After a war in which 45,000 people died, Anastasio Somoza fled the country in 1979 and was later murdered.

The junta which gained control was led by radical Left-wingers Daniel Ortega, his brother Humberto and Thomas Borge. Their Sandinista National Liberation Front (FSLN) is Marxist-Leninist and élitist. It has a nine-man Directorate, an 80-member committee and a party membership pegged at 5,000.

Immediately after taking office in 1981, President Reagan cut all US aid to Nicaragua on the grounds that Nicaraguan arms were reaching Communist insurgents in El Salvador. The CIA began a covert war against Nicaragua, which was itself strengthened by Soviet-bloc weapons. The US provided money and arms to the Contras, the name given to the Right-wingers opposing the Sandinistas. The Contras, with 15,000 men under arms in 1984, were in several groups. The most important, the Nicaraguan Democratic Force (NDF), was led by Colonel Enrique Bermudez, a former Somoza officer, and operated in the north. In the south, the Democratic Revolutionary Alliance (ARDE) was led by Eden Pastora Gomez, 'Commander Zero', who had 3,000 fighters.

The Contras were vastly outnumbered by the army. Humberto Ortega, as Defence Minister and nominal commander-in-chief, in 1984 had 60,000 regular and 120,000 reservists. The army restricted Contra activity to the mountains, river valleys and coastal swamps. Soviet-bloc activity increased and the number of Cuban advisers grew to 7,000. In 1985 Ortega forcibly moved 50,000 peasants from the northern provinces to restrict the Contras still further.

Miami, Florida, was the Contras' political and financial capital. Saudi Arabia, the Gulf States and Portugal backed them with money. In 1987 about 1,000 guerrillas, after a 45-day trek across the mountain ranges, pushed back the army and killed forestry workers and co-operative farmers. In retribution the Sandinista army raided neighbouring Honduras, where the Contras have their camps.

In 1987 major clashes took place within Nicaragua, with the Contras winning battles at Siuna, Rosita and Bonanza. They also used US shoulder-fired Redeye missiles to shoot down Sandinista helicopters. Despite Contra successes, the government held the balance of power and several changes occurred in the leadership of the United Nicaraguan Opposition (UNO). The Sandinistas undercut the Contras still further by rescinding the ban on the opposition daily newspaper, *La Prensa*, and allowing banished priests to return.

64

Areas where Contras operated

Main Contra base camp

Las Trojes

HONDURAS

Tegucigalpa

Wiwili

Recent Contra infiltration routes

Coco R.

Caribbean Sea

Matagalpa

La Trinidad NICARAGUA

Bluefields

Managua Lake Nicaragua

Monkey Point

Pacific Ocean

0 Miles 80

El Castillo

San Juan del Norte

COSTA RICA

Nicaragua: Sandinistas versus Contras

JAMAICA CUBA HAITI DOMINICAN REP.

BELIZE HONDURAS Caribbean Sea

GUATEMALA EL SALVADOR NICARAGUA COSTA RICA

VENEZUELA GUYANA SURINAM FR. GUIANA

PANAMA COLOMBIA

ECUADOR

PERU

BRAZIL

BOLIVIA

PARAGUAY

CHILE

URUGUAY

ARGENTINA

Summary of the War in 1988

Recovering from setbacks, the Contras penetrated deep into Nicaragua. At Rama Road, in the central province of Chontales, they killed 200 Sandinista soldiers and wounded 300. However, following the Guatemala (Arias) Accord, the Contras had to negotiate with the Sandinistas. This process caused tensions among the Contra leaders. In March, the rebel leaders signed a truce and agreed in principle to move their men into ceasefire zones inside Nicaragua by 30 May. Instead, they withdrew into Honduras. In March, the US Army flew a airborne brigade into Honduras as a show of support for the Contras.

By now, the Contra command was riven with discord and feud. Enrique Bermudez was elected to the seven-man directorate. A group of moderates, led by Alfredo Cesar, split from the Bermudez group. It seemed that as an effective opposition force the Contras would lose all credibility.

The War in 1989

The eight-year war ground to a halt when the US Congress cut off military aid late in 1988. The conflict had exacted a high price, with 23,000 people killed and twice that number injured. Damage to property was estimated at $12 billion. *Hurricane Joan* added to the nation's problems, causing $800 million worth of damage. On top of that, the US trade embargo initiated by President Reagan in 1985 has paralysed the economy.

After 10 years rule by the FSLN the misery that characterised life under the Somoza regime has not abated. The single success of the FSLN is holding on to power. Alfredo Cesar, having left the Contras to return to Managua as opposition leader, said: 'The Sandinistas are good fighters, but they have not made the transition from being guerrillas with guns to a government with laws'.[1]

In mid-1989 inflation was 36,000 per cent (10,000 per cent in 1988) and the national currency, the cordoba, was virtually useless. Public transportation barely existed. Diplomats in Managua say that much of the country's plight rests with the Sandinistas' administrative incompetence and ideological intransigence. Loans and credits from once-generous benefactors, such as West Germany and France, dried up as the regime failed to adopt basic political and economic freedoms. Disillusionment became clear during President Ortega's fund-raising tour in Europe, during April-May 1989. He sought $250 million but returned with only $32 million.

The FSLN remains firmly in power because of the unshaken support of the Sandinista People's Army. It is a formidable, well run and well led force. During the Contra war its leaders became proficient in tactics. All ranks attend compulsory political education classes. The FSLN had promised to root out corruption but several ambassadors have reported to their governments that the party has developed a cadre of top leaders who live much better than anyone else. As the regime began its second decade it was almost totally isolated.

Hoping to fare better with President Bush than President Reagan, Daniel Ortega offered fresh promises of reform, such as ending the confiscation of private property and holding fair elections in 1990. The Bush administration had bowed to Congress's refusal to continue financing the Contras but it has not been impressed with Ortega's reforms.

What troubles the Nicaraguan opposition is that the Sandinista directorate, which is not elected or answerable to anyone, makes the most important decisions in the country and all in total secrecy. In their defence, the Sandinistas can cite their majority in the National Assembly won in the last elections. But President Ortega has also said repeatedly that if the Sandinistas were to lose an election they would give up office but not power.

The real reason behind the Sandinistas' reluctance to relinquish power is that the Right-wing opposition will not accommodate themselves to what is essentially a social revolution. The Sandinistas believe that there is a faction that would actively try to overturn the tenets of the revolution if it won an election.

Officially, the Contra war is over but the Contras themselves have not been disbanded. Large numbers remained in camps and under training in 1989. While Contra politicians were ready, like Augusto Cesar, to return to Nicaragua and engage in a political life, the hardliners, such as Colonel Bermudez and others, prefer to live off American 'sustenance money'. Brooklyn Rivera, a Miskito Indian leader, waged war against the Sandinistas long after most other Nicaraguan leaders had either given up the fight or joined with Colonel Bermudez.

Disturbingly, Nicaragua continues to arm and train foreign insurgents from Guatemala to Argentina. Also the Sandinistas are continuing to increase the size and strength of their armed forces, regardless of global trends.[2]

US policy on Nicaragua has been slow to take definite shape. A key element appears to be persuading the Soviet Union to press the Sandinistas to undertake democratic reform. The Bush administration may be unwittingly relying on a set of wishful myths regarding the nature of the changes affecting the Communist world.[3] For instance, it is a myth that economic pragmatism has replaced Stalinist ideology as the driving force behind Communist intentions.

Why the Contras Failed

The Contras won some battles and successfully harassed the Nicaraguan army but failed to win the long war. Yet, in so heavily supporting the Contras, the Reagan administration believed that they could win. The CIA, with its massive covert aid, predicted that they would win. But such a victory was never remotely possible. The main reasons for the Contra failure are these:

Lack of unity Political divisions within the Contra command adversely affected the conduct of the war. There were times when field commanders not only failed to co-operate with one another but actually refused to do so.

Limited field of operations The Contras wanted to take the active war into the urban areas but in this they failed totally. They could not safely extend their lines of communication such long distances and they had no expectation of popular support in the cities. While they showed their ability to win major skirmishes in the more remote regions, these victories had no political effect in Managua. Often they were not even reported there.

Contra atrocities Both sides were guilty of atrocities with the Sandinista army more culpable in the number of crimes committed against civilians. However, the Contras needed all the support they could get in villages and rural areas. They alienated much of it by killing people they suspected of informing the government about their activities or of working for the government. The killing of forestry workers discredited the Contra cause.

Lack of air support The Contras did not develop an air arm and without direct US help probably could not have done so. In contrast, the Sandinista forces had, in 1988, 12 helicopter gunships and 50 other helicopters. In addition, they had 16 combat aircraft as well as 11 transport planes. The advantage which the aircraft gave the commanders in reconnaissance rapidity of movement and attack from the air was considerable. While the Contras lost few men to air attack, they felt constantly threatened and vulnerable. Despite their great skill in movement, they were frequently spotted from the air while moving towards attack areas.

Lack of reinforcement From 1985 the Contras lacked an adequate intake of recruits. Many young Nicaraguans, who might have joined the conflict in the earlier years, had now decided that the Contras could not win. The government was also successful with its propaganda campaign to induce men not to join the Contras. Defections were a constant worry for the Contra commanders.

And the War Begins Again

On 1 November 1989, President Ortega announced the end of a 19-month ceasefire and said that a new military offensive against the Contras had already begun. Ortega said that the decision had been forced on Nicaragua by continuing US support for the Contras. Certainly, throughout October the Contras mounted a series of attacks against military and civilian targets in violation of the ceasefire.

According to Ortega, the Contras were determined to sabotage any effort to have them demobilised and were intent on wrecking the Nicaraguan elections planned for February 1990. At the beginning of November the Defence Ministry published details of increasing Contra violence. The rebels had killed more than 700 people since the ceasefire came into effect and during October 1,500 Contras had infiltrated from Honduras. The Contras themselves claimed in November to have 6,000 fighters in Nicaragua.

The Bush administration condemned Ortega's action in beginning a new offensive and denied that it had considered re-arming the Contras. Conservatives in Washington called on President Bush to give the Contras the means to defend themselves but although the Senate voted unanimously to condemn Ortega's decision the chances of Congress passing legislation to renew military aid for the Contras was slim.

References

1. In a statement to a European journalist, 3 January 1989.
2. Diplomatic sources in Managua.
3. The opinion of Max Primorac, research fellow at the Council for Inter-American Security.

Chad and Libya

A CEASE-FIRE HOLDS—JUST

Background Summary

Colonel Gaddafi of Libya interfered in the affairs of his neighbour, Chad, after his coup in Tripoli, in 1969. There was already a civil war in Chad. Hisseine Habré and his *Forces Armées du Nord* (FAN) opposed Goukouni Oueddei, leader of *Forces Armées Populaires* (FAP). In 1973 Libya backed Habré and occupied the 60-mile wide Aouzou Strip. The opportunist Gaddafi switched his support to Queddei when he founded the *Gouvernement d'Union Nationale de Transition* (GUNT). In June 1982, FAN troops captured the capital, N'djamena, and Queddei fled.

When Habré formed a government, Gaddafi supported GUNT in its capture of Faya-Largeau, May 1983. France, the US, Sudan and Egypt supported FAN. Gaddafi staked his claim to part of Chad by establishing six bases. In December 1986, he launched an offensive to capture Fada and Zouar but Chadian troops routed the better-armed Libyans at Bardai. In January 1987, the Chadian National Armed Forces (FANT) defeated the Libyans at Fada and recaptured Zouar. Queddei's GUNT disintegrated. On 13 September 1987 the Organisation of African Unity (OAU) negotiated a cease-fire but nobody expected Gaddafi to observe it fully.

Summary of the War in 1988

Gaddafi strengthened his hold on the Aouzou Strip, building fortifications and bringing in more tanks and anti-aircraft batteries. Chadian units captured Libyan soldiers in the Sudanese region of Darfur and claimed a military victory. Gaddafi responded by announcing that there were Chadian prisoners in Libya and displayed them for the Press. In fact, this was a deception. He merely showed off men who might reasonably be taken as Chadian.

Sporadic fighting occurred, mostly small-scale and in remote border areas. On several occasions Gaddafi trucked his Islamic Legion of foreign mercenaries to the Chad border and crossed it with much fanfare and publicity. These border crossings were 'symbolic warfare', the President announced, to show that he could take the offensive at any time.

On the whole, Gaddafi was temporarily satisfied to end the war with possession of the Aouzou Strip. He was conciliatory towards his North African neighbours, especially Egypt. The war showed that while Libya had enormous advantage in military manpower and *matériel*, the Chadian commanders showed superior tactical skill. Also, Chad troops were more effective in close combat than the Libyan soldiers.

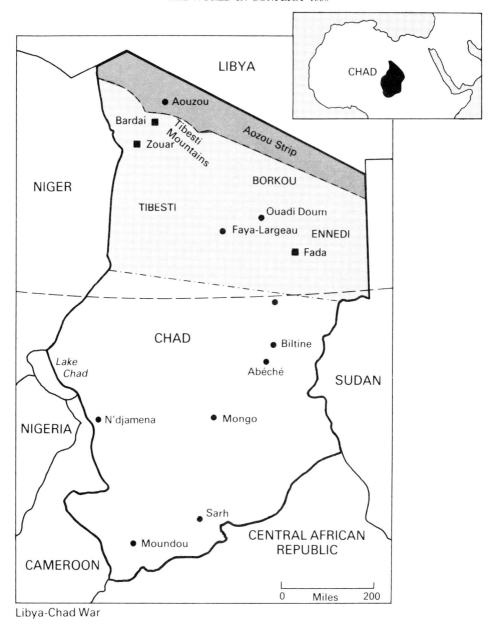

Libya-Chad War

Annexed by Libya

Chad Rebuilds after 25 Years of War

Chad's wars cost the country 20 years of economic development. In 1989 the country was among the 10 poorest nations and was surviving on international aid. Military spending swallowed up a quarter of the published budget. Unknown to the outside world, Chad has a second, unpublished, defence budget. President Habré lives in expectation of a further Libyan attack and spends massive amounts of money on arms to protect Chad against it.

The World Bank stated, in August 1989, that Chad needed $400 million just to repair roads. Outside N'djamena, there are only 25 miles of paved highway in a country the size of France and Spain combined. 'For the next 10 years Chad needs generous aid to reach the level of other Sahelian countries', according to Horst Scheffold, the World Bank director in Chad.

Despite Chad's many problems brought on by war, several foreign analysts believe that it could develop into a much more prosperous nation. The discovery of oil around Lake Chad will lessen its dependence on imports from Nigeria and Cameroon.

It may be some years before foreign investors are convinced that Gaddafi will not inflict another ruinous war on Chad. Libya and Chad restored a form of diplomatic relations late in 1988 but peace talks are only in an early stage.

Prisoners in Chad

Libyan prisoners in Chad are Habré's bargaining counters. More than 2,000 Libyans are held in remote compounds and denied contact with international organisations. Most of the prisoners were captured in the spectacular Chadian thrust in late 1987 to end Libya's occupation of northern Chad. About 5,000 Libyans were killed in that operation.

On 1 July 1989, Habré said: 'It is a real dialogue of the deaf. Libya wants only one thing, to get its prisoners of war back. They do not even want to discuss the rest, hence the stalemate in the talks. But it is a simple matter. Gaddafi should hand back the Aouzou Strip and stop interfering in Chad's politics.'

The Chadians refuse to publish a list of prisoners, a tactic designed to heighten anxiety in Libya and increase pressure on Gaddafi. Gaddafi's problem is that he has few friends willing or able to influence Chad to free his soldiers. Even if he did, it is unlikely that they could move Habré, whose only leverage over Gaddafi is the captives.

US–Libyan Air Conflict

In January 1989 American and Libyan fighter aircraft fought a strange battle over the southern Mediterranean, 70 miles from Tobruk. The incident is included in this book to show that such incidents, while not constituting war, are indeed warlike and can lead to larger conflict.

The eruption came in the dying days of the Reagan administration. It was applying pressure on Gaddafi, and on US allies, to prevent the production in Libya of poisonous gases that could be used in chemical warfare. The US insisted that a huge chemical plant at Rabta, 50 miles south-west of Tripoli and ringed with anti-aircraft batteries, was primarily intended to produce mustard gas and chemical nerve agents.

Two US Navy F-14 (Tomcat) fighters were protecting the aircraft carrier, USS *John F. Kennedy*, in its Mediterranean manoeuvres. Flying at 20,000 feet, the F-14s picked up two Libyan MiG-23s (Floggers) on their radar screens at 11.57 am on Wednesday 4 January. The F-14s turned away from the approaching aircraft, a signal that the American pilots were not seeking a fight. The Libyan pilots moved abruptly to return to a nose-to-nose line up with the Americans.

In a second evasive manoeuvre, the F-14s dived to 3,000 feet. This gave the US fliers a tactical advantage. Their radar could now look up for a clear view of the approaching Libyan planes. The less sophisticated radars on the Libyan aircraft had to contend with the clutter of the sea. At 11.59 am the radar intercept officer behind the lead Tomcat pilot armed his plane's long-range Sparrow missiles and the short-range Sidewinder missiles. The US pilots made three more efforts to shake off the Libyans. On each occasion, observers in a US Navy E-20 control plane flying nearby heard the Libyan ground controller order the MiG pilots to revert to potential collision courses.

At 12.01 pm the lead F-14 pilot reported: 'Bogeys have jinked back at me again for the fifth time. They're on my nose now, inside of 20 miles'. He launched two Sparrows and both missed the Libyan aircraft. Instead of fleeing, the MiGs continued to close. One was shot down with a Sparrow, the other a Sidewinder. The two Libyan pilots parachuted into the sea, from where they were rescued.

Some analysts, both American and European, suggested that Gaddafi may have deliberately engineered the incident in the expectation that world opinion would turn against the US. This is what happened. Gaddafi was portrayed as the 'innocent victim'. At the time, 142 nations were about to meet in a five-day conference in Paris to discuss means of halting the spread of chemical weapons.

Following the purchase of Soviet Su-24 'Fencer D', Libya now has a potent anti-shipping capability. While the Fencer in Libyan service may not be equipped with anything more powerful than conventional iron bombs, the aircraft is capable of carrying a combination of weapons ranging from the AS-7 Kerry to the AS-14 Kedge medium-range air-to-surface weapons. Together with Fencer's precision naval-attack avionics, Kerry and Kedge would give Libya a previously unmatched capability to strike US shipping in any future skirmish off the North African coast.

In mid-1989, France relaxed its 1983 embargo of defence equipment to Libya. Libya already has French all-terrain vehicles, trucks, tank transporters, light arms, anti-tank missiles, mortars, communication equipment, land-based radar, missile patrol boats, amphibious landing-craft, combat aircraft, transport planes and air-defence missiles. The easing of restrictions means that Gaddafi can buy much-needed parts for this equipment.

References

War Annual 3 carried a full description of the armed forces of Libya and Chad.

Colombia Civil War

STILL FAINT HOPE OF PEACE

Background Summary

The conflict in Colombia began as a struggle between liberals and conservatives. This soon brought in the Colombian Revolutionary Armed Forces or *Fuerzas Armadas Revolucionarias Colombianes* (FARC), the military wing of the Communist Party. The pro-Cuban Army of National Liberation (ELN) and the Maoist People's Liberation Army (EPL) joined in the war in 1960. A group known as 19th April Movement, but called M-19, entered the conflict in 1973. With Leftist-Nationalist-Castroite ideologies, M-19 soon became the most powerful fighting force. Workers' Self-Defence, known in Colombia as ADO, joined the guerrilla war in 1982. By the end of 1985 more than 40,000 people had died in the war.

Virgilio Barco, a liberal who became President in 1986, promised peace but could not deliver it. He also offered amnesties, pardons, scholarships and small-business loans to the rebels, but found no applicants.

ELN displaced M-19 as the most formidable group and changed its name to National Guerrilla Co-ordination (CNG). Led by a former Roman Catholic priest, Father Perez, it became powerful enough to give instructions to M-19, EPL and the other groups. The Patriotic Union, a Right-wing organisation of government officials and supporters, became ENG's main target and 500 of its members were killed.

FARC, under Manuel Marulanda, remained the most powerful organisation in rural areas. The multiple wars were made even more complex by the private armies owned by the drug barons.

Summary of the War in 1988

The leading drug baron, Pablo Escobar Gaviria, declared 'total war' on President Barco, his government and the armed forces. One of the many outrages committed by Gaviria was the murder of the Attorney-General, Carlos Hoyos Jiminez. In 1988 the rule of law broke down. Death squads killed 700 members of the Patriotic Union before the elections of March 1988.

A new group, calling itself the American Battalion, clawed its way into the conflict in 1988. Financed by North Korea and Cuba, its members are Bolivian, Ecuadoran, El Salvadoran, Panamanian, Peruvian and Nicaraguan Sandinistas.

It became clear that Marulanda and Perez were waiting for anarchy to prevail so that they could mount a successful coup. Marulanda said that he wanted 'to cleanse Colombian society by killing all the men of violence'. The death squads and private armies are not traditional guerrilla forces, as are FARC and CNG,

Colombia Guerrilla and Narcotics War

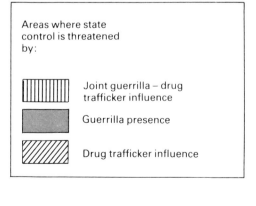

Areas where state
control is threatened
by:

Joint guerrilla – drug
trafficker influence

Guerrilla presence

Drug trafficker influence

COLOMBIA

SOUTH
AMERICA

but in 1988 they were probably responsible for more deaths than the FARC and CNG guerrillas combined.

War Control in Uraba

At the end of 1988 General Luis Armando Arisa Cabrales was sent to Uraba, Colombia's north-eastern banana-growing region, to bring peace to one of the most unsettled regions. With his HQ in Aportado, Cabrales set out to show all the warring factions that the government, through the regular army, was in control.

President Barco chose Cabrales for the job because of his reputation as a military leader who could not be frightened, unlike many of his army colleagues. He also has a reputation for impartiality. The President hoped that if Cabrales could succeed in Uraba he might establish a model for similar operations elsewhere.

The region, with a population of 300,000, was well chosen to test any general. The EPL and FARC have long been established there. In addition, the powerful labour unions are able to paralyse banana production. Assassination of union members and Leftists is routine. Right-wing death squads, backed by the drugs mafia and military officials, kill peasants and farm hands, mainly to intimidate the populace.

Cabrales quickly showed that he was prepared to be tough; according to some sources, he has been too heavy-handed.[1] When guerrillas kidnapped 22 soldiers and police, Cabrales began a military operation to recover them. Helicopter attacks and military ground patrols brought terror to several villages. The show of force apparently influenced the guerrillas to negotiate and the 22 prisoners were released.

Cabrales' major problem is the peasants' distrust of the military. Peasant leaders say the military accuses them of belonging to, or aiding, the guerrilla groups. The army often confiscates part of the food which peasants buy in the towns, claiming that it has been bought for the rebels.

In an effort to control the movements of workers, Cabrales and the plantation owners brought in a strict system of identification cards for all employees of the banana farms and their families. All are registered at the local army HQ. In response, the region's unions called a strike by 26,000 plantation workers, cutting the flow of bananas to the US and Europe. Union officials claimed that military intelligence units feed identification information to paramilitary death squads.

As in other parts of Colombia, the more strength the unions and the Left gain, the more leaders and members are killed. More than 200 union members were killed in Uraba between 1986 88.

The Segovia Massacres

The police and military have dealt efficiently with Leftist guerrilla groups but they have rarely, if ever, fought the Right-wing death squads. According to Colombia's Interior Minister, Cesar Gaviria Trujillo, 137 Right-wing paramilitary organisations are in operaton. He provided the army with a list documenting names and areas of operation; however, he says, no action has been taken against them.

The Right-wing groups were particularly angry with the activities of guerrillas in Antioquia Province. A group called Death to the Revolutionaries of the North-East announced that it would 'pacify' the capital of the province, Segovia. Another group, called The Realistic Ones, made similar threats.

Threats became reality on 11 November 1988 when gunmen arrived in several cars. They machine-gunned the streets and threw grenades into buildings. In an hour-long attack, the raiders killed 47 civilians and wounded another 200. In another massacre, gunmen slaughtered 14 peasants watching a cock fight in the town of Pinalitio.[2]

Judge Marta Lucia Gonzalez issued warrants for the arrests of three drug barons and three army officers. She also ordered the arrest of the police chief and mayor of the town of Puerto Boyaca, where the paramilitary squads have their training schools.[3] No arrests were made and Judge Gonzalez fled the country because of threats against her life. Many judges have indeed been murdered. None of the men implicated by this judge has been detained. Puerto Boyaca's mayor, Luiz Rubio Rojas, retains his post, although a government intelligence report leaked to the Communist party weekly, *La Voz*, claimed that he is the political chief of a death-squad network operating in several provinces.

Cease-fire by FARC and M-19

In January 1989, Carlos Pizarro, leader of M-19, agreed to disband his organisation and 'engage in dialogue' with the government. Pizarro had little choice but to take this step. Defection and casualties had reduced his membership from about 1,000 in 1985 to 150 in 1989 and M-19 faced extinction.

FARC idealogue and second-in-command, Jacobo Arenas, angrily accused M-19 of 'abandoning the solidarity' of CNG. However, only days later Arenas himself began to explore cease-fire possibilities with Senator Alvaro Leyva, a member of the Social Conservative Party, the traditional opposition to Barco's ruling Liberal Party. At 6pm on 28 February 1989, FARC's radio station made the following announcement: 'The Chiefs of Staff of the Colombian Revolutionary Armed Forces hereby order all our 44 fronts to cease fire unilaterally and indefinitely.'

FARC and M-19 have not won over the ELN and EPL to the idea of a cease-fire and this may take a long time. President Barco has said, 'There is hope that 35 years of guerrilla warfare may at last be coming to an end. I just hope that it is more than a mere pause to catch the breath'.[4]

By the end of 1989 more than 70,000 had died in the Colombian war.

References

1. One of them is human rights' lawyer Eduardo Matyas, based in Bogota.
2. These and other statistics from a Bogota-based, Jesuit-sponsored information agency.
3. Puerto Boyaca Press source. Both this source and the information agency are undercover until times are less dangerous.
4. President Barco to the author, 1 May 1989.

East Timor Resistance War

Background Summary

When the Portuguese abandoned East Timor in 1975, after 500 years of colonialism, several factions fought to gain control. The Indonesians already possessed West Timor, which had been ruled by the Dutch, as well as part of East Timor, known as Timor-Dili. Civil war broke out on 11 August 1975 and was won by *Frente Revolucionara de Timor-Leste Independente*, always known as Fretilin. Fretilin declared independence on 3 November 1975. Only one week later Indonesia annexed East Timor in *Operasi Keamanan*—Operation Security. Within 10 years the Indonesian army had massacred 200,000 of the population of 688,000. The East Timorese Resistance fought against occupation, but little was known about its activities until May 1986.[1] Appeals by human rights organisations for UN visits of inspection in East Timor have been ignored or refused by Indonesia.

Summary of the War in 1988

Until 1988 Fretilin had a policy of attacking enemy soldiers only in the bush or in their posts. It then decided to attack them when they were off duty in the towns as well. In August 1988 Fretilin bombs exploded in the towns of Dili, Manatuto, Beguia, Aileu and Same. Since these places are well scattered, Fretilin was warning that it had the ability to strike at will.

The London-based Minority Rights Group (MRG) reported: 'East Timor has incurred, in percentage terms, greater suffering from the Indonesian invasion than almost any other victim of invasion this century. The suffering shows no signs of easing. It seems very much that the government is seeking to starve East Timor into submission. Indonesia's invasion has been marked by a degree of barbarity which many people outside the area find it difficult to comprehend.'[2]

The War in 1989

There was no respite for the people of East Timor or for Fretilin. If anything, the occupation became even more barbarous following an order to the army commander, at his HQ in Dili, that 'resistance must be crushed by the end of 1989'. The same order noted that 'our military actions are attracting too much attention in the outside world'.[3] This was at least an admission that information was getting out of East Timor, despite stringent efforts by the authorities to prevent its happening.

East Timor is now virtually sealed off. Goods destined for East Timor must be sent to Indonesia, where they are trans-shipped to Indonesian vessels. Malay fishing boats are no longer allowed to call at Indonesian ports. Foreign journalists

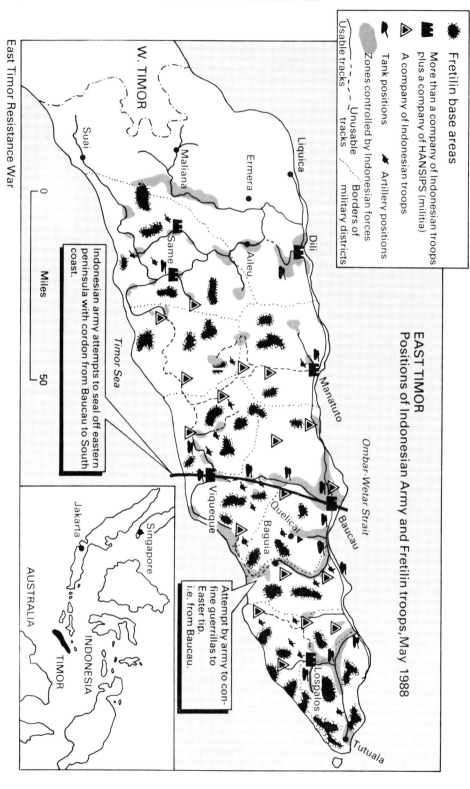

East Timor Resistance War

EAST TIMOR
Positions of Indonesian Army and Fretilin troops, May 1988

Legend:
- Fretilin base areas
- More than a company of Indonesian troops plus a company of HANSIPS (militia)
- A company of Indonesian troops
- Tank positions
- Artillery positions
- Zones controlled by Indonesian forces
- Usable tracks
- Unusable tracks
- Borders of military districts

Indonesian army attempts to seal off eastern peninsula with cordon from Baucau to South coast.

Attempt by army to confine guerrillas to Easter tip. i.e. from Baucau.

W. TIMOR

Suai
Maliana
Ermera
Liquica
Dili
Same
Aileu
Manatuto
Timor Sea
Viqueque
Quelica
Baguia
Baucau
Ombar-Wetar Strait
Lospalos
Tutuala

Miles
0   50

Jakarta
Singapore
AUSTRALIA
INDONESIA
TIMOR

are prohibited from entering East Timor, but some reporters, notably from Australia, made illegal entry during 1989.

The increasingly oppressive administration of East Timor is influenced by foreign Islamic fundamentalists. Indonesia is an Islamic nation with the largest Muslim population in the world. However, about half of East Timor's people are Roman Catholics, the result of Portuguese colonisation. As reported in **The World in Conflict 1989** (*War Annual 3*), Indonesian soldiers on duty in East Timor have been told by fundamentalists that they are engaged in a *jihad* or holy war against infidels, *ie* non-Muslims. During 1989 this was stressed by the arrival of Pakistani and Iranian Islamic extremists. These men have told the army that the East Timor Christians must be induced to convert to Islam or accept *dhimmi* (inferior) status. Should they refuse both options, 'the inevitable must apply'.[4]

Fretilin was able to receive several consignments of modern small arms during 1989. At least one consisted of Chinese Kalashnikovs and another of American M-16s. Explosives were smuggled into the country, apparently aboard an Australian-registered ship chartered by an American Christian organisation. The quantities are too small to suggest that a popular uprising is imminent. In any case, Fretilin leaders know all too well that they could not defeat the Indonesian army in open confrontation.

The guerrillas are highly efficient after 14 years of bush and urban warfare and not one has been caught during 1989. However, the army took reprisals against the populace. At least three villages were destroyed during the year and some civilians were tortured for information. The army's frustration is understandable. In the first six months of 1989 it lost 70 soldiers in Fretilin ambushes. In Dili, a naval patrol boat was blown up and on Dili airfield a helicopter was damaged.

East Timor is largely mountainous and forest-covered and armour cannot operate there. Even jeeps are useless in such terrain. The army tries to use mounted patrols but their horses are generally stolen during the night. Scout helicopters sometimes locate a Fretilin base in the mountains but the guerrillas are not tied to bases and by the time a helicopter calls in bombers the quarry has disappeared.

It is interesting to note that the Fretilin guerrillas are using precisely the same tactics as those developed by the 2/2nd Australian Independent Company, which operated in East Timor against the Japanese invaders throughout 1942. The commandos were never defeated and it is unlikely that the Indonesians will conquer the Fretilin guerrillas.

It also seemed unlikely that appeals from foreign leaders would have any effect on Indonesian policy. The Pope himself urged the Indonesian government to adopt a 'more humanitarian' approach to East Timor and its problems, but his words were ignored.

No government of a Western industrialised nation wants to run the risk of offending a country which needs a vast amount of Western technology and products as it becomes more developed. Indonesia is seen by the world's international business community as a potential 'gold mine'. According to a French diplomat in Djakarta, Western embassies in the Indonesian capital are under strict orders not to endanger good relations by referring to East Timor.

References

1. The report in **War Annual 3**, *The World in Conflict 1989*, discloses how the information reached the outside world.
2. *East Timor and West Irian*, Report No. 42, published by Minority Rights Groups, London, December 1988.
3. From a copy of the order which reached Portuguese army intelligence, Lisbon. This order carried no date but it reached Lisbon at the end of January, 1989.
4. *Dhimmi* people are second-class citizens within Islam. They are accorded 'protection' on the understanding that they accept their submissive status. The 'inevitable' and final option is death. It is all too obvious since 1975 that genocide has been the Indonesian aim. Information about the Muslim fundamentalists at work in East Timor comes from Roman Catholic sources, notably the Roman Catholic Institute of International Relations, London.

Ethiopia–Eritrea–Tigre–Somalia

Background Summary

The conflicts in all four of these regions are inter-connected and largely stem from the Ethiopian refusal to grant independence to its minorities. The Eritreans have long regarded themselves as a separate people. Much of Eritrea's identity as a nation was imposed by the Italians, who ruled the area from 1880 until 1941. The British threw out the Italians during the Second World War and the United Nations agreed, in Resolution 390A, that Eritrea should be an autonomous territory in federation with Ethiopia. The predominantly Muslim Eritreans claimed that they should have a separate State from the mainly Christian Ethiopians.

Ethiopia annexed Eritrea in 1961 and sent an army of 80,000 to occupy the area. The Eritrean Liberation Front (ELF), with 40,000 fighters, fought off the Ethiopians. The Soviet Union then entered the conflict. The Russians had been arming Somalia with the aim of using it as a surrogate to dominate the Horn of Africa, but in 1977 dropped Somalia and backed Ethiopia as a better prospect. With Soviet support, the Ethiopians expelled the ELF guerrillas from parts of Eritrea.

The Tigrean People's Liberation Army (TPLF) was simultaneously fighting the Ethiopians for their own autonomy. In the south, the Ogaden tribes rose to fight for reunion with their countrymen in Somalia. Overall, Ethiopia faced massive military operations and Colonel Mengistu, the dictator-president, increased the size of the Ethiopian army to 306,000. The ELF changed its name to Eritrean People's Liberation Front (EPLF) and, as the main force opposing the Ethiopians, inflicted several defeats on Mengistu's army.

By 1986 EPLF was in no sense a guerrilla force. It had become a regular army, with British, French, US, Italian and West German equipment. In 1987 the EPLF army had 26,000 fighting men and women and was manning 340 miles of trenches from the Red Sea to the Sudanese border. The TPLF was even more success ful than EPLF. Claiming control and support in 80 per cent of Tigre, it brought 100,000 refugees back from Sudan.

In December 1987 the EPLF defeated an Ethiopian brigade in a pitched battle and overran the defended towns of Maidama and Areza. Large quantities of stores and armaments fell to the EPLF.

Summary of the War in 1988

The war was so eventful during 1988 that readers are advised to refer to **War Annual 3**—*The World in Conflict 1989*. Briefly, the EPLF defeated the Ethiopian

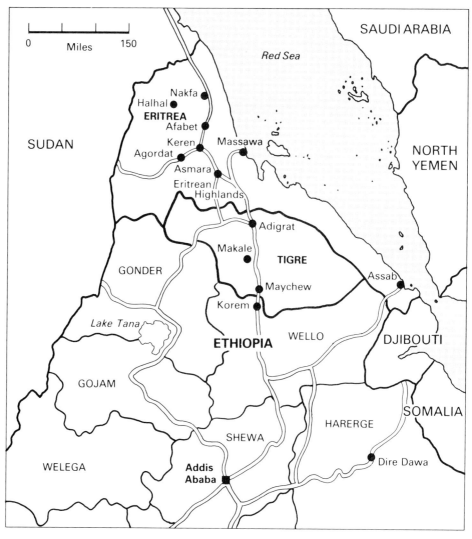

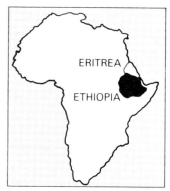

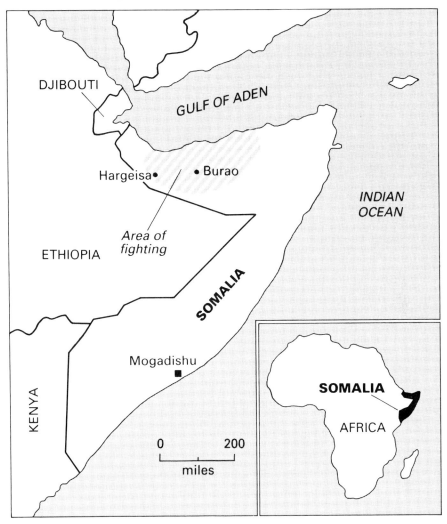

Somalia

army in the major battle of Afabet and then repulsed a three-column Ethiopian counter-offensive.

The Ethiopians resorted to revenge attacks on undefended Eritrean settlements. In addition, President Mengistu executed several of his senior commanders and imprisoned others for their failure to defeat the EPLF.

The War in 1989

Rebel Groups Drift Apart

The EPLF has drifted away in ideology, military strategy and lifestyle from the guerrillas of the TPLF. In 1988, the two groups healed a three-year rift and agreed to co-operate in military campaigns, but great differences separate them. When the EPLF split away from the main Eritrean rebel alliance in 1970, it did so under the Marxist banner. It was still formally Marxist in 1975 when it set up training programmes for the student radicals of the new TPLF. Since then, the teachers have moderated their policies while their pupils have become more extreme.

Most guerrillas in Tigre are members of a political party which advocates Stalinist policies and strict Marxism-Leninism. The TPLF continues to rely on hit-and-run guerrilla strategy and says its infrastructure is mobile, spread throughout Tigre.

In 1977, after a series of defeats, the EPLF abandoned the guerrilla tactics it had taught the TPLF. In a considered and planned change of military thinking rare among guerrillas, it adopted a strategy of a country defending its borders. It fights an almost wholly conventional war based on its system of trenches and fortifications. In the far north it has settled in a permanent community with factories, offices and hospitals.

Both movements have won remarkable victories since the beginning of 1988. These triumphs have left a vast area of craggy mountains, highland plateaux and wide deserts in rebel hands. Camouflaged factories, hidden in the rocky gorges of the EPLF's heartland, owe something to the Italian industrial legacy. They churn out plastic sandals, pharmaceuticals, clothing and weapons.

Tigrean rebels brand the EPLF 'reactionary' for disowning guerrilla warfare, and accuse the EPLF fighters of being isolated from their population. Worse still, from a Tigrean point of view, the Eritreans have eliminated all denunciations of 'imperialism' and 'Zionism' from their EPLF programme. They have decided on a mixed economy, foreign investment and a multi-party system for the future Eritrea. The EPLF foreign affairs spokesman, Girma Asmerom, has said: 'We have learnt from the negative experience of other liberation movements'.[1]

Despite the differences, the EPLF and the TPLF still have many important matters in common. Children of both groups, including the 4,300 students at Zero University in Eritrea, study Marxist history. Women make up 30 per cent of the fighters of both EPLF and TPLF. Both groups provide agricultural, medical and social services to civilians. Most important of all, they have a common enemy, President Mengistu.

War as a Way of Life

In 28 years' continual conflict, war has created an extraordinary economy in Eritrea. It has an underground and virtually cashless society, but the EPLF nevertheless has a Minister of Commerce, Tadesse Yohannes. Because EPLF victories have brought many thousands of people under rebel administration, Yohannes's Commerce Commission works to supply a wide variety of goods. Many of the businessmen who have come to the fore were once smugglers.

With EPLF backing, one smuggler has become an import-export dealer with considerable capital. His money is in an EPLF-owned bank. He followed the victorious EPLF into conquered Afabet to find that hundreds of shopkeepers no longer had any access to their former Ethiopian wholesalers. Now, by truck, camel and donkey he transports sugar, coffee, soap, shoes, veils and other consumer goods into Afabet. Minister Yohannes encourages other businessmen to sneak in great truckloads of goods from Sudan and boatloads of cargo from Saudi Arabia and North Yemen.[2]

EPLF members rarely visit merchants because they hardly ever use cash. While the EPLF is no longer Marxist, the pressures of survival have made possible an unlikely classless and cashless society. The thousands of non-military EPLF members labour in factories, build roads and drill wells under the control of various ministries and commissions. Nobody is paid a salary but all receive free basic necessities. Transport in EPLF buses is free, as is medical care. EPLF drivers use vouchers to buy petrol from the EPLF's own chain of camouflaged petrol stations.

Ethiopian Military Strength

The Ethiopian army maintains 180,000 troops in Eritrea, 40,000 in Tigre and 30,000 in the Ogaden. It has another 250,000 troops elsewhere. The army is Africa's second largest, after Egypt, but the second poorest, after Mali. The country is able to support such a vast army only because of Soviet aid, worth about $1 billion annually. The presence of 3,000 Soviet and Cuban military advisers and instructors has not helped the Ethiopian army to win a major campaign. Such success as has been achieved is due to sheer weight of numbers and air superiority. The most recent Ethiopian offensive was that of 13–23 May 1988, launched to coincide with the 25th anniversary of the Organisation of African Unity meeting in Addis Ababa. The Ethiopians were driven back after suffering 9,100 casualties and losing 300 soldiers and prisoners and 50 tanks. In May 1989 the army began a drive to bring in 100,000 more recruits, mostly by force. Many boys of only 13 and 14 were rounded up by press gangs—and some have since been captured by Eritrean and Tigre fighters. Parents who can afford it send their sons abroad.[3]

The Failed Coup

While Colonel Mengistu was on a state visit to East Germany on 18 May 1989 a coup to overthrow him began at Debra Zeit base, 37 miles from the capital. Army units in Harar, east of Addis Ababa, joined the rebellion and before long mutinous soldiers also controlled Asmara, Ethiopia's second city.

In a radio broadcast, the EPLF command announced that they were calling a two-week truce in the north as a way of supporting the rebellious troops. This was an astute political move. All 12 divisions of the Ethiopian army in Eritrea—more than 150,000 men—backed the coup attempt. The TPLF also said that it would support the coup, though it had no effective way of doing so.

Ethiopian military leaders in the north had good reason to feel bitter about Mengistu's management of the war. He not only had several officers executed after defeats in 1988 but he personally shot dead a regional commander when he returned to the capital.

Two days after the coup began, units of the loyal Second Army reached Asmara and recaptured the radio station. They also killed the senior rebel officer in the area, Major General Denissie Bulto. Mutinous élite paratroopers had flown to Addis Ababa in four Antonov transport planes to take part in the coup. Some of these men surrendered without resistance at the international airport. Others, at the old airport outside the city, put up a fight before they gave up.

Mengistu quickly returned from East Germany but even before he reached Addis Ababa the coup was in its death throes. The Industry Minister, Fanta Delai, was found to be one of the principal conspirators. The Defence Minister, Habte-Mariam, was killed when he refused to join in the plot. The EPLF, which had hoped that Mengistu's overthrow might lead to an end of the 28-year-long war, cancelled its unilateral cease-fire.

Mengistu was obviously in control again but the rebellion, especially among the units facing the Eritreans, shook his faith in the army. As a result, on 5 June he presented a 'peace initiative' to the EPLF and TPLF. He offered to talk to rebels in Eritrea in the presence of international observers. He made it clear, however, that he was not prepared to discuss full independence. Both the EPLF and TPLF rejected the Mengistu offer as being 'without substance'.

A diplomat in Addis Ababa said: 'The timing and particular circumstances under which Mengistu acted illustrate that his main purpose was to curb the growing pressure from the Ethiopian people and the army. He was buying time.'

The EPLF Operations

Each January, the EPLF command publishes a military report concerning its actions against the Ethiopian army.[4] In January 1989 it claimed to have carried out 118 military operations, 'excluding those of our engineer corps'. The report sets out its successes against the Ethiopians in this way:

- 60,000 troops killed, wounded and captured.
- 76 tanks and armoured cars destroyed.
- 200 military vehicles destroyed.
- 20 fighter planes and helicopters destroyed.
- 34 army depots and garages destroyed.
- 7 navy ships damaged.
- 55 tanks captured.
- 200 military vehicles captured.

'Moreover, millions of ammunition, bombs, BM 21, 122-mm, 130-mm and 23-mm guns were also captured.'

It has been impossible to verify some of these claims. A comparison with figures available in Addis Ababa shows that the casualty figures are correct. Visiting journalists have seen at least 55 tanks in good condition as well as many trucks made in Eastern Europe. The ships and aircraft are more questionable. Many of the aircraft would have been destroyed on the ground, either by artillery fire or demolition charge, and it is not unreasonable to suppose that EPLF units overran an Ethiopian airfield, but there is nothing to substantiate this.

Diplomatic inquiries reveal that EPLF commando units in speedboats attacked the Ethiopian naval base in Massawa on 6 September 1988 and damaged three warships. The weapons used and the extent of the damage is uncertain.

The major EPLF attack against the Ethiopian forces occurred at Assa Illa, in the province of Dankalia, on 2 January 1989. In this six-hour battle, the Ethiopians had 355 soldiers killed, 90 wounded and 12 captured. The EPLF shot down one M1-24 helicopter. The EPLF command decided on the operation because the Assa Illa garrison had been harassing the population of the town. The attack was a considered response to this harassment, intended to ensure that garrisons in other areas would think twice before such acts.

Somalia—'Genocide is the only word for it'

Following meetings in January 1986 and March 1988, President Mengistu and President Muhammad Siad Barre of Somalia agreed to resume diplomatic relations and remove border forces. This withdrawal began on 15 April 1988 and the pullback was completed a month later. The Ethiopian–Somali Accord had an unforeseen consequence. The Somali National Movement (SNM) launched a major assault on northern Somalia, hoping to overthrow President Barra. They captured the radio station at Hargeisa, the country's second city, and overran part of the garrison at Dhubto.

The government response was immediate. The garrison at Hargeisa counter-attacked from an underground complex near the airport and killed 1,500 people, many of them uninvolved civilians. The fighting cost thousands of lives and pushed 400,000 refugees into Ethiopia. For President Barre and his Marehan clan the war then became a matter of revenge and retaliation.

Community Aid Abroad (CAA), an Australian agency, in November 1988 pulled out of a health-care programme it was running in conjunction with the Somali Ministry of Health. The CAA charged the government with systematically killing civilians. 'Genocide is the only word for it', said CAA worker Peter Kieseker. 'They were conducting turkey shoots from the backs of Land-Rovers.'[5]

The targets were members of the Isaq clan, which dominates the SNM. The CAA describes the government's actions as brutal. Medicine and vehicles were misappropriated and there was widespread beating, torture and rape. On eyewitness evidence, the CAA stated that, when two soldiers were blown up by a landmine, the local army commander ordered 200 Isaqa killed in retaliation. Troops lured 37 Isaq males, including three small boys, to a 'peace meeting'; they were taken to the site of the mine explosion and machine-gunned. To fill their quota of 200, troops drove into the bush to search for other victims.

Despite pleas from Somali officials, the British government withheld $9 million in aid pending progress on human rights and on reconciliation in northern Somalia. This had not come by July 1989. Clashes occurred in Mogadishu between security forces and Muslim worshippers on 14 July. More than 400 civilians were killed, many when military vehicles armed with machine-guns opened fire on houses in heavily-populated residential districts. Two days later Somali soldiers rounded up 46 men, took them to a beach and shot them.

Barre Regime in Ruins

In mid-1989 Somalia was in an advanced state of disintegration as President Barre lost the grip he had held on Somali politics for more than 20 years. His ability to balance Somalia's disparate groups with a mixture of patronage and repression was waning as a serious succession battle involved most of the country. Despite the President's claim that tribalism had been abolished, Somali politics remains rooted in the balance of three tribal groupings. They are the Isaq in the north, the Haweih who dominate the south, and the Darode who live in the middle and hold the balance. Barre's Marehan clan is part of the Darode, as is the numerous Ogadeni clan which makes up most of the army.

Facing both the Indian Ocean and the Gulf of Aden, Somalia has great strategic importance. Superpower interests in the region have been to balance each other's bases. The US has a base for its Rapid Deployment Force at Berbera on the northern coast, matching the Soviet bases at Aden and on the Dahlak Islands belonging to Ethiopia.

The Predicament of President Mengistu

By November 1989 it was clear that President Mengistu's days were numbered. Abandoned by the Soviet Union, in need of the generals he had liquidated and with his troops holding only three towns against the Tigrayan People's Liberation Army, his fall was imminent. The formidable state security apparatus put in place by East Germans, had broken down and united rebel forces, stiffened by defecting army officers, were within 100 miles of Addis Ababa.

Heavy fighting brought serious losses to the Ethiopian army—25,000 casualties in October 1989 alone. Government aircraft based at Gonder, in the west, were indiscriminately bombing men engaged in hand-to-hand fighting, regardless of which army they belonged to. Mengistu strengthened his palace bodyguard with tribesmen from the south, after narrowly escaping assassination by a palace official. Meanwhile, 30 generals who had led a recent coup were waiting court-martial in a palace compound. That they were still alive and had not been shot out of hand was an indication that Mengistu felt that he might yet need their support to save his own life.

References

1. In a talk with the author.
2. An admission by the Minister.
3. Diplomatic sources in Khartoum.

4. It is distributed in several languages and is also published in *Adulis*, journal of the EPLF foreign relations department.
5. Peter Keiseker speaking at a CAA Press conference.
6. Information on the atrocities is confirmed by the African human rights organisation, Africa Watch.

India–Pakistan War

NO QUARTER ASKED

Background Summary

India and Pakistan share a 2,000-mile border that stretches from the Arabian Sea in the north-east to the great mountains of the Karakoram Range. Since 1947, the Indian and Pakistan armies have been in a state of war, though fighting has been intermittent. The fundamental conflict is over Kashmir. India holds two-thirds of the region and Pakistan the other third. But Pakistan claims the entire area, on the grounds that two-thirds of the population of Kashmir are Muslims. A secondary dispute is over water, since the rivers that flow through Pakistani Kashmir have their source in India. Pakistan is also worried that India could isolate Pakistan from its ally, China. India holds the strategic Siachen Glacier, which overlooks the strategic 800-mile Karakorah highway from Peking.

The permanent presence of UN observers in Kashmir cannot prevent fighting between Pakistan and India. In 1985 infantry fought near Siachen Glacier and aircraft from the belligerent countries fought above it. In 1986 there was face-to-face tension in the Jammu section of Kashmir. In September 1987 sharp actions at company and special unit level took place and UN observers reported that tension and conflict had reached danger point. Neither side was quite prepared to introduce air power—beyond dog-fights—or to expand the conflict to the south. The following year, 1988, three engagements took place and each side suffered hundreds of casualties from long-range shelling.

During 1988 the Pakistani army strengthened its positions in areas where the Indians might try to push even deeper into Pakistan-controlled Balistan, the region adjoining the conflict area. Skardu, the administrative capital of Balistan, is headquarters for Pakistani military operations.

The War in 1989

That the conflict over the Himalayan boundary really is a war needs to be stressed. The General commanding the Indian sector told Edward W. Desmond of *Time* magazine in July 1989: 'This is an actual war in every sense of the word. No quarter is asked and none is given'. The point needs to be made because India and Pakistan are supposedly at peace. Prime Ministers Rajiv Gandhi[1] and Benazir Bhutto are trying to reach a more friendly relationship. Ms Bhutto said that she wants to eliminate the 'irritant' of the Siachen Glacier problem. However, the problem is difficult because of national prestige. Bhutto once taunted General Zia al-Haq, the late President, for losing the territory in the first place. The slightest sign of compromise with New Delhi produces vehement criticism from her political enemies, who accuse her of 'submission' to India.

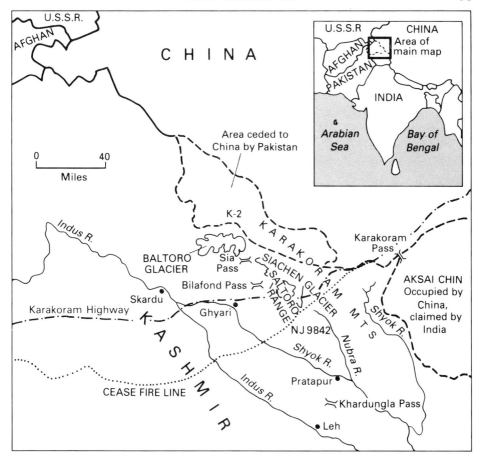

India-Pakistan Confrontation

At the front, the rules of engagement are clear-cut on both sides and well understood by all ranks: if there is a target, fire. Artillery observers, on peaks and ridges, keep watch day and night, with night-vision equipment after dark. They are there to spot the other side's patrols and supply columns and bring gunfire to bear.

The terrain and weather cause more casualties than combat. Temperatures drop below minus 43°F, blizzards are common and soldiers are sometimes lost in avalanches and down crevasses. The UN observers classify eight out of ten casualties as 'non-combat'. Pulmonary edema, brought on by high altitude, strikes a few Indians each day, as they hold more higher posts than the Pakistanis.

The Pakistani commander, Brigadier S. A. R. Bukhari, says that his strategy is to make it difficult for the Indians to hold Siachen Glacier and claims that this has worked. The assertion is undeniable but no amount of difficulty has inclined India to make any concessions on the boundary.

'Battle' at 21,000 feet

Where Indian and Pakistani bunkers are only a few hundred yards apart there are frequent exchanges of machine-gun and rocket fire. Infantry assaults are infrequent, mainly because it is difficult for the soldiers to move at heights of 18,000 feet and higher, and over crevasse-ridden ice.

The most serious incident during 1989 was near Chumic Glacier, where a 'battle' went on from mid-April to mid-May. According to Indian reports, the clash began when the Pakistanis tried to establish a new post from which to direct artillery fire against Indian positions. The Pakistani response is that the Indians had merely discovered an old observation post. Both sides sent men off in a race to the high ground, an icy peak 21,300 feet high. Since it was clear that the Indians would reach the peak first, the Pakistani command took a desperate step. Two soldiers were tied to ropes and suspended from a helicopter's runners for a seven-minute ride to the peak, They survived the intense cold, landed on the summit and held off an Indian patrol. As more Indians attacked, so the Pakistanis flew in reinforcements. Over the next month, the Pakistanis claim that six of their men died and that at least 34 Indians were killed. This figure cannot be confirmed. Local commanders met face to face to reach an agreement. Both sides pulled back and the Indians agreed to accept that two Pakistani posts were 'legitimate'— that is, they had been there for a long time.

The respective army commands are content to have the war continue as a way of training troops under extreme conditions. Both armies frequently change their garrisons. The Kashmir experience has greatly improved India's capacity for high-altitude warfare. This has a bearing on India's dormant dispute with China over the mountainous area of Aksai Chin. India lost this territory in a brief war in 1962. Should that conflict again erupt India will be much better prepared in training, experience and equipment. The Siachen operations have also pushed Pakistan back from the Nubra Valley, which leads to Leh, and widened the stretch of Indian territory between Pakistan and Aksai Chin that leads to the Karakoram Pass.

The major Indian base at the foot of the Siachen Glacier is at an altitude of 11,400 feet and is 75 miles from Pratapur, HQ of the 102nd Brigade. Dozens of daily helicopter flights, mostly with M1-17s, take ammunition and other supplies to the 75 forward posts. For high-altitude missions smaller Cheetah helicopters are used. Troops need six or eight days to reach the forward posts from the base camp. They move on foot rather than in helicopters to acclimatise and toughen them.

References

1. In national elections in November 1989, Rajiv Gandhi was unseated as Prime Minister. However, there was no indication that India's policy over its conflict with Pakistan would change under a new leader.

India's Other Wars

Turmoil in Assam

Less than a decade after a violent Assamese-rights campaign brought turmoil to India's north-eastern state of Assam, a new war began in February 1989. It was started by young militants of the Bodo tribe who believe that the Bodos were not given adequate rights in earlier settlements of ethnic grievances.

The militants, drawn largely from the All-Bodo Students' Union, are facing a relatively new State government headed by former guerrillas of the All-Assam Students' Union. It waged an earlier war on behalf of the State's Assamese-speaking people, who are made up of several ethnic groups.

The Assamese, under the Chief Minister, Prahulle Mahanta, are now being accused by the Bodos of being as insensitive to their aspirations as the central government in New Delhi once was to those of the Assamese. The Bodos want a separate homeland, although they form at most 40 per cent of the population in the areas they claim. Assam has about 20 million people, of which Bodos and other tribal groups are thought to account for 15 per cent.

The Bodo guerrilla insurgency is concentrated in Upper Assam, north of the Brahmaputra River. The tea-growing areas of Tezpur, Darrang, Goalpara and Kokrajhar have been most severely effected. Railways, roads and bridges have been blown up. The Bodo insurgents prevented the transport of tea after the summer harvest of June, July and August 1989. The rebellion and the consequent fighting follows the pattern that has become familiar in South Asia. The militants want to prevent all economic activity, thus forcing the army to use brigade-sized formations in attempts to crush the guerrillas.

The Maldives

At 2.15pm on December 1988 the capital of the Maldives Islands, Male, was attacked by a force of Sri Lankan Tamils. Using machine-guns, rockets and grenades, the sea-borne raiders struck the HQ of the local militia, the President's residence and the radio and TV station. The President, who was at once rushed to a hideout, frantically appealed to the US, UK, Sri Lanka, Pakistan and India for military help. Within 90 minutes the Indian cabinet approved the sending of an Indian force.

By 9pm a company of the 50th Parachute Brigade, the HQ Group of the 6th Battalion Parachute Regiment and some artillery were airborne in Ilyushin transports. After a flight of 1,200 miles, the troops landed at Hulule, the Maldives' international airport, and secured it. Two platoons crossed to the coral atoll of Male and recaptured the government buildings. After brief skirmishes some of the attacking Tamils surrendered while others escaped in a hijacked ship. The

India's Sikh-Hindu War

seized ship was buzzed by helicopters and depth charges were dropped near it. When it still failed to stop, a destroyer crippled it with gunfire. The attempted coup was over.

The brief 'war' is interesting because of the rapid and efficient Indian response and military build-up. Within hours not only troops but several types of aircraft and naval vessels were on the scene. The preparation was so comprehensive that an Indian army field hospital was ready in the Maldives to receive patients within six hours of the alarm. The point that emerges is that India is prepared to assume the role of regional policeman. The acquisition of strategic airlift capability, the growing navy and a focusing of Indian security concerns southwards into the Indian Ocean confirms the trend. The Maldives operation brings out the critical element of India's South Asian doctrine, which assumes US acquiescence in its actions in the region of the Indian sub-continent, with the exception of Pakistan.

The Sikh War

The Sikhs of the Punjab embarked on a civil war against the central Indian government in 1980. This was the result of a dispute which began in 1947, at the time of independence and when India and Pakistan were divided from each other. The Sikhs gained the impression that they would be given a Punjabi-speaking State which they would call Khalistan. India could not meet the Sikhs' 45 demands. The nationalist *Akali Dal* party turned the Golden Temple of Amritsar into a great fortress. Indian commandos captured it, in *Operation Blue Star*, in summer 1984. This led to Mrs. Gandhi's assassination at the hands of her Sikh bodyguard.

In the Sikh–Hindu war which followed, Hindus slaughtered about 2,000 Sikhs and the Sikhs began a 'holy war' of unbridled terrorism. Many groups, such as the Khalistan Liberation Army and the Khalistan Commandos, became prominent. During 1988 the Golden Temple again became the site of a pitched battle between Sikhs and the Indian National Protection Group, which includes the Black Cats, a paramilitary police force. By May 1988, Hindu migrant workers were in full flight as refugees from Punjab.

During 1989 the war continued with fearful atrocities. On 9 August a bomb planted by Sikhs in a passenger bus travelling between Chandigargh and New Delhi killed 22 people and wounded 33 others. The attack was one of many made in the weeks preceding the 42nd anniversary of India's independence from Britain, on 15 August. During 1989, 1,640 people were killed by Sikh separatists.

The Indian government and army regard the conflict as a war and their response to the actions of the Sikh fighters is to treat them as a foreign enemy. Despite this forceful reaction, Indian army intelligence seems unable to capture the leaders of the Sikh 'armies', or to pre-empt their attacks.

Sri Lanka: See Sri Lanka Civil War.
    War Annual 3 carried a full description of the causes and course of the Hindu–Sikh war.

Iran–Iraq (Gulf) War

TRUCE WITHOUT PEACE

Background Summary

On 17 September 1980 the Iraqi President, Saddam Hussein, attempted to capture Iranian territory which he claimed really belonged to Iraq. This was the beginning of the Gulf War. The Iranian army was weak, largely because Ayatollah Khomeini's religious zealots had killed its best Generals. Iraq's powerful armed forces were expected to have an easy victory.

The surprise assault brought the Iraqis an initial tactical success but the Iranian lines did not break and Ayatollah Khomeini and his government did not accept defeat. The first year was a war of artillery duels and patrol actions, but in 1981 the Iranians went on the offensive and drove the Iraqis from some of the captured territory.

Both sides attracted allies. Egypt, Saudi Arabia and Jordan backed Iraq; Syria and Libya supported Iran. The Syrian–Libyan alliance with Iran caused friction in the Arab world as Iran is not an Arab state.

Iran launched *Operation Ramadan* in July 1982. This was a massive infantry assault by waves of Pasdaran (Revolutionary Guards). They recovered some territory but at immense cost. *Operation Ramadan* set the pattern for the great battles of 1983, 1984, 1985 and 1986. Iran, with plentiful manpower—and boypower—threw its infantry against barbed wire, minefields, machine-guns and tanks. The losses were colossal.

The conflict had gone far beyond a dispute over territory. Iran's fundamentalist leaders presented it as 'a war between Islam and heresy'. Iraq declared that it was fighting as a champion of the entire Arab race against 'the vile Persian aggressors'. With 40 nations selling arms and equipment to one side or the other—or to both—the war could continue indefinitely.

Iran's success in *Operation Dawn* (1986) provoked Iraq into using mustard and nerve gas. In May that year the 2nd Iraqi Army Corps captured Mehran, inside Iran. The Iranians counterattacked and caused an Iraqi rout. Sadam Hussein executed the Iraqi General held responsible for the defeat.

Despite overwhelming Iraqi superiority in tanks and airpower, the Iranians lost little ground. Their air defences were efficient and during one Iraqi attack they brought down 100 bombers.

International shipping became caught up in the war. In May 1987 the American destroyer *Stark* was hit by an Iraqi Exocet missile, supplied by France. The navies of the US, Britain, France, Belgium, Italy and the Netherlands sent ships to the Gulf to protect international shipping.

The Long Front

Summary of the War in 1988

Strategies and tactics changed, the 'war of the cities' intensified and internal tensions were evident in Iran and Iraq. For the first time in seven years, the Iranians did not mount a winter offensive in 1987–88. They were unprepared for the Iraqi assault of April 1988 to retake the Faw Peninsula. This offensive marked a new Iraqi policy—a change from static defence to hard-hitting offence. The Faw Peninsula was not strategically important but its loss was a psychological blow to the Iranians.

The Iranian government ordered mobilisation of all males of military age— 16–55 years— from its population of 45 million. However, by mid-1988 Iran was gripped by war-weariness and two senior mullahs called publicly on Khomeini to negotiate an 'honourable peace'.

At 10.54am on Sunday 3 July 1988 the US navy in the Gulf made an error of judgement. The captain of the USS *Vincennes*, the ship with the most advanced air defence system afloat, mistook a civilian Iran Air-Bus for an Iranian F-14 and destroyed it with two missiles. All 290 people aboard perished.

On 18 July 1988 Iran accepted UN Secretary Council Resolution 598 calling for peace between Iran and Iraq. Even so, Saddam Hussein sent his armies into Iran in an attempt to win more ground before the commencement of cease-fire talks. A delegation of seven Arab Foreign Ministers induced Hussein, on 20 August, to accept the cease-fire.

Iraq claimed to have won the war and in that Khomeini felt himself ashamed to have failed to win it—ending it was 'bitter poison' he said—there was some justification for the claim. Iran's acceptance of a truce resulted from the collective impact of economic, military and diplomatic pressures. These pressures were applied by the US, the Soviet Union, Saudi Arabia and Kuwait. They were given extra weight and drive by Iraq's use of chemical weapons.

In fact, neither side 'won' the war. It really ended in stalemate. For year after year Iraq made military blunders. These mistakes have been obscured by the change in the final year from static defence to fast-moving offensive operations. In 1989 'the value of quickly moving onto the offensive' was being pressed in the military colleges. The years in which no such philosophy was followed are glossed over as 'periods necessary to establish a solid base for the offensive'. Lecturers never refer to Saddam Hussein's strategic mistake in 1980 when, having overrun a large part of south-western Iraq, he stopped and sought to negotiate.

Lessons and Conclusions

One of the longest large-scale wars of the 20th century, the Iran–Iraq War provides interesting lessons, the most general and obvious of which might be that the superpowers can neither prevent nor stop regional conflicts. However, the US would claim that its navy's intervention in the Gulf was a factor in Iran's eventual acceptance of the UN cease-fire resolution.

Sacrifice as a Weapon

Iran, though critically short of weapons, held off an enemy with vastly superior firepower through the use of innovative tactics, profoundly motivated forces and a readiness to make large-scale human sacrifice. Probably only in Islam could such grotesque battle losses be tolerated. Iranians could not accept the word 'grotesque'; for them, those who die in battle against a foe declared to be an 'enemy of God' are martyrs. However, ideological commitment is no substitute for advanced weapons systems. It is doubtful whether Iran has learnt this lesson. As late as March 1988, Mohsen Rezai, leader of the Iranian Revolutionary Guards Corps, said: 'It is sufficient for us to bring to the battlefield four times more infantry forces with light weapons than Iraq's forces'. A more sober judgement is that lack of access to advanced weapons cost Iran a clear-cut victory.

Use of Chemical Weapons

Iraq's use of outlawed poison gas and nerve gases was the most disturbing military development. Iran also used gas but on a much smaller scale and only in retaliation. Even these Iranian troops bent on martyrdom were afraid of facing gas attacks. Since it is infinitely cheaper to develop and manufacture chemical agents than other weapons, any country's use of them is likely to provoke similar use by unstable or poor national leaders.

Air Supremacy must be Exploited

At the start of the war Iraq had about 340 combat aircraft and Iran had 450. At war's end, the Iraqi air force had more than 500 Soviet aircraft, including MiG-25s and SU-20s, as well as French-supplied Mirages. Iran then had only 60 operational aircraft of which only a handful were modern. The disparity is instructive. It was no secret that Iran could not buy spares for its aircraft, so that its initial numerical superiority was meaningless. Yet the Iraqi command did not use its air force intelligently. When Iraq was forced on the defensive after 1982, Saddam Hussein and his Generals did not use their air superiority which had reached a ratio of 8:1. From time to time the Iraqis bombed Iran's industrial base but each of these attacks seemed speculative and more vengeful than purposeful. Not one attack was sustained long enough to cause irreparable damage to Iran's war effort. Systematic destruction of Iran's oil facilities would almost certainly have shortened the war. Even in the 'tanker war', which began in 1984, the Iraqis failed to cut Iran's oil exports. This was not due to Iranian resistance but to the West's resigned willingness to accept losses of its own ships. About 11 million tons of shipping were sunk or declared to be commercially useless. This was the most serious campaign against shipping since the battle of the Atlantic, 1940-44.

Missiles Against Cities

For the first time in the history of warfare, two belligerents systematically attacked each other's capital cities with missiles. This had a deeply demoralising effect. Between January and April 1988, Iraq's daily missile bombardment of

Teheran drove half the population of 8 million from the capital. The use of medium-range missiles, apparently mostly Scud-Bs, killed thousands of civilians. Baghdad, closer to the Iran–Iraq border than the Iranian capital, was also frequently hit. Iraqi propaganda minimised the damage and civilian deaths.

Unified Command is Essential

Iran had—and still has—a parallel command structure, with the army and the Revolutionary Guards under different operational control. During the war, liaison between the two was so poor that sometimes they found themselves attacking the same objective without previous co-operation. Constant friction between the two forces damaged the entire war effort, since co-ordinated planning was impossible. Even at tactical level there was no uniformity. The army had its trained Generals but the Revolutionary Guards were led by fanatical mullahs. The army genuinely tried to get an adequate return for its casualties; the Revolutionary Guards seemed to measure success by the immensity of their casualties. Not until 1986 did they substitute infiltration for human wave assaults and seek to inflict more casualties upon the Iraqis than they themselves suffered.

Use of Sea Mines

Iran's use of mines was well publicised. They were antique types; some had 80-year-old Russian-made contact devices. However, they were effective. While Iran's use of mines was no surprise, Iraq's failure to use mines was a surprise. The Iraqi Command could have more effectively damaged Iran's oil movements by laying mines in the well-defined tanker routes off the Iranian coast. These routes are not widely used by neutral shipping. The air strikes against neutral shipping were damaging but the objective should have been to bring Iranian production to a halt.

The Breakthrough Mentality

The Iranians were innovative and even imaginative, as in their capture of the Faw Peninsula and in getting through the 'impossible' marshes south of Basra. However, they futilely battered themselves against the layered defence works around Basra. Iraq had built its version of the Maginot Line around Basra and it had an extraordinary effect on the Iranian leaders. Mindlessly, they mounted several major offensives to break through this line. There is no evidence to show that they ever considered outflanking it. The ram and ram again tactics prevailed until the end. They were stupid and ignorant, since lessons abound about the effectiveness of outflanking such strong defences. Had Iran put as much effort and as many men into attacks against Baghdad from the east as it did from the south the war might have ended differently.

Measuring the Cost

In human terms, the cost of the Gulf War was colossal. Iran suffered 600,000 dead, with wounded estimated at 800,000. Iraq lost 400,000 dead. Wounded are difficult to estimate but the government's ban on information about them suggests that they were considerable. The damage to Iraqi society is probably greater than to the Iranian people, who more readily accepted casualties. In building up its armed forces and their arms and in maintaining them, Iraq incurred foreign debts of $110 billion. It is unable even to pay the interest on these debts. Iraq is therefore to a large extent dependent on its still unpaid suppliers. Iran is not nearly so dependent. It diversified its sources of supply during the war and found some countries, notably China and North Korea, willing to give rather than sell supplies. Also, Iran developed its own armaments industries. Despite all the obstacles, Iran managed to export enough oil to cover its basic war costs. It lost virtually its entire navy, which was destroyed by the US fleet in the Gulf, but the ships are being replaced. Iran's ability to export the Islamic revolution was unimpaired and it remains more of a regional superpower than Iraq, despite the struttings of Saddam Hussein as the 'conqueror of Persia'.

Truce Without Peace

At the time of writing no genuine peace talks or negotiations had taken place. Between them, the belligerents still held 200,000 prisoners of war and could not agree on a procedure for resolving the consequences of the conflict. Rivalry might have left the battlefield but it is now entrenched in diplomatic intrigue and bargaining.

Both sides maintain large forces at the front and Iran is pressing ahead with efforts to rebuild its armed forces, increasingly with weapons from Warsaw Pact countries. These supplies are linked to the availability of large numbers of tanks because of conventional force reductions in Eastern Europe. According to a Pentagon analysis, in 1989 the Iranian government had made firm plans to spend $20 billion on arms by 1993.

Unchanging Hatreds

The spirit of *glasnost* that emerged in Iran after Ali Akbar Hashemi Rafsanjani succeeded Ayatollah Khomeini in 1989 clearly did not extend to Iraq and its leader, Saddam Hussein. Teheran continues to demand that Baghdad should withdraw its troops from 2,600 square kilometres of occupied Iranian territory before talks about a firm peace can resume. Iraq says priority must go to clearing debris blocking the Shatt Al Arab. This would open the way to restoring the moribund city of Basra to its prewar eminence as a major trading port.

Caught in the middle are the prisoners. Attempts at the end of 1989 by the International Red Cross to arrange the repatriation of sick and wounded prisoners collapsed in acrimony as Baghdad and Teheran accused one another of bad faith after the exchange of only a few hundred prisoners.

Monitoring the Cease-fire

The United Nations Iran-Iraq Military Observer Group (UNIIMOG) was established on 9 August 1988, under the command of Major General Slavko Jovic of Yugoslavia. His deputy in Iran is Brigadier James Kelly of Eire and the deputy in Iraq is Brigadier Venki Patil of the Indian army. UNIIMOG's strength consists of 350 unarmed military observers from Argentina, Australia, Austria, Bangladesh, Canada, Denmark, Finland, Ghana, Hungary, India, Indonesia, Ireland, Italy, Kenya, Malaysia, New Zealand, Nigeria, Norway, Peru, Poland, Senegal, Sweden, Turkey, Uruguay, Yugoslavia and Zambia. New Zealand provided an 18-man air unit, Ireland 37 military police and Austria a small medical unit.

UN observers are based in four sectors on the Iranian side: Saqqez, Bakhtaran, Desful and Ahwaz. On the Iraqi side they are at Suleimaniyeh, Baquba and Basra. Their duties are to establish agreed cease-fire lines along the 950-mile frontier. They investigate violations of the agreement and supervise and verify withdrawals. In the first 12 months of its existence UNIIMOG received 2,600 complaints of violations and confirmed about 25 per cent of them. The observers patrol by vehicle, helicopter, boat, on horseback and on foot.

Amnesty's Revelations

Late in October 1989, Amnesty International's annual report brought to light aspects of the war which Iraq and Iran have tried to obscure. The report stated: 'On 28 August 1988, Iraqi government forces reportedly entered several villages near the town of Dohuk and arrested 1,000 people, some of whom were suffering from wounds sustained in chemical weapon attacks. Those detained were allegedly summarily executed and then buried in mass graves.' This was one week after the ceasefire and Dohuk, the site of the atrocity, is being developed as a tourist centre.

Amnesty reported that in Iraq thousands of political prisoners continued to be arrested and detained. Many were held for long periods without trial and torture of political prisoners was widespread. Large numbers of people had disappeared and were feared killed.

Amnesty did not accuse the Iranians of indiscriminate attacks on civilians—which Iraq inflicted on its Kurdish population—but pointed to other atrocities. 'Over 1,200 political prisoners were executed, some of whom were said to have received only prison sentences. Torture of political prisoners remained widespread and opponents of the government were sentenced to imprisonment or execution after unfair trials.'

Aspects of the War discussed in War Annual 3 include:
    The sea war
    The Iranian National Liberation Army
    Iran's chemical weapons
    The nuclear future
    US error of judgement
    Elimination of minorities by Iran and Iraq

Holy War–Jihad

BOMBS, RIOTS AND RUSHDIE

Background Summary

Holy war—*Jihad* in Arabic—has several forms. It is fought openly and conventionally as in the Iran-Iraq war; covertly through assassination and in terrorist form through kidnappings and bombings, some of them suicide bombings. It is also fought through propaganda and economic warfare. *Jihad* is as old as Islam itself, that is more than 13 centuries. The current phase of holy war is being waged under the direction of Shia Muslims of Iran and southern Lebanon, together with the more extremist of individual Sunni Muslims, such as Colonel Gaddafi, President of Libya.

Jihad is not merely a war waged by fundamentalist Islam against the Christian West and against the Jews. It is also aimed at all Muslim monarchs, as monarchies are anathema to strict Shia Muslims. Regimes declared to be 'reactionary', such as Egypt, are enemies to be fought and destroyed. Various current wars have an element of *jihad*; they include the Bangladeshi war of genocide against the Shanti Bahini tribes; a similar war waged against the Christians of East Timor by the Indonesian army; the Syrian-Muslim war against the Christians of Lebanon, and the Afghanistan War. In the latter case, all participants are Muslim but the Mujahideen tribesmen regard the government and its followers as apostates.

Summary of Holy War 1987-88

Holy war operations and attacks were planned and co-ordinated within the Iranian embassies in London, Rome, Vienna and Paris. A group of terrorists arrested in Paris on 22 March 1987 were found to be under the direct control of the Speaker of the Iranian parliament, Hojatolislam Rafsanjani (later to become President of Iran). The Iranian ambassador to the Vatican, Ayatollah Khosrow-Shahi, was believed to control a network of operations in Spain, Italy, West Germany, France and Britain.

Throughout 1987 and the early part of 1988, Libyan missions in several countries recruited mercenaries for Gaddafi's Islamic Legion and its offshoot, the Pan-American Islamic Legion. Co-operation between Libya and Iran extended to Western Europe, where their intelligence teams worked closely together.

Leaders of extreme Islamic groups held a conference in London in January 1988 to plan further moves in the holy war. More than 400 delegates from 40 Islamic countries gathered for the three-day meeting. Delegates discussed plans to 'liberate the Islamic *umma*'—that is, Muslims throughout the world.

A Holy War Brigade, comprising volunteers from several Arab countries, fought with the Afghanistan Mujahideen against the Afghan regime and its Soviet allies. When the Soviet army withdrew from Afghanistan, this Brigade turned its whole attention to fighting the regime.

Holy War in 1989

Bahrein Security forces uncovered an underground holy war group with ties to *Hezbollah*, the Lebanese-based 'Party of God'. Investigations showed that the group had organized subversive cells in several Shia villages in Bahrein. During 1988–89 it was forming terrorist cells to carry out attacks against US officials and Gulf businessmen. The American target is larger than might be thought. The US navy maintains support facilities in Bahrein and used Manama as a frequent port-of-call. An estimated 1,200 US businessmen and their families live in Bahrein. Some members of the holy war group were trained in Lebanon. In the past, most activities by Gulf-based Shia extremists were encouraged and at times directly supported from Teheran. Diplomats in the Gulf say that relationships are changing and that Beirut is the main centre for support, finance and encouragement.

Algeria Muslim fundamentalists preaching holy war had been looking for an opportunity to gain power in Algeria. They want to turn Algeria into an Islamic state on the Iran model. Their opportunity arose in October 1988 when a protest against the scarcity of goods turned into a riot. The key figure in what rapidly became an uprising was a preacher, Sidi Ali Bel Hadj, aged 32. Bel Hadj, who operates from a mosque in the Algiers slum of Bab el Oued, soon had mobs stampeding through Algiers and other cities shouting *Allahu Akbar!'* (God is great). In the consequent bloody upheaval more than 1,000 people were shot dead by police and troops. The government later admitted that it had underestimated the strength of the *jihad* which Bel Hadj had evoked.

Syria Although maintaining close links with the Iranian regime and allowing *Hezbollah* to operate from Syrian-controlled areas in Lebanon, the Assad regime has applied the severest of measures against Islamic holy war fundamentalists at home, as seen in the 1982 Hama massacre. According to various estimates, more than 20,000 people were killed. Occasionally, similar steps have been taken against overly assertive *Hezbollah* elements in Lebanon.

Iraq Small Islamic holy war underground groups, the leading one being *ad-Da'awa*, receive assistance from Iran and Syria.

The Arabian Peninsula Although Islam is a pillar of government policy in Saudi Arabia, this has not prevented outbreaks of severe violence at the instigation of extremist *jihad* elements, backed by Iran. An attempt by fundamentalists from Iran to seize the Kaaba (Islamic 'Holy of Holies') during the annual pilgrimage to Mecca in August 1987 resulted in the deaths of hundreds.

Sudan Islamic *jihad* is strong in this country. With a large following among students, and to some extent in the army, it is the third-largest political force in the nation's parliament. Enforcement of Islamic law is one factor in the continuing civil war between the non-Muslim blacks of the south and the Muslims of the north.

Jordan Growing manifestations of Islamic holy war among the population have caused the Jordanian government to respond on two levels: preaching an enlightened and tolerant Islam in an attempt to neutralise extremism and vigorously suppressing dangerous Iran-backed fundamentalist elements.

Pan Am's Flight 103

Just before Christmas 1988 Pan Am Flight 103, a Boeing 747, was destroyed by a bomb at 31,000 feet above Scotland, killing all crew and passengers. Much of the wreckage fell on the rural town of Lockerbie, where other people died. The total death toll was 270. The bomb had been expertly placed in the aircraft's forward baggage hold, just in front of the section where the wings are attached to the fuselage. About 10lb of plastic explosive severed the cockpit and part of the first-class cabin from the rest of the aircraft. The most likely group responsible for the outrage was that of Ahmed Jibril, the Popular Front for the Liberation of Palestine—General Command. The Jibril terrorists have a history of aerial bombings. Various Islamic groups claimed that they had arranged the bombing in retaliation for the destruction by USS *Vincennes* of the Iranian airliner over the Gulf in July 1988. It is doubtful whether these groups have the technical knowledge necessary to carry out such an operation, but their readiness to claim responsibility was an indication of their wish to destroy Western planes as acts of holy war.

Gaddafi's Continuing Role

In September 1988, Gaddafi told an Italian interviewer: 'My mission is Islam. It is Allah's will that I should triumph. It is my duty to fight against all those who try to prevent this triumph.' In another interview that month he said that he would not reduce his support for groups who practise what he referred to as 'so-called terrorism'. When asked if he would be willing to withdraw backing from the Abu Nidal terrorists in order to improve his relations with Washington, he said 'If you want to stop what you call terrorism and I call holy war, the British should withdraw from Ireland, and the Zionists must go back to the countries they came from'.[1]

In 1989 the British Foreign Office published a briefing paper, *Libya's External Relations and Activities*. The document, while not a declaration of British policy, clarifies for foreign diplomats and others what Britain finds so objectionable about Gaddafi. It states:

> Libya's foreign policy has been characterised by an obstinate, erratic pursuit of Arab unity and by hostility towards the US and Israel. For all his professed pan-Arabism, Gaddafi has won few friends in the Arab world, while Libyan-inspired subversion and terror acts have alienated numerous countries.

One of these countries was Australia, which closed the Libyan People's Bureau in Canberra and expressed concern about Libya's destabilising role in the South Pacific and Australia. The Prime Minister, Robert Hawke, said: 'There is no plausible explanation in terms of geography or legitimate national interest for Libyan activity in this region.'

For Gaddafi, holy war gives him a legitimate interest in all regions. Most recently, his terrorists have been active against Britain, West Germany, France,

Italy, Greece, Belgium, Spain, Turkey, Chad, Kenya, Uganda, Egypt, as well as in Central America, the Caribbean and West Africa. In July 1988 the Benin government ordered the head of the Libyan People's Bureau to leave the country.

Gaddafi wants a world society based on a mixture of precepts from the Koran and from Marxism. He justifies all his aims on the basis of *jihad*.

The Rushdie Affair

The Muslim uproar which greeted the publication of Salman Rushdie's *The Satanic Verses* was a manifestation of holy war. Muslims said that the book was blasphemous and should be banned. The author was condemned to death by Ayatollah Khomeini, a sentence reaffirmed by other senior Muslim clerics and renewed by Khomeini's successor, President Rafsanjani.

Rushdie was brought up as an Indian Muslim and holds a Cambridge degree in Islamic studies. In an attempt to dilute Islamic hostility, he protested that he was a lapsed Muslim. Islam does not recognise such a status while a Muslim who converts to another religion is considered guilty of apostasy, a crime punishable by death.

This episode has probably done more in the Western world to draw attention to the fierce strength of holy war than anything else.

Reference

1. Gaddafi was speaking to Lenard Valpino, a freelance journalist who has known him since 1976. Gaddafi makes the same statement to nearly every journalist who gains access to him.

Aspects of Holy War discussed in War Annual 3 include:
> Saudi Arabia—a major enemy of *jihad* warriors.
> The Haramine Conference to plan holy war worldwide.
> Challenge to Egypt and President Mubarak
> *Jihad* in Afghanistan

Israel and the Palestinians

THE *INTIFADA*—A NEW TYPE OF WAR

Readers are referred to War Annual 3 *for a detailed description and analysis of the uprising or* Intifada *(Arabic for 'shaking free') from its beginning until towards the end of 1988. The report in* War Annual 4 *deals with aspects of the* intifada *which are currently more relevant.*

Palestinian Organisation

The *intifada* differs from previous disturbances in Gaza and the West Bank in its intensity, its pervasiveness and its leadership. In earlier years sporadic protests were headed by intellectuals and members of municipal councils. Many of these people were deported and their organisations suspended by the Israelis. At the beginning of the *intifada* random groups of Palestinians threw stones, illegally displayed colours and patriotic slogans and insulated the security forces. Within weeks, the grass roots nature of the *intifada* was taken over by a decentralised, clandestine leadership—the Unified National Leadership of the Uprising (UNLU). UNLU was not as unified as its name suggests but it extended participation to practically the entire Palestinian community in the occupied territories. It issues pronouncements in a series of leaflets and by *Voice of Palestine* radio.

UNLU's tactics include calls for an economic boycott of many Israeli products, non-payment of taxes to Israel, mass resignation of Israeli-appointed Arab police and local government officials, strikes up to a week long, involving transport, trade and education. It decided to refrain from using firearms and explosives—though petrol bombs have been used. 'Popular committees' were set up in almost every village, town and refugee camp to organise distribution of food, fuel and other resources. It has aimed to create an alternative administration to provide a medical, agricultural, commercial and educational infrastructure. Much of this, especially the strikes, damaged the Palestinians more than the Israelis.

Increasingly, the *intifada* has been 'taken over' by a Muslim fundamentalist group, the Islamic Resistance Movement. Known by its Arabic acronym *Hamas* (zeal), it is particularly influential in the refugee camps of the Gaza Strip. The aims of *Hamas* are the destruction of Israel and its replacement by a model Islamic State. It opposes any move by the Palestine Liberation Organisation (PLO) to recognise Israel. UNLU, in contrast, is unequivocal in its allegiance to the PLO. At first UNLU and *Hamas* were aware of the dangers of a split in the *intifada* but later, *Hamas*, wanting to dominate the uprising, issued separate leaflets and strike calls, often conflicting with those of UNLU. Another Muslim fundamentalist group prominent in Gaza is *Ilamid Jihad*, though it is not linked to groups of the same name in Egypt and Lebanon.

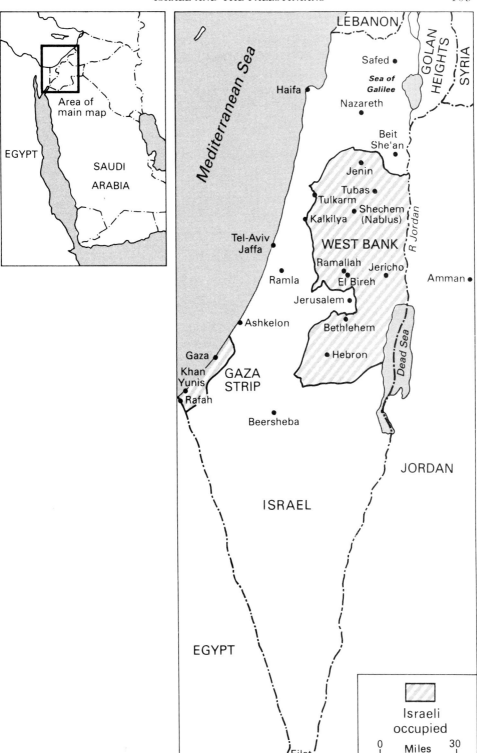

West Bank and Gaza: Areas of Tutifada

Economic Effect of the *Intifada*

Twenty years of Israeli administration created a great degree of integration of the economies of Israel and the West Bank and Gaza. Real *per capita* income in the occupied territories rose steadily after 1967, largely because increasing numbers of Arabs were travelling into Israel each day to work. When the *intifada* began, about 125,000 were doing so. The unrest has been a disincentive to some Israeli employers to take on Arabs whose attendance at work may be erratic and who may also be troublemakers. The Israeli Finance Minister has said that the uprising has caused a drop of just over one per cent in the Israeli gross national product. He attributed the slowdown to a lack of manpower from the occupied territories, reduced trade in those territories and a fall in tourism. Even under normal circumstances the economy of Gaza is relatively poor; its industrial base, like that of the West Bank, is minimal.

Better Life Fuels Nationalism

Physical conditions of life on the West Bank and in Gaza improved enormously after Israel took over their administration in 1967. Jordan had done nothing to improve living conditions on the West Bank and Egypt had neglected the Gaza Strip. It was, tragically, the improvements made by Israel which helped fuel the *intifada*. The Israeli government introduced compulsory education and founded five Arab universities. Living standards rose, as did the feelings of nationalism. A younger, better-educated generation took over from the older generation which had been inclined to rely on UN Relief and Rehabilitation hand-outs in the refugee camps. The inclination of the young generation—as many as 80 per cent of the population under 30—was to side with the PLO. When they became aware that the PLO consistently failed to produce a breakthrough on the Palestinian issue, many turned to Islamic fundamentalism, inspired by the Iranian revolution of the ayatollahs.

The Role of Children

In an article entitled 'A Profile of the Stone-Throwers',[1] a pro-PLO journalist, Daoud Kuttab, describes in detail the role which the *intifada* organisers impose upon young children. Teachers and other leaders assign tasks to children according to their age.

- 7–10 years old: set tyres on fire in the middle of the road to block traffic.
- 11–14 years old: place large stones in the middle of the road to block traffic.
- 15–19 years old: throw large rocks; engage in activities aimed at breaking the curfew.

Young people over 19, Kuttab explains, take key positions in order to lead teams of younger children.

'They are in contact with observers on the hillsides and on high houses and they help determine which cars are to be attacked and which are to be let go.

They stand at an elevated point and direct the stone-throwers as to when and how far to retreat when the soldiers advance. They decide on the moment of a counter-charge which is carried out with loud screams and a shower of stones.'

The Israeli Army View

The officer in charge of Central Command since the beginning of the *intifada* is Major General Amram Mitzna. His Command's main duty is to safeguard Israel's border with Jordan, from the Dead Sea to the Sea of Galilee. In addition, it protects Israel's heartland, including the entire metropolitan areas of Tel Aviv and Jerusalem. Since 1967 the Central Command has been in military control of the West Bank. In an interview with an Israeli editor, General Mitzna was asked about his principles and guidelines concerning the *intifada*. His comments provide an interesting insight which might not otherwise be available.[2]

'Our actions are dictated by the Geneva Convention Agreements. The [Israel Defence Force] IDF employs its forces according to the responsibilities it has been given, specifically quelling violence by the civilian population which is involved in a nationalist uprising. In the territories today, there are restrictions which are similar to those placed on any force dealing with any civilian population which is engaged in violence inspired by nationalism. These restrictions involve limitations on permission to open fire, imposing sanctions, taking legal measures. As the senior officer in Judea and Samaria [West Bank] I work according to internationally-accepted conventions and restrictions.

'Although I receive instructions from the government leaders, I am the senior authority in the territories. The point is that we are dealing with a civilian population that, as the result of a war, is under our control. The fact is this temporary situation has lasted 20 years.

'We have been asking ourselves whether we can deal successfully with the assignments we have been given on one hand, and cope with the judicial restrictions we have on the other. This, while also guarding the border.

'Regarding what soldiers are permitted and what they are forbidden to do, the basic rules are quite natural. IDF troops have no part whatsoever in the punishment of individuals. But soldiers are required to respond with force to every violent demonstration.

'They can forcefully dismantle roadblocks, or prevent any active form of violence. But once an individual has been stopped, he is subject to the law, including a charge sheet, the right to a defence attorney, and for his case to be heard by a judge. Soldiers are entitled to use their weapons only if their lives are in danger. This determination, of course, is subjective. Rioters can put the soldiers in situations where their lives really are in danger even without weapons. An example might be someone standing on the roof of a house in one of the alleys in Nablus holding a cinder block which he is ready to drop.

'The excessive use of force is the exception rather than the rule, especially if you take into account the number of soldiers stationed in the territories, and the number of incidents to which they must respond.

'It is possible that at first we weren't clear enough in our instructions to the soldiers. As the *intifada* continued, we made our instructions much more explicit, and when infractions were exposed, we began punishing both officers and soldiers. The fact that we are so severe with our soldiers is one of the things that distinguishes us from other armies around the world confronted with similar circumstances.

'From the point of view of the IDF, the most difficult problem today is rocks. I'm referring to the more "intelligent" rocks thrown by the more selective population, that finds a tree, or house, or quiet corner, and waits. They throw their rocks mostly at civilian Israeli targets, such as buses taking children to school.

'The lessons we have learned centre around intelligence, training and preparation of units about to go into the field, and the co-ordination of all the groups dealing with the uprising. There is no magic formula. Our aim is still to disrupt the general public as little as possible, while dealing individually with the actively subversive elements of the population. In so doing, we reduced the number of active participants. With time, fewer people have been participating in the demonstrations and the violence. This is due in part to the principle of trying to let those who want to live a normal life do so, while selectively targeting our activities against those who are causing the problems.

'The most difficult thing is dealing with a civilian population, whether the issue is punishment such as destroying houses, or any other measure. The problem is the internal dilemma that you have constantly. On one side is the need to deal with Arab violence, which is in no way selective; it harms a mother and child travelling on a bus, just as readily as it harms soldiers. On the other side is the need to continue to deal properly with the majority of the population, taking into account that they are not subversive.

'The conflict between the Arab majority versus the Jewish settlers makes our lives very complicated. When I have to talk to Jewish residents of a settlement where several residents have been hurt by rocks, despite their strong emotions, I have to explain why they can't shoot at everyone who throws a rock, or demolish every house, or expel thousands of people.

'Even if there are exceptions, and there always are, our performance is definitely improving. There is neither discussion nor hesitation within the IDF about the need to maintain law, values and morality.

'The IDF never had to deal so intensively with events of this magnitude. In my view, we are carrying out our part well. I don't think there is another army or country that could face similar demonstrations with so few infractions by its soldiers.'

Arab Against Arab

During 1989, many Palestinians were labelled as collaborators with the Israelis and killed by their own people. During April, more than 20 died—beaten, stabbed, hacked to death or shot. Their deaths have been portrayed by Palestinian apologists as a 'purging of undesirable elements'. Sometimes the crime of collaboration is not mentioned; instead, the victims are said to have been guilty of social and moral lapses, such as theft or drug-dealing. The catalogue of death for collaborating is gruesome. On 17 April, the body of Ribhi Bani Odeh was found in a field outside the village of Tammoun. He had been beaten to death. On 18 April, the body of Azam al-Qadi was found in Nablus, hacked to death. On 26 April, Omar Zekut was killed by fellow detention inmates at Keztiot detention camp in the Negev. On 29 April, Kamal Abu Zand was shot dead in a Nablus street. Muhammad Arif Salah of the village of Burqa was shot through the head and then decapitated so that the authorities would not realise that villagers had firearms.[3] The killings are seen by some Palestinians as an unpleasant but necessary phase of every revolutionary movement to exterminate traitors. Many others fear that the killings are leading to destructive internecine chaos. Some alleged collaborators escape death but are stoned out of their towns. To the end of 1989, 330 Palestinians were known to have been killed by other Palestinians.

References

1. Daoud was writing in the *Journal of Palestine Studies*, published by the Institute of Palestine Studies and Kuwait University; Spring 1989.
2. General Mitzna was interviewed by Zvi Volk, editor of the *Israel Defence Forces Journal*, No. 16, Winter 1988.
3. This catalogue was compiled by Charles Richards of *The Independent*, London, and published on 12 May 1989.

Kurdish War of Independence

AS ALWAYS, ON THEIR OWN

Background Summary

The Kurds are the world's largest ethnic minority without a homeland and with little hope of obtaining one. Handicapped by having no desire for unity in the 3,500 years of their known history, the 16–22 million people of Kurdish origin began their own split with the break-up of the Ottoman Empire in 1919.

They occupy an area which lies across the borders of Iraq, Iran, Syria, Turkey and the Soviet Union. None of these States has any sympathy for their nationalist aspirations and the Kurds have been bloodily repressed. Unfortunate alliances have also damaged the Kurds' cause. Mustafa Barzani, leader of the Iraqi Kurdistan Democratic Front (KDP), allied himself to the Shah of Iran in the early 1970s and fought against the Iranian Kurds. In 1975 the Iraqi government induced the Shah to abandon the Kurds by bribing him with territorial concessions. The KDF was then caught between the Iraqi and Iranian armies and suffered heavy losses. In 1983, with the Gulf War in progress, the KDP helped Iranian troops to cross into Iraq. The rival Patriotic Union of Kurdistan (PUK), led by Jalal Talabani, trained anti-Khomeini Iranian Kurds to fight the government's troops. These actions, and others, brought retaliation against the Kurds.

The Kurdish Workers Party (PKK), nationalist and Marxist-Leninist in ideology, has had much influence in Turkey. 'Apo' Abdullah Ocalan formed the PKK in 1978 and its militants became Apoists. The PKK was outlawed in Turkey in 1980 and Ocalan found refuge in Syria. Trained in Syria, the Apoists have crossed into Iran and Iraq to wage war against Turkey.

After 1985 the KDP, led by Idris Barzani—son of the famed Mustafa Barzani—fought as guerrillas against the ruthless Iraqis. The much-divided Kurds have other groupings, including the Socialist Party of Kurdistan (Pasok), the Iraqi Dawe Party, which is a Shia Muslim group, and the Turkish Workers' Party of Kurdistan.

When Idris Barzani died during an Iraqi air raid on 31 January 1987, his brother Massoud became leader of the KDP and tried, without much success, to unify the Kurdish factions. In Turkey, the heavily-oppressed Kurds became more militant, despite the absence of their leaders in prison. In the remote eastern provinces of Turkey the conflict between the Turkish army and the Kurdish insurgents became full-scale war. At the same time, many Kurds were fighting with Iran against Iraq and another 11,000 were fighting against Iran in Iranian Kurdistan. These guerrillas are members of a breakaway group of the Kurdish Democratic Party led by Abdorrahmen Qassemlou. Wherever they have fought, the Kurdish guerrillas or *peshmergas*, have won a formidable military reputation.

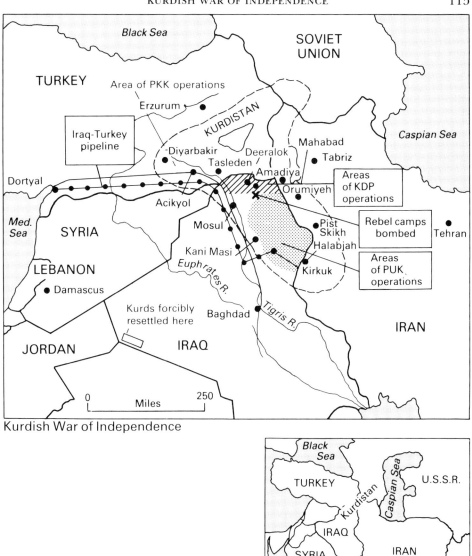

Kurdish War of Independence

Summary of the War in 1988

The KDP decisively defeated Iraqi forces at Deeralok in northern Iraq in January. In a six-day battle, the Iraqis suffered 600 killed or wounded and had 600 men and 1,000 rifles and machine-guns captured. Throughout the year, the Iraqi government acted brutally and ruthlessly against its own civilian Kurds. At least 500,000 families were forcibly resettled in regions close to the borders with Kuwait and Jordan.

The PUK and KDP formed a tactical alliance, as the National Front of Kurdistan (NDF). This gave them a joint strength of 45,000 experienced fighters as well as a militia of 15,000. Between them, PUK and KDP controlled 30,000 square miles.

In Turkey, the biggest reported encounter of the four-year Kurdish insurgency occurred on 1 April in the mountains north of Nusaybin. After a 17-hour fight, the Turks were victorious.

The ceasefire in the Gulf War did not help the Kurds. The Iraqis no longer needed their Kurdish-Iranian allies and abandoned them. Similarly, the Iranians abandoned the Kurdish-Iraqis who had so stoutly supported them. President Saddam Hussein, with the war against Iran suspended, could turn his attention to crushing his Kurds.

The War in 1989

Some of the events described here took place in 1988 but were not known about until 1989.

Iraq began chemical bombing of the Kurds in an onslaught at Halabja in March 1988. This marked a period of unrestricted chemical warfare. The Kurds, undeterred by attacks which they understood, were shocked by the gas attacks and their morale sank, probably to the lowest level ever.

A fresh Iraqi onslaught against the Kurds came soon after Iran accepted the UN Resolution to stop the war against Iraq. On 5 August, Hussein sent 12 armoured brigades and 18 light infantry battalions, supported by artillery and aircraft, against the Kurds. The KDP defended Shirwan and Sidakan.

The next day, the Iraqis used chemical weapons at Kani Rush, Deryasour, Ari and Deshte Bagester. Casualties were widespread among guerrillas and civilians. Worse was to come. On 20 August, with the implementation of the cease-fire agreement in the Gulf War, Hussein used four army corps against the Kurdish area. Liberal use of rockets and gas bombs brought guerrilla resistance to an end.

On 25 August, Iraqi aircraft dropped gas bombs on 70 Kurdish villages between Zahko and Amadiya and near Shadlawa. More than 100,000 civilians, mainly women and children, left their villages and began to walk towards the Turkish border. Other refugees fleeing Iraq took refuge in the Iranian town of Pist Skikh, where many Kurds live.

Not all the Kurds reached safety. Several thousands were trapped in the Basi Valley when the Iraqi army cut the Batufa–Amadia road. On 28–29 August these people were bombed with gas canisters. People on a nearby ridge, who watched helplessly as these attacks were made, said that about 500 families were wiped out. Many thousands more Kurds were captured by Iraqi troops as they fled into the hills and valleys. Saddam Hussein, pleased with his conquests, declared an amnesty, beginning on 6 September, for all Kurds who surrendered within one month.

Some desperate Kurds felt that they had no choice. Bands of *peshmergas* who surrendered near Barmaneh were taken first to Sarsang and then to the provincial capital of Dohok. All leaders were repeatedly interrogated by officials of Iraq's numerous intelligence agencies. Those who refused to answer questions were stoned to death. Atrocities were commonplace. In the village of Kureimeh, 30 *peshmergas* who had surrendered with their families were shot on the spot.

About 30,000 rounded-up Kurds were herded together at Beherkeh, near Irbil, a major Kurdish town. The only relief came from the people of Irbil, who brought food and tents. Even so, thousands of people had to sleep in the open on the ground and many died. Saddam Hussein and the Iraqi government widely publicised their claim that those Kurds who surrendered after the amnesty was announced were not punished.

It is now known that many who surrendered just *before* the amnesty proclamation were not so fortunate. About 10,000 *peshmergas* who did so in the first few days of September were separated from their families and transferred to a prison camp at Salamiyeh near Mosul. They have not been heard of since. Throughout 1989 there were reports that these men have been killed or 'allowed to die' through starvation and exposure.

Saddam Hussein won the 1988–89 phase of the Kurdish war with his use of chemical weapons. He had calculated that the *peshmergas* would fear for the lives of their families—and thus lose their traditional spirit to resist. This proved to be the case. Men who were still quite unafraid of the Iraqi army were thrown into despair about the safety of their families who now, for the first time, were acutely vulnerable.

Battle of Kuarkouk

On 19 July 1988 about 500 *peshmergas* held a strategic position close to where the Iraqi, Iranian and Turkish frontiers meet. In command of the Kurds was Jamil Goran, a former colonel in the Iraqi army, before the purge against the Kurds lost him his job. Anticipating attack, Goran had placed his men in superbly defensive positions behind *sangars* (defences of stones) in shallow trenches.

The Iraqi High Command parachuted the crack 68th Commando Brigade of 1,800 men into places where, it was supposed, the Kurds had their rear. In fact, Goran's force had no rear; it was ready to face an attack from any direction. The Kurds caused such heavy casualties that the Brigade ceased to function. Some reports say that it was wiped out.

On 27 July, the Iraqi High Command sent in fresh units but they could make no impression on the Kurds' defences. After a week the Kurds began to withdraw, in a steady, disciplined way, towards the Turkish border. Further Iraqi units could not halt the Kurds' movement and could not break their formation. When the pressure became too great Goran called a halt and his Kurds quickly prepared defences.

On 2 September, the Iraqi Air Force dropped gas bombs on the *peshmergas* but this activity ended after only 30 minutes. It was later discovered that the Turks had vehemently protested, at top political level, that bombs had dropped in Turkish territory. Saddam Hussein reluctantly ordered the gas bombing to stop.

Finally, on 5 September, Jamil Goran, running short of ammunition and with no way of getting any further supplies—unlike the Iraquis, who were constantly re-supplied—decided to cross the border.

The Turks, who were within observing distance of the battle, confirmed that the Iraqi casualties ran into thousands. The Kurds lost 28 fighters. Their stand had been magnificent but it was their last opportunity for such a display of fighting spirit.

Change of Tactics

Jalal Talabani of PUK said, in Spring 1989, that the *peshmergas'* military capabilities had not been destroyed. They had simply had to change their tactics. One tactic Talabani adopted was to create small, special units, roughly along the lines of the British SAS. Talabani has high regard for the SAS and has read everything he can find about the unit.

Massood Barzani of KDP also believes that he has the answer to tactical problems. Like Talabani, he favours using small, highly-trained commando groups—10–60 men—for hit-and-run operations against Iraqi military bases, depots, dumps, communication centres and isolated outposts. Such units, Barzani knows from experience, are hard to detect, even from helicopters. In addition, the Iraqis would be unlikely to use chemicals against small groups simply because there is little chance of hitting them.

By February 1989, Kurdish leaders were planning to start operations against sensitive targets in Iraqi cities and towns. Interestingly, none of them favours broadside terrorism on the Palestinian model. They realise that their own civilians are too vulnerable to indiscriminate counteraction, especially from a leader as merciless as Saddam Hussein. As targets, the Kurds choose pilots who took part in chemical raids on Kurdistan, men belonging to Iraq's state security apparatus, and anybody known to have had anything to do with the gas attacks.

Barzani publically announced that the war of independence would move south, towards Mosul, Baghdad and Basra. Whether he could live up to his threat was open to question. Guerrilla strength in August 1989 was probably no more than 5,000.

Weapons now used by the Kurds are limited to captured AK-47 Kalashnikov automatic rifles; light and medium machine-guns; 60 mm, 81 mm and 82 mm mortars; and RPG-7 rocket launchers. Before the end of the Iran–Iraq war the Kurds also had heavier weapons but these are not suitable for the new, rapid, deep penetration tactics.

The guerrillas' problem is to find a way of conducting future military operations. One handicap is that the 55,000 Kurds in Turkey will not be permitted to take up arms against Iraq. Willing fighters would be glad to get out of Turkey and the Turkish government would like them to go—provided they go to Iran. But Iran has made it clear that it wants no more Kurds.

The long-term viability of Iranian territory as a Kurdish base is open to question. The harsh reality is that while Iran will back anything that might damage the Iraqis, the Kurds cannot trust Iran. An Iranian government sold them out in 1975.

Massoud Barzani visited Britain in June 1989 in an attempt to persuade the government not to grant export licences for the sale of 62 British Aerospace Hawk trainer aircraft to Iraq. He was successful. The British government condemned Iraqi atrocities against the Kurds but would do nothing else for them.

Many Kurds believe that Turkey will be the first nation to grant some form of self-rule to the Kurds because of Turkey's pro-West policies, its membership of NATO and its desire to join the European Economic Community. The leaders, notably Barzani, demand that Kurdish refugees from Iraq be recognized as political refugees by the UN High Commission for Refugees and other international bodies.

A superpower solution to the conflict is unlikely. The Soviet Union, the US and Europe have their own interests in the region and none of these interests has any relevance to a solution to the Kurdish problem. The US promised to be a guarantor of Kurdish rights and freedoms but has done nothing to protect them. The Kurds, as always, are on their own.

Kurds' Suffering Continues

Abdorrahmen Qassemlou was assassinated in Vienna on 13 July 1989 during peace talks with Iranian representatives in what Kurds say was a trap set by Teheran. Shortly before his death he gave an interview in which he said, 'One doesn't hear enough about the Kurds because we have never taken hostages, never hijacked a plane. But I am proud of this.' Such restraint has won the Kurds some influential friends. An international conference on Kurdish human rights in Paris, in October 1989, was chaired by Danielle Mitterrand, wife of the French President, and one of the speakers was Andrei Sakharov, who proposed a UN General Assembly session on the plight of the Kurds. Sakharov's death in December dismayed the Kurds.

In Turkey, during the winter of 1989–90, security forces evicted Kurds from their mountain villages and burnt their homes in an attempt to stamp out an insurgency in the south-east. The army wants to destroy potential hiding places for guerrillas of the PKK. The conflict has increased in intensity and the death toll has been high—2,000 between 1986 and 1990. According to reliable reports, one Turkish area commander awards a bounty for killing guerrillas, providing Kurdish heads are produced as proof of death. Not surprisingly, the Turkish situation has made the PKK the most hardline of the Kurdish movements. It will settle for nothing less than national independence.

References

Iraq's gas attacks. The evidence that Iraq has used chemical weapons against the Kurds is overwhelming. The International Red Cross, the Turkish Red Crescent, Amnesty International, Western and Turkish journalists and teams of Western doctors confirm it. The Iraqi government, through its ambassadors abroad, continues to deny it.

Battle of Kuarkouk. Information about this remarkable encounter comes from Turkish military sources and from the Kurds' leader, Jamil Goran. Turkish officers were in touch with the Kurds by short-wave radio throughout the action. They also monitored Iraqi communications. Two young Turkish officers unofficially joined the Kurds to observe the course of the battle.

Massoud Barzani expressed his views during a Press conference in London and to several Western journalists who, individually, have managed to reach his HQ.

Anarchy in Lebanon

ALLIANCE AGAINST CHRISTIANS

Background Summary

The conflict has many parts but its basis is the civil war which began in 1975. The principal belligerents were then the 'Lebanese Forces'—the Maronite Christian militia—and terrorists of the Palestine Liberation Organisation (PLO). After bloody expulsion from Jordan in 1970, the PLO settled in southern Lebanon, where it became a State within a State. The main PLO region was known as Fatahland, after Yasser Arafat's faction. When the Christians appeared to be losing to the PLO, the Syrian army went to their aid. Later, the Syrians changed sides and backed the PLO.

As other groups entered the conflict it became complex. Those involved were: Shia Muslims of the south, Sunni Muslims of centre-west Lebanon, and the Druse of the hills, notably from the Shouf Mountains. In the next eight years more than 100,000 Lebanese were killed, mostly in massacres.

In 1978, PLO raids into Israel brought retaliation with *Operation Litani*. The UN sent in a multinational force, the United Nations Interim Force in Lebanon (UNIFIL). When raids and cross-border shelling continued, Israel launched *Operation Peace for Galilee* (6 June 1982) and defeated both the PLO and Syrian forces. The PLO split into two and the Arafat faction evacuated Beirut in October. Christian militiamen massacred Palestinians in two refugee camps, Sabra and Chatilla.

Iranian Shia Muslim agitators had reached the Bekaa Valley in large numbers and here established the extremist *Hezbollah* (Party of God) movement. US Marines, French paratroopers and Italian and British soldiers were sent to Beirut as peace-keepers. They were out of their depth in what had become a holy war. American and French casualties were heavy as a result of Shia suicide bombing attacks and all four Western nations withdrew. Israel also made a phased withdrawal but suffered casualties in attacks made by suicide 'martyrs' driving cars primed with bombs. In alliance with the South Lebanese Army (SLA), the Israelis seet up a security zone along the Israel–Lebanon border.

During 1985, Maronites, Druse, Shia Muslims, Sunni Muslims and Syrians, in shifting alliances, fought ferociously in Beirut. The Sunni militia was practically wiped out. In a siege operation which became known as the Camps War, the Shia militia, *Amal*, with Syrian help, tried to destroy the camps in which 50,000 Palestinian refugees lived. Meanwhile, gunmen from Arafat's PLO faction filtered back into Lebanon and took control of territory from Sidon to Maghdousheh Heights.

During 1987 two wars took place concurrently. *Hezbollah* fought *Amal* in south Beirut and both fought the SLA and Israeli forces in the security zone. The Beirut

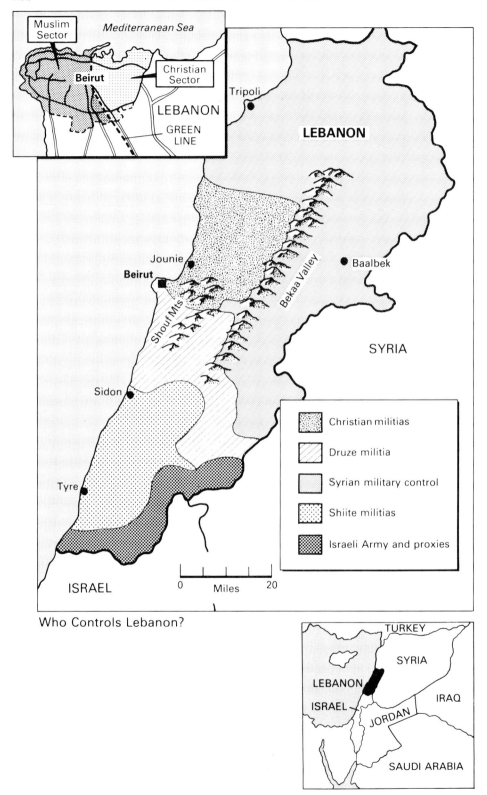

Who Controls Lebanon?

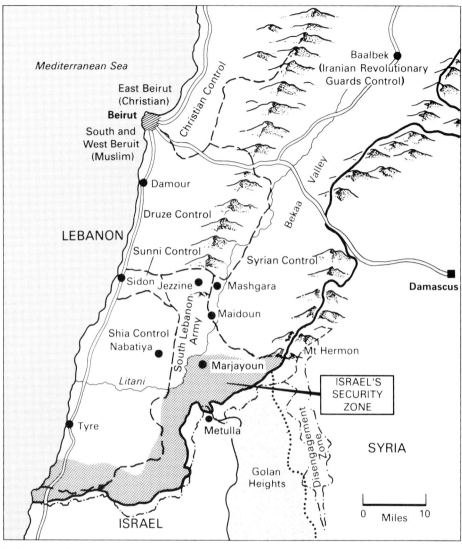

Lebanese Regions

fighting was so savage that the Syrian army imposed intermittent ceasefires. To protect their *Amal* protegées, the Syrians executed scores of *Hezbollah* fighters. In the north of Lebanon, the Syrian army fought *Taweed*, the Islamic Unification Movement.

Summary of the War in 1988

Amal lost to *Hezbollah* nine of the ten Beirut localities it had controlled. Syria intervened to protect *Amal* but, while *Hezbollah* briefly put its weapons aside, it remained in control. Members of the Supreme Shia Islamic Council of Lebanon attacked the role of Iran in Lebanon. According to *Amal* sources, *Hezbollah*, in alliance with 2,000 Iranian Revolutionary Guards, killed 11,000 civilians and wounded many thousands more between January 1987 and June 1988.[1]

In the period September 1987 to May 1988, PLO raiders made hundreds of attempts, most of them futile, to cross the security zone into Israel. The Israeli Defence Forces retaliated, on 2 May, with a large scale attack on the *Hezbollah*-held town of Maidoun.

The Lebanese Army, which is the national force, clashed with the Lebanese Forces, the Maronite militia, in mid-1988. The Syrian navy blockaded the coast of the Christian-held part of Lebanon in an attempt to prevent supplies and arms reaching the Christian fighters. Syrian artillery in the hills overlooking the coast frequently shelled shipping trying to breach the blockade. Passenger ferries between the port of Jounieh and Cyprus were sometimes hit. The scene was being set, during 1988, for further phases in the unending conflict.

The War in 1989

By the end of 1988 Samir Geagea, leader of the Lebanese forces, had emerged as the main strongman of Lebanon's 800,000 Christians. He challenged the divided Christian-Muslim Lebanese Army, the Syrians and their Muslim and Leftist allies. He seemed to be aiming for the partition of Lebanon into sectarian States. When President Amin Gemayel's six-year term expired on 23 September Geagea, by devious political manoeuvring, eliminated him as a challenger to Geagea's growing power in the shrunken Christian enclave north of Beirut.

Geagea allied with the Lebanese Army commander, General Michel Aoun, who had been named by Gemayel as Prime Minister. His legitimacy was challenged by a rival Muslim Prime Minister, Selim Hoss, and his cabinet. Aoun and Geagea detested each other and only the common Syrian threat held them in an alliance.

Divisions within the Shia community showed up in fighting which broke out between *Amal* and *Hezbollah* in early January 1989. At least 150 people were killed and 300 wounded as *Amal* and *Hezbollah* sought to dominate Lebanon's 1.5 million Shia Muslims. *Hezbollah* was fighting to regain villages lost to *Amal* in the 1988 clashes. *Amal*'s aim was to eliminate the challenge from *Hezbollah*. The inter-Shia hostilities embarrassed both Syria and Iran, who for most purposes are allies. After intensive negotiations in Damascus, presided over by senior Iranian and Syrian officials, a truce was signed on 30 January.

Another regional power, Iraq, now entered the Lebanon arena. The halt in the Gulf War allowed Iraq, Syria's long-standing rival in the Arab world, to resume its efforts to undermine Syria's influence in Lebanon. To do this, Saddam Hussein chose to back the Christians, specifically the Lebanese Forces, with its 6,000 fighters and 30,000 reservists. He gave Geagea equipment valued at about $200 million. The most significant arms were 100 artillery pieces, ranging from 105 mm to 155 mm guns. Also included in the hand-out were T-34, T-55, M-48, M-4 and AMX-13 tanks. With the materiel came a promise of limitless ammunition, together with replacement guns and tanks as needed.[2]

General Aoun had been thought of as a rather dull and unimaginative man but he soon showed that, militarily at least, he could be ruthlessly effective. The four Christian brigades of his national army attacked Geagea's Lebanese Forces on 14 February in four days of fighting. Aoun's 15,000 men captured most of Geagea's Beirut bases. A total of 76 Lebanese Forces men were killed and 200 wounded in the worst fighting in the Christian sector for three years. The Forces used the Iraqi-supplied equipment but Geagea's units were tactically outclassed by the Army. Commando battalions did most of the heaviest fighting. It was brought to an end only by intense pressure from the Maronite establishment. Part of the ceasefire agreement was that the Lebanese Forces should cede control of their area in the East Beirut port complex. This is one of several ports along the coast north and south of Beirut which are operated—illegally—by Christian, Shia and Druse militias, providing important sources of revenue and war supplies. The ports are also used for export of drugs. Aoun now controlled 75 per cent of the Christian area.

Christian 'War of Liberation'

This destructive phase of the Lebanese conflict began on 14 March after General Aoun attempted to blockade the ports to the south of Beirut controlled by Shia and Druse, without first reaching agreement with the Selim Hoss rival Muslim administration in West Beirut. The Druse, led by Walid Jumblatt, responded by shelling Christian East Beirut. General Aoun then bombarded Muslim West Beirut, the Druse areas in the hills around the city and Syrian positions in the Bekaa Valley.

Aoun accused Syria of inciting and then increasing the fighting between East and West Beirut. He stated, in a virtual declaration of war, that his aim was to force the withdrawal of 35,000 Syrian troops deployed in two-thirds of Lebanon. In the following weeks, Beirut endured some of the heaviest artillery bombardments of the entire war. More than 400 civilians died in April and May and thousands were injured. Thousands of homes and cars were destroyed and electricity and water supplies were almost completely disrupted.

The Ministerial Committee of the Arab League led efforts to negotiate a ceasefire. On 16 April the Spanish ambassador and members of his family were killed by a Syrian shell, a tragedy which led the European Community to repeat its call for a cessation of hostilities. On 28 April a cease-fire came into effect but it broke down on 6 May.

On 11 May another cease-fire was negotiated but the Syrians announced that they regarded it only a 'land cease-fire'. They continued to bombard the coast to prevent seaborne supplies from reaching the Christian enclave. Further recriminations between the two communities were caused by the car bomb assassination, on 16 May, of Sheikh Hassan Khaled, Grand Mufti of Lebanon, spiritual leader of the country's 700,000 Sunni Muslims. Another 21 people were killed in the explosion. The Mufti, who was renowned for his moderation and support for a united Lebanon, favoured the Arab League ceasefire plan and was an important channel for a series of agreements reached between Aoun and Hoss. It is probable that Shia extremists, possibly *Hezbollah*, murdered the Sheikh to wreck any further attempts to reunify Lebanon.

The 11 May cease-fire was broken almost daily by the Syrians and their Muslim allies. Losing patience, General Aoun gave the order, on 3 June, for unrestricted shelling of his enemies' positions. Syria called a conference of its allies in Damascus and within two days 18 Lebanese and Palestinian groups, mostly terrorist organis-ations, promised to join Syria and fight against Aoun. Carloads of gunmen and militia jeeps, mounted with recoil-less rifles, appeared on the streets of West Beirut. Some belonged to the Druse and Shia *Amal* but others were manned by *Hezbollah* militiamen from the southern suburbs. This was the first time since February 1987 that Syria had permitted armed *Hezbollah* fighters to move in the commercial streets of the capital. Syria was thus fulfilling its threat to Aoun to set its savage Muslim allies against the Christians in East Beirut.

General Aoun said: 'Our war is not against Lebanese factions. We have been fighting the Syrians for more than five months. Now they want to create facts and claim the conflict is between Lebanese groups. We do not accept this.' His state-ment was not entirely true. The Druse militia had been fighting the Lebanese Army for the same five months as the Syrians.[3]

Amal relies on Syria to protect it in large areas of Beirut where it would other-wise be crushed by Palestinian guerrillas and Druse militia. Syria relies on *Amal* to keep the PLO guerrillas in check. The Druse need the Syrians to protect them from the Christian Maronite militias.

The Soukh al-Gharb Battle

On 13 August, the Syrians massed tanks to support their 41st Brigade in an attack on the 8th Brigade of General Aoun's army at Soukh al-Gharb, on ridges above Beirut. Walid Jumblatt's Druse militia joined the Syrians for the attack. Jumblatt was so confident of victory that he pre-arranged a Press conference to announce his success.

Possession of the ruins of Soukh al-Gharb would allow the Syrians to aim their guns all the more effectively on targets in East Beirut. After artillery had shelled the ruins and supposed positions of the 8th Brigade, the Syrian tanks advanced, closely supported by Syrian and Druse infantry. The Christians held firm and wrecked a number of enemy tanks with fire from field-guns and rockets. The over-confident Syrian and Druse foot soldiers were then caught in machine-gun crossfire. About 40 Syrians and 80 Druse were killed. General Aoun's HQ did not reveal its Christian casualties but claimed victory. In that Aoun's lines did not crack, he was undoubtedly the victor. Significantly, the Druse Press conference was cancelled and the Syrian Army denied that its forces had been involved. The Christians had merely beaten the Druse, a Syrian communiqué announced.[4]

The following afternoon, Syrian armour massed in another ruined village, Douat-Chweir, in the Metn Hills. Mortars fired on Lebanese Army positions for five hours, while Aoun's officers redeployed their own tanks. This phase of the battle did not develop but it was only a matter of time before other fierce clashes developed. President Assad felt compelled to destroy Aoun, the most dangerous political and military enemy he has faced in Lebanon. And this particular enemy has, as his ally, the 'beast of Baghdad', as the Syrians call Saddam Hussein.

The Syrians could readily storm Christian north Beirut and crush Aoun's forces but even Assad could not face the storm of international condemnation that would follow. In Aoun's 'War of Liberation', the safest place to be was on the front line. Civilian casualties from the protracted night and day shelling far exceeded those of the Lebanese Army.

Apart from the French, who sent a fleet to stand off the Lebanese coast, the international Christian community was strangely uninterested in the Christian plight.

Disposition of Lebanese Army Brigades

Late in 1989 four mainly Christian brigades—the 5th, 8th, 9th and 10th comprising about 15,000 men in all—were loyal to General Aoun. Five brigades, predominantly Shia Muslim—18,000 men—had either sided with the Muslim anti-Christian alliance or remained on the sidelines.

The 1st Brigade, based in the Syrian-controlled Bekka Valley, of east Lebanon, is made up predominantly of pro-Syrian Shia. The 2nd Brigade, a mixture of Muslims and Maronites, was stationed in northern Lebanon, where Syria is in control.

The 3rd and 4th Brigades disintegrated. Most of the 3rd allied with the 6th, together with half of the 4th. About 1,500 Christian soldiers from the 4th escaped by sea to join Aoun's forces in the Christian heartland.

The 6th Brigade, which is predominantly Shia Muslim, was in East Beirut and allied with the Syrian-backed Shia Amal militia. The 7th Brigade, comprising Christians loyal to former President Suleiman Franjieh, one of Syria's closest Christian allies, controlled the Batroun region, north of Samir Geagea's territory.

The 11th Brigade, mainly Druse, was based in the Shouf Mountains and, in 1989, had not taken part in any action since February 1984. The 12th Brigade, mainly Sunni Muslim, was loyal to acting prime Minister Selim Hoss, and was based in the southern provincial capital of Sidon.

'Enough agony, enough blood, enough destruction'

After months of difficulty, the deputies of the Lebanese Assembly at the end of October 1989 elected a president to succeed Amin Gemayel whose term of office had expired. He was René Moawad, a mild man of high principle. Unfortunately, he represented everything which many of his fellow Christians hate—Syrian influence, Syrian dominance, occupation by the Syrian army. Moawad appointed Dr. Hoss as Prime Minister and planned, once he had a cabinet in place, to replace General Aoun as army commander.

On 22 November, President Moawad attended a reception and parade to mark Lebanon's 46th year of independence. He also appeared on television and reminded his people of the suffering they had endured over the previous 15 years. 'Enough agony, enough blood, enough destruction,' he said. 'Enough impoverishment, enough adventures. Let us at long last close ranks and build the new Lebanon.'

Having greeted ambassadors, Moawad left the prime minister's office and climbed into his armoured Mercedes. His motorcade, guarded by three jeep-loads of Lebanese paramilitary police and six Syrian escorts, drove towards the presidential palace. A bomb of 550lb of TNT, hidden in a shop, exploded as his car passed by. It killed the president and 23 other people and injured scores more. Since no country in the Middle East desires Syria's humiliation more than does Iraq, it was logical to suspect Iraq of complicity in the killing. The Syrian leadership blamed General Aoun for the murder.

The deputies chose Elias Hrawi as the new president. Hrawi, who is also a 'Syrian man', sacked Aoun and told him he was no longer commander of the army. To prevent Aoun's eviction from his HQ at Baabda, scores of thousands of his supporters formed a human shield around Baabda. His soldiers remained loyal and 39 right-wing French deputies flew from Paris to join his local followers.

The Arab world still tried to bring about some form of peace in Lebanon on the lines of the Taef Accords agreed on in October 1989 in Saudi Arabia but Aoun and the Lebanese Christians reject the accords. Most foreign observers remaining in Lebanon say that the peace will come only with the withdrawal of the Syrians, the Iranian Revolutionary Guards and the PLO. After this, these observers say, the Christians must be allowed to have a separate independent state in their enclave of 800 square kilometers. If peace depends on such a list of conditions it remains impossible to bring about.

*   *   *

Israeli troops, backed by tanks and helicopter gunships, made their deepest raid into Lebanon for a year on 26 December 1989 when they raided the head-quarters of the Lebanese Communist Party (LCP) at Nabi Safa in the Bekaa Valley. The Israeli Defence Ministry claimed that LCP terrorists used the base from which to launch attacks against Israeli troops and the South Lebanon Army. The paratroop raiders destroyed the base without casualties to themselves.

Despite the raid, the Israeli Chief-of-Staff, Lieut-General Dan Shomron, said that as a matter of 'principle and policy', Israel would not involve itself in Lebanon, as long, as there was no direct Syrian threat to Israel's northern border.

References

1. Hospital sources in Beirut said that these figures are 'more or less' accurate. However, it should be noted that all figures from Lebanon are suspect. Those from hospitals and certain Western embassies are generally the most reliable.
2. These details were verified by a diplomatic source in Baghdad.
3. General Aoun was available to Western journalists throughout the 'War of Liberation'. It was also possible to talk to Walid Jumblatt. The Syrians issued 'official statements' but would rarely provide a spokesman to answer questions.
4. Details of this action were verified from a variety of sources, principally a foreign aid worker who happened to be in the Soukh al-Gharb area when the fighting began.

War Annual 3 used three maps of Lebanon and its conflict. The main subjects described and analysed were:

Details of the border raids against Israel.
The essential nature of UNIFIL's role.
The Syrian action in attempting to control *Hezbollah.*

Morocco–Polisario War

A FAINT HOPE OF PEACE

Background Summary

The war concerns the ownership of Western Sahara, a former Spanish colony. When Spain announced its imminent withdrawal in 1975, Morocco and Mauritania claimed the territory. The International Court ruled that neither had a legitimate claim and that the overriding principle was self-determination by the estimated 300,000 inhabitants, the Sahrawis or West Saharans.

Following Spain's withdrawal in 1976, Morocco and Mauritania partitioned the 30,000 sq. mile country. The Popular Front for the Liberation of Saguia al-Jamra and Rio de Oro (Polisario) declared the whole area to be the Sahrawi Arab Democratic Republic (SADR). After military reverses at the hands of Polisario, Mauritania agreed to a cease-fire. Morocco then claimed the entire area.

The Polisario guerrilla army, a highly mobile force, made it impossible for Morocco to occupy the region. The Moroccan Army then based its strategy on the Hassan Wall, a system of defences which it began to construct in 1980. The Sahrawis were squeezed into the north-east and into refugee camps, notably Tindouf, in neighbouring Algeria, which supports Polisario. The Organisation of African Unity (OAU) recognised SADR, as did many other countries, but Morocco refused to negotiate with Polisario. The UN does not recognise SADR as a state and has not admitted Polisario as an observer delegation.

SADR leaders hoped that Islamic fundamentalism, already rife in Morocco, would bring down the monarchy of King Hassan. The Moroccan people would then reject the enormous cost of the war. While Polisario had numerous supporters it had only one powerful friend, the Soviet Union. Morocco could count on help from the United States and France.

The Moroccan army broadened its control of the disputed territory. By 1985 it held nearly all the northern part, leaving only the stony plains of Rio de Oro for the guerrillas. The ever-lengthening Hassan Wall dominated the territory and in 1985 it stretched for 1,000 miles. Made of earth packed about 12 feet high, it is protected by barbed wire, radar and ground sensors.

Nevertheless, in bold raids Polisario continued to capture enemy arms and equipment. Simultaneously, SADR became more politically and socially cohesive and by 1987 was recognised by 65 countries.

Summary of the War in 1988

The war was costing Morocco $1 million a day; the garrison of the Wall increased from 110,000 to 150,000 and the length of the remarkable defences

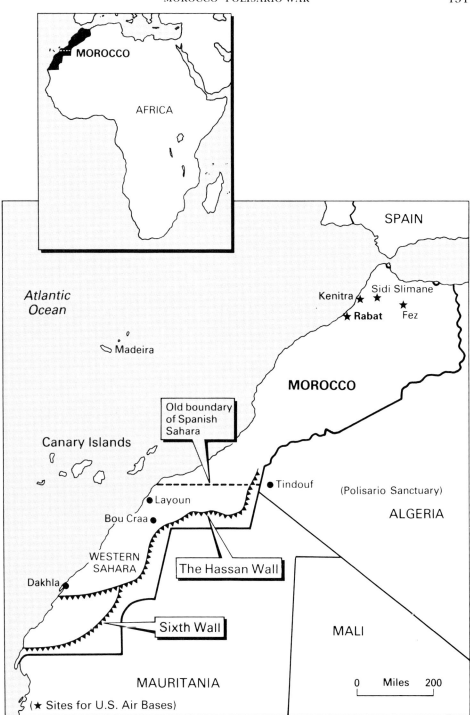

Morocco-Polisario War

stretched to 1,500 miles. The Moroccan Army used cluster bombs and napalm against the guerrillas, an indication of its desperation to secure a military victory.

During 1988 the military prowess of Polisario was impressive. With only 3,000 fighters, it breached the Hassan Wall virtually at will. This is because of the excellence of its intelligence. It uses pilotless reconnaissance drones fitted with television cameras to spy on Moroccan positions behind the wall. Astonishingly, the raiders even managed to capture Moroccan soldiers and transfer them to SADR camps before the Moroccan command could react.

In a systematic attempt to demoralise and discourage the SADR leadership, the Moroccan government was steadily settling Moroccans in areas behind the wall. By mid-1988 about 10,000 people were established in new communities. This activity was condemned by Zambia's leader, Kenneth Kaunda, and the many other statesmen who support SADR. On numerous occasions they pointed out that SADR was already a state, with an enlightened and efficient administration, under President Abdelaziz.

From time to time the Moroccan army made sweeps into Polisario territory but all were fruitless. On most occasions the army columns did not even sight a Polisario guerrilla. On one such occasion the army suffered more than 100 casualties from Polisario landmines without firing a single shot against the elusive enemy.

The War from September 1988

In an operation of astonishing boldness for a guerrilla organisation, Polisario breached the Hassan Wall on 23 September 1988. Using armoured personnel carriers, the Polisario command sent in about 1,000 fighters formed into units of 350 men each. The units were classed as 'two light infantry battalions and one mechanised infantry battalion'. This operation was a complete surprise, since nobody had known that Polisario had been training its men for a conventional assault.

Around the Oum Dreiga section of the Hassan Wall, in the north, the fast-moving attack hit Moroccan garrison units before they could completely deploy. The 3rd Regiment Motorised Infantry suffered most, losing its commanding officer, Colonel Abdelsalam Al-Abidi. Taken prisoner, the Colonel later died of his wounds. The Moroccan army took the unusual step of announcing casualty figures—51 of its men killed and 95 wounded. This was an attempt to cover up the true figures, which amounted to more than 300, including 25 taken prisoner.[1]

The Moroccans claim to have inflicted 124 casualties on the Polisario raiders but this is a gross exaggeration. Polisario itself never gives details of casualties but Algerian sources say that 'no more than a handful of guerrillas' were killed or wounded.[2]

By 1989, the US had provided Morocco with $859 million in armaments. The weapons have been purchased mainly through US military credits as well as with outright grants. Major weapons supplied by the US include 20 Northrop F-5E fighters and trainers, six Rockwell OV-10A reconnaissance aircraft and five additional Lockheed C-130 transports, three KC-130H tankers, 108 M60A3 tanks, 190 M48A5 tanks and quantities of Sidewinder, Maverick, Dragon, Chaparral, TOW and HAWK missiles. Artillery, cluster bombs and electronic equipment have also been provided.[3] Much of this equipment is useless for the type of conflict being fought against Polisario.

Apart from Soviet *materiel*, Polisario has used equipment from Libya, North Korea and Yugoslavia. Equipment in use against the Moroccans included Soviet-made BMP-1 armoured vehicles, T-55 tanks, Sagger anti-tank missiles and an array of mortars and field pieces.

Despite such spectacular strikes as Oum Dreiga, Polisario has no territorial gains to show for years of bitter warfare and the success of Oum Dreiga did not indicate that Polisario could win the war. However, it established for SADR politicians a firmer basis for cease-fire talks.

Brahim Ghali, a member of the Polisario executive committee who was SADR Minister of Defence from the beginning of the conflict until he was transferred to a military position in May 1989, said in June; 'Our independence represents no danger for Morocco or any other country. We want to be free and we want co-operation with all our neighbours, especially Morocco, which will have privileged relations with us'.

The move towards a settlement can be attributed to two factors. One is the continual heavy drain on Morocco's financial resources and its foreign debt of $18 billion. The other is the re-establishment of diplomatic ties between Algeria and Morocco, resulting in a weakening of Algerian support for Polisario. Bogged down by its own growing economic problems, which culminated in a bloody uprising in October 1988, Algeria had been forced to rebuild links with Morocco.[4]

On 26 January 1989 King Hassan and SADR leaders met in the King's palace at Marrakesh. The primary object of the meeting was to discuss a United Nations proposal to end the war by holding a referendum among the inhabitants of Western Sahara. The plan would allow a choice between independence for SADR or integration with Morocco.

Under the proposed UN ceasefire plan, Morocco would reduce its troops in Western Sahara by 100,000. Those remaining would be stationed in sites desig-nated by the UN Special Representative, Hector Gros-Espial of Uruguay, and placed under the surveillance of a UN observer group. The Polisario guerrillas would be under similar surveillance. Polisario has released 200 of its 2,500 Moroc-can prisoners as a 'goodwill gesture'.

The UN, which is to supervise the referendum in December 1989 together with the OAU in Western Sahara, will send a 2,000-strong peacekeeping force to monitor the ceasefire.

By mid-1989 both sides had firm calculations on how the referendum vote would go. They know who is on the list of eligible voters, whether any given voter is in Tindouf or inside Western Sahara and more-or-less how each might vote. Each side believes with absolute conviction that it will win. It is a numbers game and both sides have strategies on how to manipulate the rules to get the results they want.

New Offensives

After nine months of calm the war erupted again on 7 October 1989 when Polisario launched a major attack on the Hassan Wall in the Guelta Zemmour sector. According to Polasario, they breached 10 miles of wall and killed 200

Moroccan troops, including the colonel commanding the sector. The Moroccan Press Agency (MPA) admitted to only 15 Moroccan soldiers being killed and claimed that Polisario had suffered 80 dead or wounded. Four days later, Polisario struck again, this time at Hausa, further north. The guerrillas occupied a 12-mile length of wall. Again, there was a large discrepancy in the respective casualty claims.

The MPA announced that the attacks were unexpected in view of the truce and Morocco's readiness to resume talks. Actually, Polisario resumed hostilities because of Hassan's refusal to negotiate. Polisario felt that its gestures of compromise had been rejected. Morocco even refused to accept 200 prisoners released by Polisario and they had to be returned to captivity.

Before the October attacks, Hassan had been under the impression that Polisario's resistance was crumbling. He had reached this conclusion after the defection from Polisario, on 8 August 1989, of Omar Hadrami, a founder member of Polisario and for several years its intelligence chief. The Moroccans exploited Hadrami's defection and paid for an expensive eight-page advertising section in *Time* Magazine in which Hadrami explained that the idea of total independence 'had now become impossible'. He said, 'Our brothers in Morocco have become prosperous while we have been rotting away under tents.'

In the same advertisement, King Hassan was quoted as saying that 'the Saharan issue has become a grain of sand'.

References

1. From a foreign observer who was present as a guest of the CO of the 3rd Regiment. He said:'The Polisario fighters impressed me with their battle discipline'.
2. Algeria has consistently given information which has proved to be reliable.
3. US Congressional sources.
4. The five countries in the region—Morocco, Tunisia, Algeria, Libya and Mauritania—hope to re-establish the Greater Arab Mahgreb, which would include Western Sahara. The union would be modelled on the lines of the European Economic Community.

Mozambique Guerrilla War

ATROCITY AS POLICY

Background Summary

In 1975 Mozambique became independent from Portugal and the Mozambique Liberation Front (Frelimo), a Marxist faction, won control. Its economic and social policies brought the new nation close to ruin. In 1977 Ken Flower, chief of the Rhodesian Central Intelligence Organisation, created the Mozambique National Resistance (MNR), better known as Renamo. Through its control of Renamo, white-ruled Rhodesia intended to sabotage the assistance which black regimes, such as Frelimo, might give to Zimbabwean resistance within Rhodesia.

Gradually, fighting between Frelimo and Renamo destroyed Mozambique's society. In 1982 South Africa, which has a long border with Mozambique, began a campaign to ensure that its neighbour would never become a threat to South African security. Units of the South African Defence Force (SADF) engaged in guerrilla warfare against the Mozambique army while the South African government financed, trained and armed Renamo fighters.

Portugal, Morocco, Saudi Arabia and Zaire also supported Renamo, which claimed to have 18,000 men in 1982. Frelimo, by 1986, had 15,000 soldiers supported by 3,500 Zimbabwean troops on railway protection duty. Mozambique's President, Samora Machel, relied on Soviet and Chinese aid. Renamo controlled two-thirds of the country's nearly 304,000 square miles.

The Renamo leader, Alfonso Dhlakama, claimed that 2,000 of his men were members of 'conventional battalions'. In fact, Renamo was nothing more than a collection of large gangs. They operated from Malawi for much of 1986 until President Hastings Banda yielded to Zimbabwean and Tanzanian pressure to drive them out.

When President Machel was killed in a plane crash on 19 October 1986 he was succeeded by Joaquim Chissano. Under Chissano, and with Zimbabwe's help, Frelimo reversed Renamo's gains, but Renamo remained active thoughout 1987 in 13 of the 14 provinces.

Summary of the War in 1988

In April 1988, the US Assistant Secretary of State for Africa, Roy Stacey, made an assessment which summed up much of Renamo's military activity for the year as a whole. He said: 'What has emerged in Mozambique is one of the most brutal holocausts against ordinary human beings since World War II'. Stacey accused Renamo of 'waging a systematic and brutal war of terror against Mozambican civilians through forced labour, physical abuse and wanton killing'.

This hostile American attitude was significant, since the US had up till then

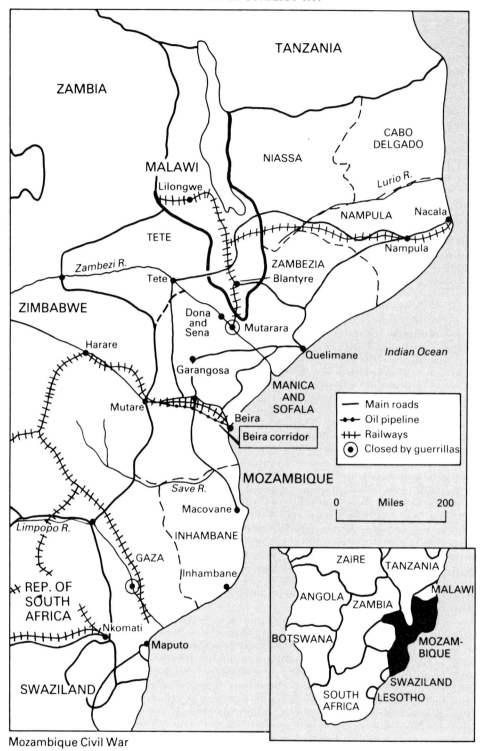

Mozambique Civil War

supported Renamo against the Marxist regime. The change came about as a result of a report by Robert Garsony, consultant to the US State Department's Bureau for Refugee Programs.

Despite Renamo's proven atrocities, throughout 1987–88 a small, wealthy and influential group of American businessmen and evangelical Christians lobbied to persuade the Reagan administration to aid the rebels, on the grounds that they were fighting a resistance war against atheist Marxists.

Since 1986, the US religious involvement has centred on Thomas Schaaf, a fundamentalist who worked in Zimbabwe before moving to Washington. He uses missionaries in Malawi to co-ordinate logistics support for the rebels. It is likely that Mr. Schaaf has worked closely with former CIA and US army officials to aid Renamo.

The first troops to be trained by British military advisers in Zimbabwe finished their 12-week course in December 1987. During 1988 they were regarded as probably the best of Frelimo's soldiers but they were handicapped by the lack of modern transport and all forms of supplies, including food.

The War in 1989

The ferocity of the Renamo guerrillas had long puzzled Western observers and diplomats. The opposition of Right-wing groups to a Marxist regime was understandable but their slaughter of peaceful peasants was irrational. In a rare interview, Alfonso Dhlakama explained his policy. For him, military strategy was nothing more than 'making problems for the enemy'. The Renamo command therefore encouraged its fighters to make problems by butchering civilians and by forcing hundreds of thousands to become refugees.[1]

In January, two Renamo leaders, Mateus Lopes and Joao da Silva Ataide, were killed while returning from a meeting with Dhlakama. They were said to have died in a road accident but murder is more likely. The murderers were probably members of a group of senior Renamo officials who oppose efforts to negotiate an end to the war.

A Mozambican official told a British reporter: 'This is a war from the Middle Ages. In some areas the government is seen as an intruder into a world of age-old traditions. It breeds a very vicious reaction, a desire to destroy any vestige of central or modern authority'.[2]

This authority was not helped by the announcement, in June, that the 800 Soviet experts and advisers would pull out of Mozambique over the next two years. Nevertheless, the dramatic turnabout was applauded when announced by Mozambique's Foreign Minister, General Alberto Chipande. A few months later East Germany and Cuba told the government that they, too, would cut back their military and security teams.[3]

The Soviet Union did not intend to abandon Mozambique. Training in conventional warfare and deliveries of heavy weapons is being replaced by increased supplies of helicopters, trucks, communication equipment and light weapons. The savings to the budget-conscious Soviet Union will amount to 40 per cent of its annual military aid budget in Mozambique, which totalled £80 million in 1988.

Even more significantly, in July, F.W. de Klerk, shortly before he became South Africa's president, conferred with President Chissano in Maputo. Chissano obtained de Klerk's public support for his new peace initiative. Mr. de Klerk said: 'Renamo should stop violence and become part of the efforts for peaceful development in Mozambique'. This was a remarkable statement from the leader of the country responsible, for a decade, for much of Renamo's military prowess. As a token of friendship South Africa has promised to help Mozambique repair the giant Cahora Bassa hydro-electric complex in the north-western province of Tete. It has also lent £1.2 million to improve the port of Maputo, which is the best outlet for South African coal and citrus exports.

President Chissano agreed to support South Africa's reintegration into the southern African community of nations, 'provided that South Africa dismantled apartheid and introduced significant degrees of equality'.[4]

President Daniel arap Moi of Kenya, acting as a mediator, also had talks with Chissano about ending the war. 'I have some information about those struggling against your government', Moi told Chissano on 21 July. 'They are willing to take part in these peace talks.' This announcement came as a surprise, since fierce fighting had been going on for 10 days in the central region of Gorongosa.

The new phase of conflict had been initiated by the army, without Chissano's authorisation. How and why such an assault could be launched at precisely the time Alfonso Dhlakama was scheduled to depart for peace talks has not been satisfactorily explained.

Nevertheless, Dhlakama did turn up in Nairobi for peace talks. His presence was an indication that for the first time in Renamo's 15-year history its leaders within Mozambique had assumed supremacy over the shadowy external chiefs. The power of these men, closely linked with Right-wing Portuguese and South African circles, has significantly decreased.

After the Nairobi meeting it became known that the peace-feelers between Renamo and the Mozambique government had begun in February 1989, when two young rebel leaders secretly met Mozambican church leaders.[5] The Renamo men were Raul Domingos and Vincente Ululu, neither of whom is a member of the Ndau tribe which once dominated the movement.

Domingos's association with Renamo is interesting. In 1980 he was kidnapped in central Mozambique while returning from a visit to relatives. After being given military training in South Africa he quickly rose to become number two in Renamo, as well as chief of staff of its army. He is now 'Minister of External Relations'.

Despite the tentative approach towards peace, Renamo is a formidable army. Its units are a strange mixture: some wear clean, regulation uniforms and are well armed, while others are little more than machete-wielding savages in ragged bush clothing. In a pitched battle, the army would win. However, no such confrontation is likely. Renamo's organisation has improved, with a network of 10 provincial military command posts linked by a sophisticated radio network.

Inducing the rebels to give up their weapons and accept peaceful administration will be an enormous task. By 1989 they numbered 30,000, many of them merciless killers of civilians. Those Renamo leaders who want to see their unhappy nation restored to peace and prosperity may be forced to turn on their own worst elements and destroy them.

The Unhappiest Nation on Earth

In July 1989 the Population Crisis Committee of New York, in its *International Index of Human Suffering* classified Mozambique as the 'unhappiest nation on earth'. The *Index* uses figures of infant mortality, life expectancy, the provision of medical care, drinkable water, diet and public safety to make its assessments.

Behind Mozambique, in the table of most unhappy nations, were Angola, Afghanistan and Chad. According to the *Index*, Mozambique surpassed even Lebanon in its suffering from genocide, civil war and terrorism. Its infant mortality rate is 35 per cent, the highest in the world. The country's *per capita* income is $95 a year. More than 3.5 million refugees, a quarter of the population, subsist on foreign charity abroad or in refugee camps inside the country. Agriculture can feed only six per cent of the urban population. In addition to the 100,000 killed in the period 1979–89, at least another 300,000 died of starvation.

The *Index*, quoting the Mozambique Ministry of Education, stated that since 1981 Renamo had destroyed more than 2,500 schools—two-thirds of the total—and 600 clinics.

Negotiations in Sight

On 8 December 1989, the two African presidents who had undertaken to mediate in the Mozambique dispute—Robert Mugabe of Zimbabwe and Daniel arap Moi—urged both sides to drop pre-conditions. While Alfonso Dhlakama still rejected Mugabe as a mediator because of the presence of 7,000 Zimbabwean troops fighting Renamo in central and southern Mozambique, he agreed to drop pre-conditions.

Renamo would not have to recognise the constitution and state, as President Chissano had demanded. Acceptance of talks would also imply Chissano's recognition of Renamo as a party. One of the sticking points is that Chissano and Frelimo insist on a one-party state while Renamo wants a constituent assembly and a multi-party system.

In a statement on 18 December 1989, Dhlakama insisted that Renamo is no different from UNITA and other movements fighting Marxism in their countries. He painted a picture of Renamo as a movement with widespread popular support in its crusade against Marxist tyranny, despite reports from refugees which contradict this picture.

It seemed possible, early in 1990, that after 12 years of fighting, direct negotiations between Renamo and Frelimo were within reach.

References

1. Quoted in a report by Richard Dowden in *The Independent*, London, 24 February 1988.
2. *Ibid.*
3. Diplomatic sources in Maputo.
4. Mozambique Prime Minister's office.
5. Roman Catholic Church sources in Maputo.

Aspects of the war covered in War Annual No. 3 include:

Food convoys without escort

Renamo's view of strategy

The army's equipment

The special forces trained by foreign governments and security firms.

Details of the Gersony report, which changed the US government's attitude towards Renamo.

Northern Ireland Terrorist War

SEEKING SOFTER TARGETS

Background Summary

The basis of the confrontation between the rival communities in Northern Ireland is the demand by the nationalist organisation Sinn Fein, whose members are Roman Catholics, for the union of Northern Ireland with Eire (the Irish Republic), and the insistence by the Protestant Loyalist community that Northern Ireland remains part of the United Kingdom.

Sinn Fein split in 1969 and since then its military arm has been the Provisional Irish Republican Army, often known as the Provisionals or the Provos. In practice, Sinn Fein and the IRA have the same command. The IRA wages a terrorist war against the Protestants' 'defence' groups, some of which are also terrorist. In 1969 the British Army entered Ulster to protect both the Catholic and Protestant communities and to fight the terrorists.

The Hillsborough Agreement between Britain and Eire in 1985 was designed to reduce terrorism by improving co-operation between the two countries. The Protestant majority in Northern Ireland—62 per cent of the population—saw the agreement as a step towards unification of Ireland and opposed it. The IRA also opposed it; it threatened their freedom of action.

On 8 May 1987 the IRA lost eight of its most experienced members in a single incident—the most serious loss in terms of numbers since the Provisional IRA was formed in 1969—when an élite murder squad of the IRA's 'East Tyrone Brigade' were killed in a clash with the security forces in Loughall.

By mid-1987 the British army had 10,200 men in Northern Ireland. The IRA, finding its operations limited, sought targets among the British armed forces in West Germany. The first of a series of attacks occurred in March 1987 when a car bomb injured 31 people at Rheindalen. In Enniskillen, Ulster, as several hundred people assembled on 11 November for Remembrance Day ceremonies, the IRA exploded a 40lb bomb. Eleven civilians were killed and 63 were injured.

A major reverse for the IRA came on 30 October when French Customs seized the *Eksund*, which was carrying Libyan-supplied arms and explosives worth £15 million for delivery to the IRA.

Summary of the War in 1988

On 6 March three IRA convicted terrorists were shot dead in Gibraltar by soldiers of the British Special Air Service (SAS). They had been planning to detonate a 400lb bomb during a parade by the Royal Anglian Regiment's band.

On 19 March, two British corporals, trying to make their way from one military

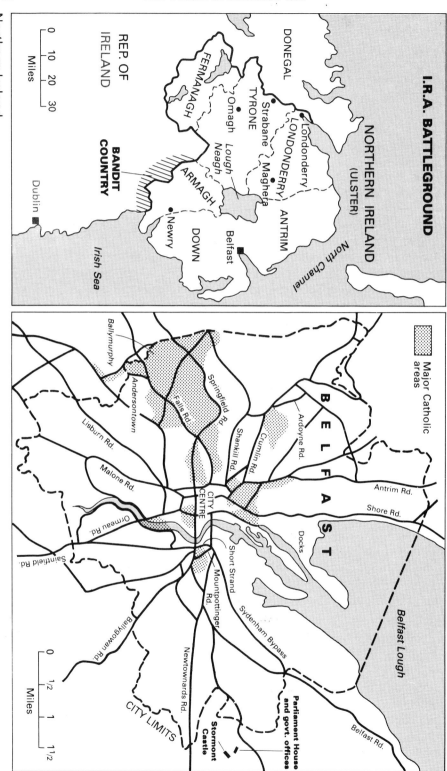

post to another in Belfast, became caught up in an IRA funeral procession. They were dragged from their car, beaten and shot dead.

In two attacks in Holland, on 30 April, four RAF men were killed and others seriously wounded. On 15 June, six soldiers were killed when a bomb destroyed their vehicle in Lisburn in Northern Ireland. In other attacks, IRA gunmen attacked army helicopters, on one occasion damaging one and forcing it to land.

The IRA's attempt to portray itself as an efficient organisation dedicated to attacking military targets had a setback in June when its terrorists bombed a school bus carrying Protestant and Catholic schoolgirls. Earlier, the same group had shot a young Protestant woman in a case of mistaken identity.

Worse was to come. A landmine meant for a senior High Court judge, a Catholic, killed a family of three who had travelled from the US on the same aircraft as the judge. Again the IRA conceded that an operation had ended in 'most unfortunate circumstances'.

Evidence emerged of serious divisions within the IRA over tactics. In documents leaked to the *Irish News*, IRA sympathisers spoke critically of 'contradictions' between the IRA's campaign of violence and their work as Sinn Fein politicians. Other Republicans quoted in these documents argued that the IRA should intensify its operations. Some called for indiscriminate car bombings in Belfast and on the British mainland.

On 13 July nine British soldiers were hurt when two IRA bombs blew a hole in the perimeter fence of a barracks in Duisburg, West Germany.

In July the IRA bombed the British army's Mill Hill postal depot in London, killing one soldier. Soon after, an off-duty soldier was shot dead at Ostend, Belgium. In August, the IRA unit in East Tyrone made a roadside bomb attack on an unmarked bus carrying British soldiers at Ballygawley. Eight servicemen were killed.

Encouraged by success, the IRA announced a new wave of car bombings aimed at blowing up offices and commercial premises in Northern Ireland—what it termed 'economic targets'. Over one weekend in late August the security forces dealt with 24 shootings, 17 bombings, 56 hijackings and 193 attacks on soldiers and police.

The security forces had some successes. On 30 August three members of the 'Mid-Tyrone Brigade' of the IRA were about to kill the driver of a lorry near Drumnakilly when they were intercepted and shot dead. A further success for the security forces came a few days later when two IRA suspects were arrested by German police when they crossed the Dutch border.

The War in 1989

The IRA set out to step up the range and number of its attacks in what its leaders call 'diversification'. At one level the objective was merely to cause casualties. The political strategy was to try to force the British government to introduce punitive measures which the IRA could label as repression. It would like to see the reintroduction of internment without trial, which would be sure to arouse international opposition. Internment, the IRA believes, would generate greater support for it, especially among the Irish Americans who finance the organisation. Ultimately, the IRA would like to see the British public demand the withdrawal of the troops so that the people of Ulster and Eire could fight out their differences in a civil war.

Campaign of Rail Attacks

Throughout 1988, the IRA seriously disrupted rail services on the main north–south rail link between Belfast and Dublin. By planting bombs on or near the line and by engineering a large number of hoaxes and scares, the terrorists closed the line for more than 50 days in a six-month period. Safeguarding the line between Belfast and the border became a major problem for the security forces, especially in south Armagh.

The line closures led to a substantial drop in the number of passengers. Nobody was seriously injured in the campaign but the risk of derailment by a bomb and the near-certainty of disruption caused many travellers to abandon the railways for the road.

Northern Ireland's small railway system is accustomed to terrorist interruption. Between 1970 and 1989 more than 1,500 incidents were directed against its operation. The 1989 IRA campaign was the greatest sustained level of attack. In addition to attacks on the Belfast–Dublin route, the line between Coleraine and Londonderry was bombed.

The IRA and Sinn Fein apparently did not see the irony of seeking to 'unite' Ireland by attacking one of the main north–south communication routes. Widespread complaints that jobs and lives were being put at risk were discounted by the IRA in favour of a wish to demonstrate its disruptive capacity and the inability of the security forces to protect the line completely.

The Secret War

The IRA's war against the security forces is almost entirely one of covert operations and it is by covert operations that the army and the RUC achieve their most important successes.

The Provisional IRA has no more than 400 active service men and women—people prepared to plant bombs and carry out shootings. Probably 90 per cent of these terrorists are known by name to the security forces. This hard core uses many more people to transport weapons, raise funds and log movements of transport and patrols. The so-called 'Active Service Units' consist of three to ten people.

Most of these activists are known for what they are in the Republican communities. They are considered safe within these communities, if only because special punishment squads kneecap or kill people suspected of informing. Nevertheless, there are many informers. The difficulty for the security forces is that very few of them are willing to give evidence in court.

The RUC Special Branch, of up to 350 officers, runs a complex web of informers, a few of whom are top-ranking IRA or Sinn Fein men. Officially, the army has no independent informer system but it could hardly operate effectively without its 'touts', as the army calls its informers. After 20 years of vicious IRA killing, more people than ever before are prepared to provide the security forces with information.

The director of intelligence is a senior MI5 officer, who chairs a weekly meeting of army and Special Branch agents. Much of this committee's work is aimed at preventing attacks against British targets in mainland Britain and on the Continent. IRA successes in 1989 showed that the committee is not omniscient.

The Intelligence and Security Group consists of a small SAS sub-unit, other army specialists and highly trained surveillance experts. Many terrorists are watched almost constantly—and are well aware of this surveillance.

Surveillance in certain parts of Northern Ireland has several aspects. Powerful TV cameras mounted in helicopters provide a flow of information about possibly suspicious activity in parts of Belfast, Londonderry and 'bandit country' on the border.

Some observation posts are prominently placed on tops of large buildings from which observers with high-powered telescopes can peer into areas where on-the-spot surveillance would be dangerous or impossible. Hidden observation posts are numerous and collectively they produce large amounts of intelligence, which is analysed by computer. Phone taps and bugging results in good information but evidence acquired in this way is rarely produced in court.

The great dilemma facing security chiefs is that few known IRA terrorists can be successfully prosecuted since they must at all costs protect their sources of information. As a result, terrorists must be picked up in the process of carrying out an attack but as they are nearly always armed a shoot-out takes place. It is widely supposed that the SAS, which is brought in at such times, has a policy of shoot-to-kill. This is not so. Armed terrorists have been arrested but such is the fanaticism of IRA attackers that when trapped they reject demands to surrender and even keep firing when wounded. In self-defence, the security forces have no option but to open fire and, sometimes, to sustain their fire.

Extremist Protestant terrorist cells have their own intelligence system. One of its objectives is to penetrate the security forces in order to obtain classified information about the IRA enemy. This has apparently been successful, since reports on IRA suspects, which were supposed to be seen only by security officers in Northern Ireland and in Eire, are known to have fallen into the hands of the illegal Ulster Defence Association. About 40,000 men have been members of Protestant paramilitary groups.

Despite IRA successes during 1989 there can be no doubt that the high level of British intelligence, together with overt and covert surveillance, has limited the IRA's operations. Intelligence has shown that the IRA has aborted many operations because its chiefs believed that they had been compromised.

The IRA's campaign of 'diversification' continued in September 1989 with the shooting of the German wife of a British soldier in Germany. She was killed while sitting in her car. Two weeks later, on 22 September, an IRA bomb exploded at the Royal Marines' depot in Deal, Kent. It killed 10 soldiers, most of them bandsmen, and wounded others. From both these atrocities it was clear that the IRA was seeking softer targets. This policy reached a new depth of ruthlessness in October when a gunman shot dead an RAF corporal and the baby he was holding in his arms. Soon after, a car bomb explosion in Colchester resulted in a soldier losing both legs.

On 8 December, an IRA party chose an operational target. They attacked a military border post and shot dead two British soldiers. They had intended to blow up the post but a truck bomb failed to detonate.

Twenty years after British troops went into Northern Ireland, Dr. Garret Fitzgerald, a former Primer Minister of Eire, noted that the IRA had two 'achievements' to its credit. First, it had shifted the centre of Irish policy away from reunification. Second, 'it had created for the first time in history a unity of purpose and policy between the governments of Ireland and Britain'. Its common and primary purpose was the restoration of peace and stability.[1]

The War in Statistics

A journalist with nearly 20 years of experience in Northern Ireland says that in proportion to the size of the population—1.5 million—the people of Northern Ireland have more direct experience of military activity, of terrorism and counterterrorism than anywhere else in the world.

Statistics for 1989 support his statement. In the first place, more than 30,000 members of the security forces are on active duty—10,000 British troops, 13,000 members of the Royal Ulster Constabulary and 6,000 members of the Ulster Defence Regiment, which comes under army command. Another 35,000 men and women have passed through UDR training. In addition about 6,000 people work for the RUC in a civilian capacity, thus releasing police officers from desk jobs. Recruitment has never been a problem in Ulster, despite the risks to life and limb. During 1988–89 more than 9,000 men and women applied to join the RUC.

Private security is a growth industry in Ulster. The dozens of firms employ about 2,500 men and women to guard public buildings and private homes, while others are engaged in checking and surveillance.

The Territorial Army has 4,400 members in Northern Ireland, though it has no security function. The 3,000 officers of the prison service are authorised to carry firearms for their personal protection, unlike prison officers elsewhere in the United Kingdom, who are unarmed.

The overall security budget for Northern Ireland is a massive £4 billion. Maintenance of the RUC takes up £414 million of this total.

Since 1969, more than 2,700 people have been killed and many more wounded in 30,000 shootings and 8,000 bombings. At least 250,000lb of explosives have been used and another 200,000lb seized. About 10,000 firearms together with one million rounds of ammunition have been uncovered and confiscated. In all, the 1.5 million people of Northern Ireland own 126,000 licensed firearms, apart from those handled by the security forces when on duty.

References

1. Dr. Fitzgerald was writing in *The Observer*, London, 13 August 1989.
2. David McKittrick of *The Independent*, London, 12 August 1989.

Major aspects of the North Ireland Terrorist War covered in War Annual No. 3 include:
   A description and analysis of the shooting of IRA terrorists in Gibraltar by SAS.
   A survey of IRA arms and ammunition.

American Invasion of Panama

Despite the trauma which afflicted the United States after the Vietnam War experience, the administration of Ronald Reagan and that of George Bush have shown themselves ready to intervene militarily in other countries. This is one of the most interesting and significant trends not only of 1989–90 but of the decade. It should be noted that in the 20th century the US has engaged in military adventures 40 times in Latin American countries.

Under President Reagan, the US put Marines ashore in Lebanon, invaded Grenada, sent a massive fleet to the Arabian (Persian) Gulf and bombed Libya. President Bush stationed the US Sixth Fleet off Libya and off Lebanon at times of crisis and invaded Panama.

The Panama crisis began on 12 December 1989 when President Manuel Noriega ordered his parliamentary assembly to proclaim him 'Maximum Leader'. On the 15th he declared that a state of war existed between Panama and the US. On 16 December, Marine Lieutenant Robert Paz was killed at a Panamanian roadblock and a US Navy officer and his wife, who saw the attack, were detained and terrorised. On 17 December President Bush secretly ordered the Pentagon to invade Panama, capture Noriega and establish a democratic government. Command of the operation devolved to General Maxwell Thurman.

Professor John Norton Moore, former adviser to the State Department on international law, justified the invasion by international law. He said, 'Here is a situation where Noriega indicated publicly that his country was in a state of war with the USA. There was an immediate increase in the number and variety of incidents of attack on US servicemen and citizens. In these circumstances alone, President Bush was perfectly justified, in international law, in acting to defend American lives.' This argument is based on Article 51 of the UN Charter, giving each country the right to defend itself from foreign aggression. Other US legal experts pointed out that the right of self-defence must be exercised in a 'necessary and proportional manner'. Could the death of one marine and other non-fatal attacks justify the invasion of a tiny country?

Bush had three other justifications: US treaty rights to defend the Panama Canal; US duty to restore democracy and assist the government cheated from office by Noriega in the violent and fraudulent May 1989 elections; the right under US law to apprehend Noriega to face charges of drug trafficking in US courts.

Over the next two days tensions heightened and on the 18th a US Army lieutenant wounded a Panamanian corporal who was reaching for his gun. On the afternoon of 19 December US military transport planes began arriving at Howard Air Force Base, in the US-controlled Canal Zone, at 10-minute intervals. The

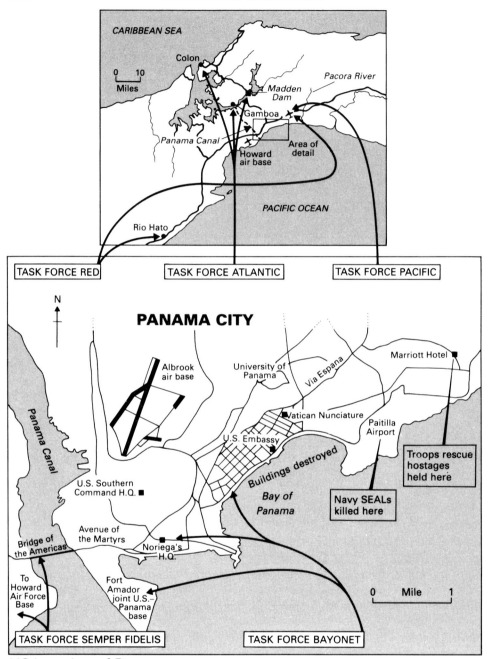

US Invasion of Panama

invasion began next day and at the same time the democratically elected Guillermo Endara was sworn in at a US base as president of a new Panamanian government.

The invasion, codenamed Operation Just Cause, was not intended to be a total surprise and could not have been so. Increased activity in the US Canal Zone military base could hardly have been concealed from Panamanian workers on the canal. In any case, Noriega was known to have a good intelligence system in the US itself. The offensive depended on vastly superior manpower, firepower and rapid execution. The American invaders were divided into five task forces. Task Force Red captured the Rio Hato barracks, where two companies of enemy troops were stationed. It also seized the Torrijos International Airport and blocked a bridge across the Pacora River.

Task Force Atlantic, of infantry and airborne troops, overwhelmed Panamanian infantry and naval infantry and secured the Madden Dam. Task Force Pacific, of the 82nd Airborne, parachuted into the international airport after Task Force Red had secured it.

Task Force Semper Fidelis, Marines and Army light infantry, secured the Bridge of the Americas across the Panama Canal as well as Howard Air Force Base. Task Force Bayonet had the important task of destroying the Panamanian Defence Forces HQ in Panama City and bottling up the troops stationed at Fort Amador. With artillery, tanks and helicopter gunships, this task force was the most crucial of the five in bringing about a quick victory.

On the eve of invasion, Panama had total armed forces of only 5,200. The great majority, 4,500, were in the army. The soldiers' personal arms were of high standard but they had no armour, only 30 reconnaissance vehicles, and the heaviest guns were 60mm mortars. The Navy's manpower of 500 included 'naval infantry', a form of land-based marines. With only 200 men, the Panamanian air force was negligible. In addition to the regular army, Noriega had created 'Dignity Battalions' of perhaps 2,000 men in all. Many of them were criminal elements whom Noriega had paid well to act as his protectors and to intimidate his political opponents.

In the first 24 hours, 9,500 US troops arrived in the combat zone and the force soon increased to 27,500. Despite American firepower, which reduced parts of Panama City to smoking ruin and caused many casualties, Panamanian resistance was not quickly overcome. Noriega's 'Dignity Battalions' were particularly stubborn. A week after the invasion, General Thurman reported that fighting seemed to be 'centrally controlled' and estimated that 1,800 'irregular troops' could be involved. Fighting did not finish until 31 December.

Noriega evaded capture, despite an offer of $1 million reward for information leading to his apprehension. As US Navy SEALS (sea, air and land capability) had seized his getaway Lear jet and his boats, it was virtually impossible for Noriega to leave Panama. Embassies where he might find sanctuary, such as those of Cuba and Nicaragua, were watched but the shrewd Noriega entered the Vatican Nunciature and asked for sanctuary. This led to a protracted diplomatic row as the US tried to persuade the Vatican to hand over the former president as a common criminal. Noriega finally gave himself up to US forces on 3 January 1990.

After a complete absence of law and order for several days, the US authorities allowed the first of the new Panamanian Public Forces onto the streets on 28

December. The new force, initially 1,000-strong, was drawn from the less criminal elements of the old military.

During the brief war, 23 US soldiers and 293 Panamanian troops were killed. Civilian deaths were estimated at 700. The Americans took several thousand prisoners and seized 44,000 weapons.

Panama exists as a nation because the US created it and the great majority of Panamanians welcomed the American invasion as a means of deliverance from a corrupt dictator. No other country in Latin America gave a genuine welcome to the invasion but after the ritual protests international opposition was remarkably muted. Predictably, Cuba and Nicaragua maintained their fierce denunciations of the US but other countries accepted the invasion as an inevitable consequence of Noriega's despotic misrule.

The American Command

Before the invasion of Panama, General Maxwell Thurman already had two nicknames, 'Mad Max,' and 'the Maxatollah'. Journalist covering the operation said that he appeared to live up to both labels.

With 36 years in the US Army, Thurman, aged 58, was due for retirement before being hand-picked in September 1989 by the Secretary of Defence, Dick Cheney, to be one of the six US regional commanders-in-chief. His appointment to Southern Command was surprising, since he had no Latin American experience, no Spanish and no command position since 1975. As supreme commander of all US forces from the Rio Grande to the Antarctic, Thurman reported only to the US Secretary of Defense and the President.

The general arrived in the US Canal Zone with a reputation for demanding standards but respect waned when he appeared indecisive during the failed coup attempts against Noriega in October. Military commentators in Washington, Panamanian officials and some senior US officials in Panama City admitted to being disturbed by General Thurman's behaviour following the invasion. They considered his handling of the Vatican Nunciature siege to be eccentric. It was the general's decision to surround the building with speakers playing loud rock music and to rattle the mission's gates with armoured vehicles.

Admiral Gene LaRocque, Director of the Center for Defense Information in Washington, said on 28 December, 'This is the most atrocious, barbaric and unsophisticated act I have ever seen from an US military commander. It's so childish, like one kid standing on the street corner and yelling names at another one.' Nevertheless, there was evidence that Noriega was rattled by the noise. It was important to get him out of the nunciature and Thurman was bound to try every form of intimidation.

The American Performance

The possible need to invade Panama had long been foreseen at the Pentagon and plans had been drawn up. It was not surprising, therefore, that when President Bush gave the order for invasion they required nothing more than final adjustments. With a long-standing American military presence in Panama, the ground was known thoroughly to the Pentagon staff and the objectives were clearly defined. Rarely in military history has an invasion had so many advantages including a nearby base, the great US Canal Zone base with its garrison of 12,000.

Once the attack was committed it made good initial headway and then faltered. This was partly because the Panamanian armed forces showed greater loyalty to Noriega than anticipated. However, there also seemed to be some deficiency in the American command. This showed itself in lack of incisiveness on the part of General Thurman and a similar lack at platoon level. Nevertheless, the fighting men involved performed well. At one point, President Bush ordered another 2,000 men into the combat zone, a clear indication that the operation was not going according to plan. However, the major political objectives were achieved, without damage to the United States' political and military prestige.

The Pentagon Staff claimed, with some justification, that the invasion of Panama was a fine example of how to wage an expeditionary war. They won, with minimum casualties, and equipment could not have performed better. The Panama invasion, the generals said, was an example of how the US could react rapidly and effectively to deal with crises leading to low-intensity conflicts.

However, there is much to suggest that the Panama operation was conceived and carried out on Second World War lines. For instance, in the use of artillery to blast civilian blocks of flats. In this shelling, at least 400 civilians were killed and 2,000 wounded and another 15,000 were made homeless. After all, Panama was a friendly country and the US campaign was not supposed to be against the people but *for* the people, in their desire to oust a dictator.

Edward Luttwak, a military strategist at the Center for Strategic and International Studies, Washington, said: 'The claim that Panama represents a rapid expeditionary force capability is hollow. The difficulty of most expeditionary interventions arises from a lack of secure arrival bases, bulk supplies in place and ancillary facilities, from radars to field hospitals. All these things were readily available in Panama.'

Peru's 'Shining Path' War

A NATION UNDER SIEGE

Background Summary

Guerrilla war in Peru began in 1980 when Abimael Guzman, a professor of philosophy, founded the Left-wing Maoist movement *Sendero Luminosa* or 'Shining Path'. Guzman's lieutenants described him as the 'fourth sword of the revolution'—after Marx, Lenin and Mao. *Sendero Luminosa*'s objective was direct—the total overthrow of the nation's Right-wing system.

In the resulting violence about 12,500 people were killed between May 1980 and October 1987. They included 410 police and soldiers and 3,500 guerrillas. Alan Garcia, elected President in 1985—at the age of 37—showed much courage in dismissing two senior generals after the army massacred 69 peasants, supposedly *Sendero* supporters, in Accomarco, in September 1985. *Sendero* and its allied urban terrorists of the *Tupac Araru* Revolutionary Movement were more difficult to deal with than the army, since neither would talk to the government.

Garcia faced a series of emergencies. The most serious occurred on 18 June 1986 after gaol riots by *Sendero* prisoners. Without the President's knowledge, the army stormed the prisons and butchered 1,000 captive guerrillas. Again Garcia dismissed senior officials.

The guerrillas held large areas of the Andes so Garcia built up a people's militia to guard the small towns and villages while he tried to find out what *Sendero* wanted of the government. The real sufferers were the peasants, caught between security forces and guerrilla terrorists. Many thousands of peasants, mostly young, poor males, disappeared.

Summary of the War in 1988

President Garcia was beset by such serious economic problems that he could give little time to the problems posed by *Sendero* and *Tupac Amaru*. His country was struggling under a $23 billion foreign debt, economic stagnation, a terrifying increase in drug trafficking and Latin America's worst population explosion. The net increase is 90 new Peruvians every hour. The intensified guerrilla war, having denuded much of the countryside, caused a rush to the cities.

While the President tried to cure his nation's economic ills and check the population increase, he also sought to reform the army. His difficulty was that the generals were intractable and the two-year conscripts, on which the army depended for much of its manpower, were incompetent. Virtually all of the guerrillas' weaponry comes from thefts from the army—and 1988 was a bad year. Lax security in the army led to the loss of 8,000 rifles, 1,600 machine-guns and submachine-guns and vast stocks of ammunition.

Garcia encouraged the formation of the Puma Special Forces Group, a supposedly élite commando unit, but its leaders were reluctant to venture into areas controlled by the guerrillas. Military intelligence was lamentable throughout the year. For instance, Garcia asked for information about the location of *Sendero Luminosa*'s HQ but the army could not tell him. 'Is Abimael Guzman still alive?' he asked his Chief-of-Staff. 'We don't know', the general said. Similarly, the military did not know the number of *Sendero* guerrillas. At the end of 1988, Garcia called his service chiefs to a meeting and said 'next year must be different'.

The War in 1989

During this turbulent year, on an average day six people died in political violence. One victim might be a government official organising peasant co-operatives, another a mayor, a third an inquisitive journalist. The rest were usually innocent peasants.

In February, the killing came to Cahuide, a private agricultural co-operative in the central Junin department. A column of about 50 *Sendero* guerrillas marched in and destroyed everything. They murdered four officials, slaughtered or stole most of the animals, ruined tractors and vanished into the countryside. The enterprise had been a thriving concern with a staff of 170 administrators and 800 workers. It had 130,000 head of livestock and a daily milk production of 2,600 gallons. After the guerrilla raid the co-operative ceased to function.

The story of Cahuide is a familiar one in Peru's vicious war. So endemic is violence that it is casually accepted. General Sinecio Jarama has said: 'It no longer causes any outcry or dismay to hear that a policeman, mayor or official has been killed. Only when there are massacres of 20 or more people do we take notice'.[2]

A mass killing took place in April. At Carhuapampa, in central-south Peru, *Sendero* guerrillas killed 26 unarmed members of a local civil defence group. Later that month the military failed to go to the rescue of a special-forces outpost under siege by guerrillas for four hours in the town of Uchiza. Ten of the surrounded security forces men were killed, three of them in public executions, after they ran out of ammunition and surrendered. The Press and public generally were outraged by the failure of the army to respond.

Outside the major cities, hundreds of policemen and mayors deserted their posts after receiving death threats. As a result, *Sendero*, which is now thought to have 5,000 men under arms, has taken effective control of at least one-third of the countryside. In these areas the guerrillas enforce a harsh order. Prostitution and drinking of alcohol are prohibited and suspected thieves and informers are summarily executed.

In response to the guerrilla menace, new and ugly forces have emerged. Early in 1989 the Rodrigo Franco Command, a pro-government death squad, made its appearance. It has killed several critics of the government. President Garcia condemns the group's activities.

Sendero is not short of money. Intelligence sources, which are now more efficient, say that it is earning $30 million a year through an alliance with cocaine traffickers. It is known to have a stockpile of 750,000 sticks of dynamite, stolen from the mines.

The capital, Lima, slowly came under siege during 1989. By May, 15 of the city's districts were without government authority and *Sendero* slogans covered the city. As guerrilla activity increased in the north and south as well as along the central mountain highway, many people only drove outside the city in daytime convoys.

A British traveller, Edward Bartley, aged 24, became a *Sendero* victim in June. He had reached the village of Olleros, in the Andean province of Huarez, and slept the night in the village hall. *Sendero* guerrillas arrived on their first raid against Olleros. Having stolen all supplies in the medical centre, they burned the archives in the village hall, where they found Bartley. They demanded that the mayor be brought to the hall and were told that he was absent. In anger and frustration, the terrorists accused Bartley of being a 'government collaborator' and shot him dead.

In early July life came to a standstill in several districts, including San Juan de Lurigancho and Canto Grande, where *Sendero* prisoners are held. Terror kept shutters down on the shops and drivers off the streets. The 'armed strike' tactic, which Sendero uses to paralyse villages, towns and cities in the Andes, had finally struck residential as well as industrial areas of the capital. 'Scab' drivers were forced at gunpoint to convey passengers without charge. Rebel groups, without bothering to mask their faces, temporarily took over shanty towns and forced people to pledge themselves to the strike and to 'the return of Presidente Gonsalo', the name they give to Abimael Guzman.

At the end of July the army hit back. In three battles, soldiers killed 110 guerrillas. Scores more rebels were wounded or captured in the fighting in the Upper Huallaga river valley, the country's most important cocaine-producing region. The decision to attack *Sendero* in this area was bold and shrewd. The Upper Huallaga is a region of rampant violence and lawlessness. In the biggest clash, at Tocache, 400 miles north of Lima, troops killed 60 guerrillas, wounded many more and captured a major *Sendero* arsenal. Officials reported that more than 200 guerrillas had been killed in July in the Huanuco and San Martin regions, other rebel strongholds.

Foreign diplomats in Lima say that it is only by such methods that President Garcia can hope to win his war against *Sendero*. Some of these diplomats report that the President has employed 'foreign' counter-insurgency specialists to help in the fight.

For the first time in years there is a belief, in government and military circles, that Abimael Guzman is alive, though no evidence exists to prove this. Some rebels captured in the July fighting report having seen him during 1989.[1]

War Annual No. 3 carried a description of the Peru Army organisation.

References

1. A diplomat who has been in Lima for several years doubts if Guzman is alive. He believes that *Sendero* is controlled by a triumvirate of Guzman's original lieutenants who, for psychological reasons, foster the mystery that he is still alive. However, a foreign journalist based in Lima considers that Guzman is alive but for the same psychological reasons prefers to remain a shadowy figure in the mountains.
2. Jarama was speaking to the author. He did not intend any irony. He was drawing attention to a simple fact of Peruvian life.

Philippines 'People's War'

Background Summary

The oppressive régime of President Marcos brought into being, between 1969 and 1972, the Communist Party of the Philippines (CPP) and its military wing, the National People's Army (NPA). Under José Maria Sison, they began a 'people's war' against Marcos, whose troops captured NPA's chief-of-training, Victor Corpus, in 1976. In 1977 the NPA formed a loose alliance with the Muslim rebels of Mindanao, only to split later. By 1984 the NPA was active in 60 of the 73 provinces.

The 20,000 men and women who made up the NPA caused the government difficulty out of all proportion to their numbers. The poverty-stricken peasants, all of whom had suffered under army brutality, supported the guerrillas. In desperation, the government formed the Civil Home Defence Force. The NPA treated its members as traitors and murdered hundreds.

When Mrs. Corazon Aquino was elected as President in 1986, and the hated Marcos fled the country, some observers predicted that the NPA and the Muslim insurgents would become conciliatory towards the government. However, President Aquino was in no position to bring in reforms of the economic, land and social systems quickly enough for the rebels, while autonomy for the Muslims was out of the question.

By 1987 the Filipino army, navy and air force had a strength of 113,000, with an additional 42,000 men in paramilitary units, 48,000 in reserve and a Home Defence Force of 65,000.

The rebel groups comprised the NPA, the *Bagsa Moro* army, which is the armed wing of the Moro National People's Liberation Front (MNLF), the Moro Islamic Liberation Front (MILF), the *Cordillera* People's Liberation Army (CPLA) as well as some private armies. Their total strength was 33,000. The NPA's strategic centre was on Samar Island, 200 miles south-east of Manila. The government planned to split the rebels regionally and to separate them from the leadership. It emphasised its acceptance of the NPA's 'genuine grievances' but insisted that they could be resolved only if the rebels accepted regional cease-fires. The ploy did not deceive the NPA.

The Muslim insurrection, mainly on Mindanao Island, created problems, but the bitter ethnic and political divisions within the Islamic community of eight million worked in the government's favour. Of the several Muslim private armies, that of Sultan Muhammad Ali Dimaporo, the 'Mad Dog of Mindanao', is the strongest with 5,000 warriors.

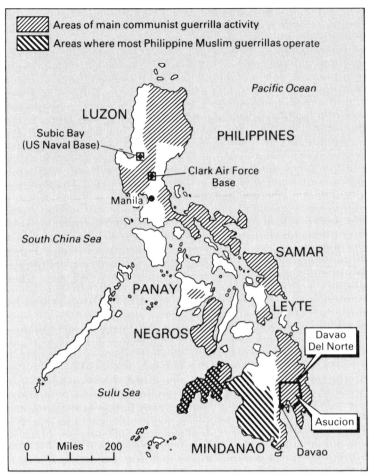

Philippines Guerrilla War

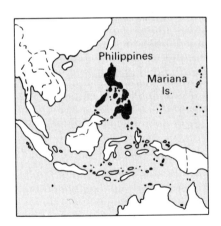

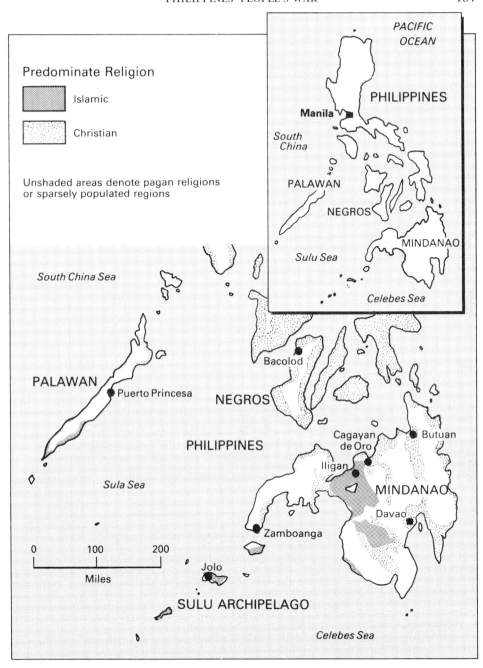

Predominate Religion

Islamic

Christian

Unshaded areas denote pagan religions
or sparsely populated regions

Summary of the War in 1988

In 3,000 reported violent incidents, 1,913 NPA guerrillas died, 912 members of the security forces and perhaps 2,000 civilians. The armed forces complained that they were handicapped by 'ridiculous restrictions', involving human rights. Officers can only gain promotion after being cleared by the National Commission on Human Rights.

The Philippine armed forces should have been able, in theory, to defeat the NPA and its Communist leadership. In April 1988 they achieved great success in capturing three CPP politburo members, including Romulo Kintanar, the official responsible for NPA activities. In May, the Ministry of Defence announced the purchase of 20 helicopters under the US military assistance programme. The plan was to equip each battalion operating against the guerrillas with at least one helicopter. At the same time, the Ministry increased the number of reservists on active duty from 45,000 to 80,000.

During 1988 the rebels were on the run and in some areas, such as northern Luzon—where their leader was Ernesto Garado—they were a spent force. By the middle of the year the only genuine NPA stronghold was the Bicol area of southern Luzon. In Manila, the CPP began a campaign of murder against members of the police force, in an attempt to conceal the NPA's failing strength. The command also issued small Casio personal computers to groups fighting in the hills and jungles, and these greatly helped in communications and code security.

President Aquino sent an emissary to King Fahd of Saudi Arabia to block an attempt by Muslim separatists to gain recognition among Islamic states. Her move temporarily prevented the MNLF from gaining 'belligerency' status in the Islamic Conference Organisation. The authorities had a success of a different kind in Davao, where Colonel Franco Calida created a vigilante group known as the *Alsa Masa* (Aroused Masses) organisation. The Colonel issued an ultimatum to the NPA in his area—surrender and live or be harried and slaughtered. His tough methods produced the surrender of 3,000 active fighters and 10,000 supporters, many of whom joined *Alsa Masa*.

Militia Gains New Status

The Defence Secretary, General Fidel Ramos, integrated the militia groups into the armed forces under the title Citizens Armed Forces Geographical Units (CAFGU), with full army reserve status. This increased army strength from 74 battalions to 130. As reservists, the CAFGU men became eligible for security assistance from the US; thus, they received M-1 and M-2 rifles. The new system is much more economical—seven CAFGU reservists can be supported for the cost of maintaining one regular soldier.

Nevertheless, there are risks in the new arrangement. In the field, CAFGU, with its high profile, is under increasing attack from the NPA. The NPA was sufficiently emboldened, in January, to raid into *Alsa Masa* territory, killing six members of a militia unit.

Under Ramos's instructions, an 'action plan' was drawn up for internal study.[1] This document ran to 168 pages and suggested that 12 or 13 of the 73 NPA fronts should be the target of a simultaneous and sustained campaign of 'gradual constriction'. Highly mobile battalions, élite special operations teams and para-military groups were to combine in any given operation

The first campaigns were in Mindanao, where militia/vigilante groups had already unsettled the NPA. More than 40 religious cults exist on the island, all of them exploited by the militias. All are committed to killing Communists.

CAFGU units will need to show continuing good results to counter the criticisms of their detractors in Manila. For instance, the Marines are annoyed about the way the High Command is using CAFGU men in small trouble-shooting units around the country, when this is traditionally considered the work of Marines and Rangers. Airmobile units also feel that their privileged function as special forces is being eroded by CAFGU. It is dangerous, the Airmobile chiefs say, to deploy small CAFGU units around the country because they are vulnerable to attack from NPA units of 100-200 raiders.

Some Defence Ministry officers believe that CAFGU men would produce better results as members of an unarmed civilian intelligence network. However, with the support of General Ramos, the CAFGU concept is likely to be given a long run in order to prove itself.

Winning Hearts and Minds

Seven-person Special Operations Teams (SOTs) are the centrepiece of the new government strategy, which calls for playing down the traditional search-and-destroy approach, which is measured in body counts. Instead, political and psychological methods are being used to woo peasants away from supporting the guerrillas. About 20 per cent of villages are classed as either infiltrated, influenced or threatened by the CPP and NPA.

Lieutenant Ding Carreon, who was produced at a press conference to help explain the new approach, said: 'Filipinos love anyone who loves their children. That's a better way of winning disputes than using guns and torture.'[2]

Much of the peasants' support for the guerrillas arises from their fear and resentment of past military misdeeds. They sometimes call the soldiers *hapon*, the derogatory word for the Japanese soldiers who conquered the Philippines during the Second World War. The SOT campaign is supposed to transform the armed forces of the Philippines into a reputable organisation, as well as defeat the rebels.

The inspiration for the SOT approach came from Major General Mariano Adalem. He got the idea after noticing that army patrols could not get information from villagers. Now his soldiers are finding it difficult to learn how to be polite and considerate. Even more, they must avoid violent retaliation against a village where a soldier has been killed.

SOTs are modelled on experience gained in the anti-insurgency programmes used by the British in Malaya, by the Americans in Vietnam and by the Thais. Under Aquino, the military is trying to 'out-promise' the Communists by convincing peasants to support the government, to act as spies and to wait patiently for land reform and development projects.

The CPP leaders take the SOT programme as a serious threat. A party internal document of August 1989 states:[3] 'The scheme is nothing less than a policy of mass annihilation or genocide of the Filipino revolutionaries and their sympathisers, hiding behind the smile of Aquino.'

One SOT difficulty has been the lack of officers able to speak well to village groups in local dialects. Many officers fail to put across the complex counter-arguments to Marxist-Leninist ideology and practices. For propaganda, SOT speakers rely on an anti-Communist manual published by *Causa International*, a group set up in 1980 by the South Korean religious leader, the Rev. Sun Myung Moon.

The SOT planners face human problems. One is that many of their handsome young officers, who address largely female audiences, have been caught womanising. Some have accepted bribes from captured NPA sympathisers to be set free; others have become boastful about their success as SOT members, thus offending officers in other branches of the armed forces.

A typical SOT presentation is a mixture of singing, eating, dancing, drama and, most potently, public confessional. Former guerrillas are asked to confess party abuses. Peasants are asked to complain about the high 'taxes'—really protection money—paid to guerrillas. Parents tell of sons killed by the NPA and an effigy of an ugly guerrilla is burned. Anti-Communist videos such as *The Killing Fields* are shown.

From these public events, an SOT team gains the trust of enough villagers to get tips on the names and organisation in the party's 'shadow government'. Soldiers then confront accused sympathisers and display a chart showing the regional CPP structure in the village square. A rally is called to parade those who have surrendered. They are then reindoctrinated to negate the Communist ideology.

The more stubborn guerrillas are forced into the hills where the army hopes it can more readily and successfully fight them.

New Threat from Muslims

In mid-1989 the Muslim leader Nur Misuari, who had been absent in self-imposed exile, slipped ashore by night to start a new guerrilla offensive. Misuari, who heads the MNLF, reached a cease-fire agreement with President Aquino in a dramatic meeting in the southern Islamic stronghold of Jolo in September 1986.

However, the MNLF did not abandon its demand for autonomy, including a separate army, for 13 provinces in an area regarded by eight million Muslims as their ancestral home. In March, the Islamic Conference Organisation went back on its decision not to support the MNLF's claim for autonomy. In fact it had agreed to this only at the request of King Fahd. Diplomats in Riyadh, Saudi Arabia, say that the King had no intention of blocking the MNLF permanently.[4] It is believed that in 1990 the ICO will give MNLF the status of government-in-exile.

New supplies of weapons reached Mindanao during 1989, most of them through Brunei and the Malaysian state of Sabah. As early as April the Mindanao army commander, Major General Manuel Cacanando, put his forces on red alert for the war which he believed would follow Misuari's return. Politicians in Manila believed that Misuari would need a year to rebuild his organisation. Nobody underestimates the dangers he poses. It is now believed that between 1972 and 1982 about 100,000 people were killed in the Philippines Muslim war.

The Philippines Muslims are supported by Libya, Iran, Syria and Pakistan, though their main financial support is believed to come from Saudi Arabia.

Aquino Masters a Mutiny

In the last week of November 1989 a serious mutiny erupted in Manila and on Cebu Island. Former senior officers who are members of Reform of the Armed Forces Movement (RAM) were behind the mutiny. They were General Eduard Abenina, Brigadier José Maria Zumel and Colonel Gregorio ('Gringo') Honason. In a tactically competent attack, rebels in stolen aircraft and helicopters sent bombs crashing around the presidential palace and military headquarters. President Aquino needed to enlist the aid of American F–4 Phantoms from US bases in the Philippines to give the government side aerial superiority.

Only moneyed right-wing opposition leaders had the authority to organise soldiers led by marines, the military élite. The armed forces chief, General de Villa, stated that the marines had been bribed to take part in the mutiny. Mrs. Aquino, who showed great resolve in the crisis, accused her political enemies, including Vice President Salvador Laurel, of colluding with the rebels. The mutiny was not quelled by force but ended by negotiation. It left 85 people dead and 500 wounded—and the certainty of more mutinies to come in an army of divided loyalties.

References

1. A few copies of this document reached London after being leaked by officers who opposed the scheme. Security over documents is extraordinarily lax in Manila.
2. He was speaking to Clayton Jones of *The Christian Science Monitor*, a well-connected correspondent.
3. A copy of this report was smuggled out of Luzon by a NPA defector. He took a great risk. The NPA has suffered so much from traitorous activities that it has set up a special killer squad to track down defectors.
4. Diplomats say that, far from wishing to hamper the Muslim fighters of the Philippines, the Saudi government supports them. It would like to see a new Islamic state set up in the Philippines, where Islamic missionaries have long been trying to stop the inroads made by their Roman Catholic counterparts.

Major aspects of the war dealt with in War Annual No. 3 include:
    An analysis of the army's success in Davao City.
    Revelations about the escape from custody of the anti-Aquino Right-wing leader, Colonel Gregario (Gringo) Honasan.
    A description of a typical raid by an NPA patrol.

The Romanian Revolution

PEOPLE POWER PUSHED TO THE LIMIT

Only the Russian Revolution of 1917 bears any parallel with the Romanian revolution of 1989 but significant differences make the Romanian experience even more dramatic than that of Russia. For instance, the Russian Revolution was planned by a group of clever politicised men who knew exactly what they were doing. The Romanian Revolution was a spontaneous uprising, completely without leaders in its early stages.

It was also a staging point in the trend towards nationalism which reached floodtide in 1989 with the downfall of Communist government and one-party states in Poland, Hungary, Bulgaria, East Germany and Czechoslovakia.

The Romanian Revolution began in Timisoara, in western Romania, on the night of 16–17 December. Its precipitating cause was the government's maltreatment of Laszlo Tokes, a priest, who had been outspokenly critical of the totalitarian régime of the megalomaniac Nicolae Ceaucescu.

Ceaucescu had exercised dictatorial power for 24 years and with his tyrannical wife, Elena, terrorised the Romanian people. He called himself the Supreme Leader—in Romanian, *Conducator*. To keep himself in power he depended on his feared Securitate or security police, with its comprehensive network of informers as well as standover men and torturers. Ceaucescu and his ministers brooked no opposition, as they showed in November 1987 in the industrial city of Brasov. The cold and starving workers went on strike, sacked the local communist party central committee building and burnt its furniture to keep themselves warm. They also burnt pictures of Ceaucescu, who sent in his troops. They killed hundreds of the workers and arrested thousands, many of whom quickly died in prison—of 'natural causes'.

Early in December 1989, Ceaucescu delivered a five-hour eulogy on the achievements of his own rule to an audience of sycophants who rose to their feet 67 times in standing ovations. In any conversation in Romania, Ceaucescu was rarely mentioned by name, just referred to as 'He', with a nod upwards. Laszlo Tokes was one of the few men in the country who dared criticise Ceaucescu openly. He had much to criticise, not least being Ceaucescu's decision to raze 8,000 villages to create agro-industrial complexes. The people of these destroyed villages were to be housed in inferior apartment buildings.

The Securitate agents harassed and terrorised Tokes relentlessly. They beat him up, ill treated his pregnant wife and announced that on the night of 16 December they would evict him from his apartment. Demonstrators, most of whom were ethnic Hungarians like Tokes himself, gathered in protest.

The officials acted brutally, bringing in tanks and machine-gunners to smash the protest on the streets of Timiosoara. The appalling bloodshed brought

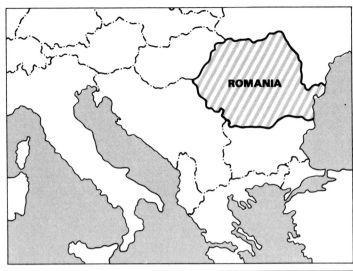

The Romanian Uprising

together ethnic Hungarians and Romanians as never before. Despite the official violence aimed at crushing the demonstration, the uprising gathered momentum and spread to some other cities in Transylvania. Bucharest was untouched and Ceaucescu went ahead with a planned three-day visit to Iran. On his return he ordered his officials to organise a rally of 'loyalty and affection' of the type which he had enjoyed for 24 years.

It took place on 21 December and began in the routine way with thousands of supporters drafted in to wave flags in the central square. The president harangued them in his dictatorial style and national television broadcast the occasion to the nation. People began to boo and jeer Ceaucescu in the first open demonstration of challenge to his leadership. The television coverage was interrupted but not before the people had seen that the president was startled and afraid. From that moment, television became a major aspect of the conflict which followed.

Demonstrations erupted throughout the capital and the panicking authorities bought in tanks and troops. Tank crews fired tear gas and then opened up with machine-guns. Many civilians were killed or wounded. That night the official Yugoslav newsagency reported: 'A massacre is taking place. Tanks are crushing students in the streets and the police are firing on everyone who is moving.' Soldiers who disobeyed orders to shoot civilians were themselves shot by the Securitate and this brought some army units into armed conflict against the Securitate.

Empty-handed students and workers stormed the Communist Party HQ. Forcing open the heavy doors, they armed themselves with weapons from the large stores found inside or dropped by fleeing Securitate. The Interior Minister, Tudor Postelnicu, who was also head of the Securitate, fled to a small office where he had several weapons but an unarmed medical student talked him into giving himself up.

The crowd built barricades and poured concrete onto the streets to stop the tanks, while troops who had declared for the new regime rushed to defend it. The airport became a battlefield and foreign aircraft bringing in much needed emergency food and medical supplies could not land. Meanwhile, in Bucharest Securitate helicopters sprayed bullets into the helpless crowds below.

Every Securitate and army atrocity brought more people onto the streets. Securitate men's summary execution of officers who refused to fire into the crowds was the root cause of the military's later change of sides.

Events happened with almost bewildering speed. Ceaucescu and his wife Elena fled, on 22 December the army changed sides and the television centre was captured by revolutionaries. Great crowds formed a human barrier to keep it secure. Ceaucescu's palace guard—modelled on the élite who protected Roman emperors—began to march on the television centre. Pitched battles began in the streets and hundreds died as policemen and soldiers fought each other. While the generals agonised over whose side they were on, tanks rolled down the streets. Ceaucescu's élite had been known as the 'anti-terrorist squad'. By mid-evening on Friday they were being called the terrorists.

The Ceaucescus were caught as they attempted to flee the country and were given a perfunctory trial, which was shown on television. Ceaucescu was charged with genocide, causing his country's economic and cultural collapse and stealing at least one billion dollars from national funds. The couple were executed by firing squad on 25 December. The rapidity of the killing was an attempt to deprive the Securitate of a cause and ensure their speedy surrender. The new provisional government announced regret for the summary justice but said that without it the bloodshed would have continued. In fact, it did continue until the Securitate men were warned that failure to surrender by midnight on 28 December would bring summary execution. Army operations after Ceaucescu was overthrown were commanded by 11 senior officers, of whom Major-General Victor Stanculescu was probably the most important.

Effectively, the Romanian uprising lasted only 10 days though isolated and frightened security police continued to snipe from vantage points. Casualties amounted to four thousand dead, nearly all of them civilians, and many more wounded.

One of the main lessons of the uprising, at both the strategic and tactical level, is that possession of the television network is vital for victory. In Romania, which had only one television channel, both sides were quickly aware of this. By holding the television centre from soon after the uprising began, the anti-Ceaucescu fighters were able to inform and to a large extent control their followers, the ordinary people. The truth of what was happening was there to see on the screen. Securitate men tried to find a way through the army's protective cordon to get into the television centre. The importance of controlling the outlet of information is not new but never before has it been so starkly demonstrated. The television stations of neighbouring countries played a part in Ceaucescu's downfall. Hungary and its media was particularly influential.

Another lesson is that in modern times an uprising does not need a conspiracy of masterminds to be successful. Ceaucescu, like the Communist leaders of Hungary, East Germany, Czechoslovakia and Poland, had been brought down by people power. And in all cases very quickly, once great crowds took the streets— and stayed there. The bloodshed made the Romanian experience different from the others, where there was no loss of life.

By any definition, the Romanian uprising was a war. The world's media called it a civil war, but it does not quite fit this label. At its onset there were no opposing armed forces and national groups. The demonstrators were unarmed to begin with and only slowly acquired a few firearms. The fighting was mostly between one part of the armed forces, the Army, against another, the Securitate. In one sense, the uprising might be termed The Romanian Youth War, since it was the young people who comprised the great mass of people on the streets. Few older people became involved.

The events in Romania differ from those in China in 1989. China had no uprising. It had merely a massive peaceful demonstration, mostly in Tiananmen Square, Peking, which in the end was quelled by massacre. No fighting occurred in China, if only because no element of the armed forces actively backed the demonstrators. However, the brutal Chinese leaders may have learned a lesson from the events in Eastern Europe—that the use of violence to suppress protests can only, in the end, make retribution more violent.

In executing Ceaucescu and his wife so rapidly, Romania's Committee of National Salvation demonstrated another important lesson—the 'strategic' need to dispose of a tyrant as soon as possible. Every tyrant has his supporters and they are nearly always fanatically loyal. They also know that, having shown no mercy, they can expect none—so they are not inclined to surrender while there remains the slightest chance of their leader regaining his authority. The people who criticise—from a safe and comfortable distance—the decision of the Romanian freedom fighters to shoot Ceaucescu out of hand, did not live through 24 years of the dictator's ruthless rule nor 41 years of repressive Communism. The war in Uganda continued long after the flight of the tyrant Idi Amin largely because his followers knew that he was safe in Saudi Arabia and expected him to return. A tyrant does not deserve the gift of a good, clean trial in which he can seek to re-establish his authority. That the Romanians killed their dictator is a measure not of their cruelty but of their desperation.

Romanian Defence Forces

On the eve of the uprising, Romania had formidable armed forces totalling 185,000, with reserves of nearly 600,000. The Army's manpower was 145,000, of which 98,000 were conscripts. The Navy had 8,000 and the Air Force 34,000. The paramilitary forces were significant, with 32,000 serving directly under the Ministry of Defence as a 'security force'. In fact, they were uniformed Securitate men. Another estimated 90,000 Securitate agents, though highly trained as commandos, were engaged on 'civic duties'—that is, spying on the people and intimidating anybody who spoke against the Ceaucescu régime. Ceaucescu also placed reliance on his Local Defence Force of 280,000. Only 15,000 were full time, operating in small groups in every city and town.

Ceaucescu's army had 1,530 tanks together with 3,500 armoured fighting vehicles and armoured personnel carriers. The Navy had a Black Sea fleet and a Danube River fleet of destroyers, frigates and corvettes. In addition, the Navy had 48 minesweepers and 72 river craft, a mixture of large patrol boats, monitors to fast patrol boats. Air Force strength consisted of 382 combat aircraft and 145 helicopters, plus transport and training squadrons.

The Securitate

The Securitate, a mixture of secret police and security police, was the Ceaucescu family's most feared instrument of repression. Apart from its own staff of 70,000, the organisation officially employed a million people, out of a population of 23.5 million and it paid at least another 3 million people as informers. The Securitate chiefs had no difficulty in gaining recruits; in poverty-stricken Romania they had only to offer more food and coal than that received by the ordinary people. Orphans were taken into the service and taught to regard the Ceaucescus with filial loyalty; they became the most fanatically loyal of all Securitate members.

The Securitate was one of the few organisations in Romania which had access to computers. Securitate inspectors saw to the registration of typewriters and even their typefaces, so that any subversive literature in typed form could be traced back to a particular machine. Photocopying machines were strictly controlled.

The Securitate had the best military equipment in the country, from tanks to personal weapons and its chiefs could get Ceaucescu's authorisation for anything they wished. The organisation was ready for any emergency—including an uprising. In several cities, notably Bucharest, it built tunnels, command centres and underground depots for storing weapons, ammunition and equipment. An underground escape route connected the complex tunnel network to a safe-house on a lake north of the city. In addition, the Securitate owned more than 200 safe-houses in the capital, each equipped to withstand a siege.

Completely unscrupulous, the Securitate members would have brought Romania to anarchy had they been able to do so. In pure spite, they set fire to the Bucharest University Library, destroying most of its great collection of manuscripts and books.

South Africa and the War in Namibia

CAN SWAPO BE TRUSTED WITH PEACE?

(South Africa's operations in Namibia should be studied in conjunction with its campaigns in Angola and its activities in relation to Mozambique.)

Background Summary

South Africa, as part of the British Empire, took over the territory known as German South-West Africa during the First World War, 1914–18. Despite opposition from many countries it held the region, now known as Namibia, for nearly 75 years.

The country has only 75,000 whites. About 50 per cent of the one-and-a-half million black Namibians belong to just one tribe, the Ovambo. Ovambo leaders, under Sam Nujoma, control the South-West Africa People's Organisation (SWAPO), declared by the UN in 1973 to be the 'sole and authentic voice of the Namibian people'.

The People's Liberation Army of Namibia (PLAN) is SWAPO's military wing. It established a base at Ongulumbashe, from where it began local recruitment and training. Seeing this as a threat to its security, South Africa sent its forces to destroy the base on 26 August 1966. Beginning from that date, the conflict is the longest bush war in Africa.

From the late 1970s the South African Defence Forces (SADF) stationed up to 35,000 troops in northern Namibia to confront the 15,000-strong PLAN.

In March 1986 the South African President, P.W. Botha, announced that a UN plan for Namibian independence, drawn up eight years before, would be implemented but only if a firm and satisfactory agreement was reached, before 31 August, on the withdrawal of Cuban troops from neighbouring Angola. No such agreement was reached. At no time did South Africa seem likely to take notice of UN resolutions about Namibia. The President of the African National Congress, Oliver Tambo, declared a 'people's war' and had 10,000 trained fighters in 1986. They made several terrorist attacks in South African cities.

Leaving Namibia made no sense to South African strategists. Withdrawal would limit South Africa's ability to dominate the southern half of Angola, either directly or through its UNITA proxy. It would lose its forward bases and radar coverage. Most of all, it would reduce South Africa's physical dominance of southern Africa almost as far as Zaire.

During talks in London in May 1988, Namibia was discussed by representatives of South Africa, the US, Cuba, Angola and UNITA. It was suggested that SWAPO, once it became the elected government of Namibia, would be required

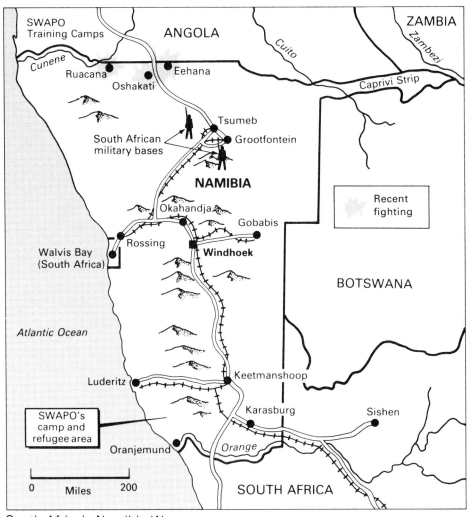

South Africa's Namibia War

to sign a non-aggression pact with South Africa. No foreign troops, including ANC guerrillas, would be allowed on Namibian soil.

On 27 June, Angolan and Cuban troops attacked the Calueque Dam, which lies at the Cunene River, on the Angolan side of the Angola/Namibia border and provides a vital source of water to Ovambaland, in northern Namibia. Angolan, Cuban and South African troops were killed, the dam wall was damaged and a water-line was destroyed. Following three separate explosions in the Windhoek area, police blamed SWAPO for one death and 18 injuries. SWAPO denied responsibility, claiming that South African agents had planted the explosives to set Namibia's white community against SWAPO.

Early in August a fourth round of talks was held in Geneva. A joint statement issued in Havana, Luanda and Pretoria indicated that the delegations had 'agreed to prepare the way for independence in Namibia and to attain peace in South-West Africa'. South Africa publicised an offer to withdraw its troops from Namibia on 1 November, provided that Cuban troops completely withdrew from Angola and the ANC guerrilla camps in Angola were disbanded.

In a statement to mark Namibia Day on 26 August,[1] Sam Nujoma said that SWAPO would cease its 22 years of military hostilities against the South African 'occupation army' as from 2 September. The cessation of hostilities would lead to a formal cease-fire in October, 'providing the occupation army does the same'.

The last contingent of SADF and South-West Africa Territorial Force (SWATF) troops withdrew from Angola on 30 August, in accordance with the Geneva Protocol of 2 August. SADF second-in-command, General Gleeson, disclosed that 50,000 Cuban troops in Angola had, in return, agreed to keep 30 to 150 miles north of the Angola/Namibia border. Less than three weeks later, SWATF issued a statement that, despite SWAPO's undertaking to cease hostilities on 1 September, 'its terrorist gangs are continuing their aggression, sabotage and intimidation in the operational area'.

After several more meetings, the Protocol of Brazzaville was signed by Angola, Cuba and South Africa. Under its provisions, the parties agreed that 1 April 1989 would be the date of implementation for Security Council Resolution 435, the UN's long-standing plan for Namibia's independence. As a final step, the South African Foreign Minister Pik Botha announced that Koevost, the Namibian Police Counter Insurgency Unit, would be disbanded 'in an attempt to gain goodwill'.

The Conflict in 1989

The United Nations Transition Assistance Group (UNTAG) came into being to move into Namibia to administer the cease-fire. A civil and military organisation, UNTAG was to deploy 7,600 troops in various parts of Namibia, not merely to keep the peace but also to assist in development projects. The Australian contingent, for instance, consists of an engineer unit.

Much controversy followed. On 6 February, the opening day of the meeting of the Commonwealth Committee of Foreign Ministers' on southern Africa, President Mugabe of Zimbabwe proposed the establishment of a Commonwealth Observer Group for Namibia and denounced the UN decision to reduce the size of UNTAG to 4,650.[2] The advance party for UNTAG arrived in Windhoek on

19 February. General Prem Chand, commanding UNTAG's military component, took up his duties on 26 February.

As early as 2 March the South Africans announced that SWAPO was contravening its own undertakings by not withdrawing north of the 16th parallel—inside Angola. On 14 March the UN Secretary General, Perez de Cuellar, wrote to the South African government and SWAPO proposing a formal cease-fire from 0400 GMT on 1 April 1989.

Inflammatory talk was ominous. On 19 March, Sam Nujoma, at a conference in Lisbon, presented a virtual threat to the South Africans. He said: 'If SWAPO wins the election in November it will not try to stop South Africans from fighting for their independence. We shall continue our support for the ANC in the framework of overall African solidarity.'

South Africa countered with the promise of 'swift counter-measures if an independent government of Namibia allows the ANC to launch guerrilla attacks from military bases in the territory'.

On 1 April, or 'D-Day', while Namibia celebrated the end of South Africa's long rule, hundreds of armed SWAPO soldiers charged over the border. Fighting erupted at once. As a result, more than 200 guerrillas and 30 police were killed and scores more were wounded. The entire UN plan was jeopardised and UNTAG faced an immediate crisis, especially as only 200 UNTAG soldiers were in the battle zone at the time.

SWAPO denied any misdemeanour and maintained that South Africa had provoked its guerrillas into fighting. This was absurd. The presence of SWAPO armed soldiers in Namibia was a clear violation of the agreement, regardless of who fired first. The incursion was either a breakdown in communication or an attempt by PLAN to assert itself.

Either explanation highlights the lack of cohesion that characterises the various internal and external wings of the organisation. Besides imperilling the transition to independence, such disarray raised questions about SWAPO's ability to run a coherent election campaign—or a government.

Since 1,200 SWAPO fighters had crossed the border, bringing with them large supplies of arms and ammunition, it was clear that they intended to establish bases within Namibia. To have an army inside Namibia is important to SWAPO. The attempt to implement Resolution 435 in 1978 fell apart because of the group's insistence on creating bases there. This time, SWAPO apparently thought that by getting soldiers over the border, it could force the UN to accept their presence. This—in SWAPO's eyes—would raise its political profile and its electoral chances. It could claim to have 'liberated' certain zones within the territory, an invaluable addition to a revolutionary's rhetorical repertoire.

The order to cross into Namibia may have been the work of Dino Amaambo, head of PLAN and a deadly rival of Nujoma. Some observers believe that Nujoma himself gave the order. A black Namibian lawyer said: 'Nujoma used to send hundreds of men to their death in offensives every rainy season just to improve SWAPO's Press image'.[3]

Peter Vale, a Rhodes University political scientist, said: 'SWAPO has a real command-and-control problem. All along, they've promised to liberate the country, by the barrel of a gun. And that's what some of their people think they're doing.'[4]

The accord got back on track, but with great misgivings on all sides. Adries Treurnicht, leader of South Africa's ultra-Right-wing Conservative Party, has called for South Africa to send home UNTAG and to abrogate Resolution 435. He said:'What must SWAPO, the Angolans and ANC do to further convince the government of the futility of 435?'[5]

In September 1989 much publicity was given to allegations that SWAPO and PLAN had tortured many of their own members. It was proved that up to 40 Namibians at a time had been imprisoned in a mud pit for weeks. Others were beaten to death. Some of the maltreated men, though of proven loyalty, were accused of being 'Boer spies'. The truth seems to be that high level officials within SWAPO and PLAN had been giving much information to the South Africans. To cover their tracks they accused lower level officers of spying.[6]

Chief of the South African Defence Force, General Johannes Jacobus Geldenhuys, said in November 1989 that with South African operations against SWAPO in Angola over, there was no justification for the Cuban presence in Angola and no reason for their withdrawal to be postponed.

He was not concerned about the possibility of a SWAPO government following the elections, since South Africa had lived with FRELIMO in Mozambique and with the MPLA in Angola. It could live with SWAPO. Nevertheless, the general said, a SWAPO victory could raise the morale of the ANC and lead to a hardening of its attitudes and those of the 'frontline states'. He was certain that the ANC would continue operations within South Africa.

Geldenhuys revealed that the SADF plans to concentrate on development programmes as the situation in Namibia becomes more stable. The army wants a new battle tank and the air force a new fighter aircraft. He stated that southern Africa was finally entering a period of negotiation rather than violence. After 20 years of what he termed low-key conflict, there was now a 'general mood to give peaceful methods a chance'.

References

1. 26 August became part of the revolutionary calendar as the day on which the first guerrillas were caught in Namibia by the security forces.
2. The force was reduced because of the cost in maintaining it. The UN could raise no more than the equivalent of $416 million. The able UN Commissioner for Namibia, Bernt Carlsson, died in the PanAm air crash at Lockerbie on 21 December 1988.
3. Despite his caustic comments on Nujoma, this lawyer is close to SWAPO and an ardent supporter.
4. Vale was quoted by Lynda Schuster, writing in *The Christian Science Monitor*, 6 April 1989.
5. Treurnicht's challenging comments were reported throughout South Africa. The Conservative Party opposes independence for Namibia.
6. The best and most comprehensive account of this aspect of SWAPO/PLAN is by Susan Brown, writing in *The Independent*, London, 29 September 1989.
7. Helmoed-Romer Heitman writing in *Jane's Defence Weekly*, 18 November 1989.

War Annual No. 3 carried several important reports about the war. They include:
    A South African Intelligence assessment of SWAPO and PLAN.
    A description of an SADF tracker-fighting team.
    An analysis of South African arms.

Sri Lanka Civil War

'A SURGE OF SAVAGERY THAT CHOKES OFF REASON'

Background Summary

The overt ethnic animosity between the Buddhist Sinhalese and the Hindu Tamils began when Sri Lanka, formerly Ceylon, became independent from Britain in 1948. In an area of 25,332 square miles, there are 11 million Sinhalese, 3 million Tamils and 1.5 million Muslims. The Tamils are mainly in the north, with smaller areas in the centre and along the east coast. From the beginning they demanded a separate state, to be called Eelam.

Open violence began in 1983. The Tamils organised many guerrilla groups to fight the army, which was wholly Sinhalese. The best known were: Liberation Tigers of Tamil Eelam (LTTE), the People's Liberation Organisation of Tamil Eelam (PLOTE), the Tamil Eelam Liberation Organisation (TELO), the Eelam People's Revolutionary Liberation Front (EPRLF) and the Eelam Revolutionary Organisation and Supporters (EROS). A wholly political body, the Tamil United Liberation Front (TULF), included members of parliament.

The government of President J.R. Jayawardene opposed a Tamil state in Sri Lanka, on the grounds that the Indian state of Tamil Nadu, just across Palk Strait, was adequate for all Tamils. Tamil Nadu's population is 55 million.

A Tigers ambush killed an army patrol. In retaliation, Sinhalese mobs murdered about 1,000 Tamils in what the Tamils call 'the Holocaust'. The conflict became savage and both sides were guilty of many atrocities. The Tigers turned against TELO in April 1986, killed 100 of its members, including all leaders, and finished it off as a guerrilla force. The Tigers were then undisputed masters of the resistance movement.

On 6 February 1987 the Sri Lankan forces launched an attack on the Jaffna peninsula and some Tamil bases were destroyed. At least 20,000 Tamils fled abroad but the guerrilla movement remained vigorous. In desperation, as his country's economic and social structure collapsed, President Jayawardene turned to India for help in suppressing the Tamils.

Following an agreement signed on 29 July 1987, the Indian government created an Indian Peace-Keeping Force (IPKF) and put into motion *Operation Pawan*. The Sri Lankan government informed the Sinhalese population that the IPKF would remain in Sri Lanka for only a limited time, but most Sinhalese viewed the Indian presence with suspicion. The chauvinist Maoist group, *Janata Vimukti Peramuna* or People's Liberation Front, known as JVP, particularly resented the Indian troops in Sri Lanka.

The JVP gained many more recruits because of heavy-handed tactics by the security forces and the paramilitary Special Task Force, which executed JVP

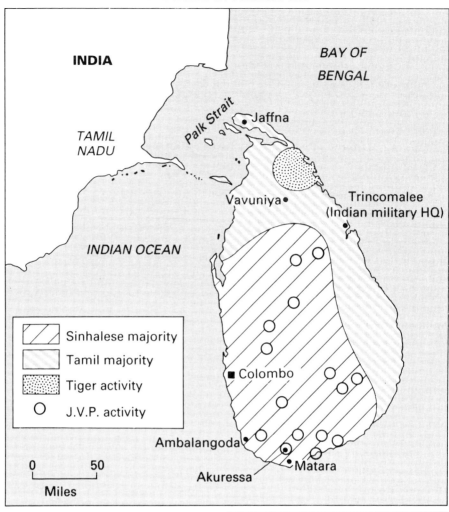

Sri Lanka: Ethnic Areas

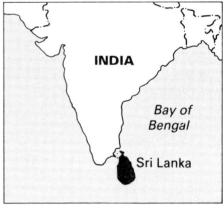

suspects. In the cause of 'achieving peace', the JVP killed scores of people between July 1987 and May 1988, mostly Sinhalese who supported the government.

In the north, *Operation Pawan* led to much fighting and further atrocities. In June 1988, India announced that the IPKF would begin to withdraw. It was obvious that withdrawal would be slow, as the Tamils, though weakened, were still militant. Their guerrilla leadership cells were intact in Sri Lanka and in Tamil Nadu, where their largest bases were situated. At the end of 1988 India's influence was so profound that Sri Lankan foreign policy was dictated from New Delhi. Despite having suffered 2,500 casualties, the Indian Army High Command was pleased with the campaign in Sri Lanka. It had given all levels and all branches of the services experience in combined service operations. However, the new Sri Lankan Prime Minister, Ranasinghe Premadase—elected in December—was anxious for the Indian army to leave.

The Conflict in 1989

The Sri Lankan government had to cope with two savage wars in 1989. One was the Tamil versus IPKF war in the north and north-east; the other was the Sri Lankan army versus JVP war in the south and west. Sometimes the two over-lapped, as the army was also committed to fighting the Tamils. In addition, Sinhalese terrorist groups and Tamil terrorist groups occasionally clashed.

The Northern War

The India–Sri Lanka accord had been flawed from its beginning, if only because no firm time limit had been set. Also, President Jayawardene had not written into the accord adequate Sri Lankan political control over the IPKF. Further, the Indian generals miscalculated the tenacity of the Tamil guerrillas in pursuit of an independent state. The LTTE has shown organisational ability, unity of aim and remarkable resilience. At the beginning of the year it commanded substantial support among the Tamils, particularly in the Jaffna peninsula, where it managed to penetrate the Indian naval screen to bring in weapons and explosives.

Rajiv Gandhi's government felt that intervention in Sri Lanka had led it into a 'no-win' situation. Its plans at the end of 1988 were to force through elections in the provincial council of the newly-united North-Eastern Province. After the elections, India could declare 'victory' and withdraw. It was not to be so easy.

In their attempt to erase the Tigers as a military threat, Indian troops gained the support of the EPRLF which, unlike the Tigers, accepts the peace accord with the Indian presence. Initially, the EPRLF alliance with the Indian Army was covert, with hooded EPRLF men identifying Tiger suspects in security sweeps. The hoods came off after the EPRLF won a majority in the North-Eastern Province council vote, having been the only significant Tamil party to defy Tiger orders not to contest the election. After that, Indian troops openly armed, sheltered and deployed members of the EPRLF.

The rebirth of EPRLF gave the Tamil conflict a new, viciously internecine aspect, resulting in a daily toll of people killed by unidentified gunmen. In three months, the EPRLF killed more than 200 Tiger fighters and civilians thought to be sympathetic to them.

In June the Sri Lankan government asked New Delhi to withdraw the IPKF from the northern and eastern provinces by 29 July. The deadline took the Indian government by surprise. A potential peace agreement between the Tigers and the government may have been the deciding factor. In any case, Ranasinghe Premadasa had been elected on a mandate to get Indian troops out of the country. A diplomatic row broke out and continued for two months, although New Delhi did begin a token troop withdrawal on 30 July.

On 17 August, LTTE spokesmen claimed that Indian soldiers had killed 6,000 Tamil civilians during the 22 months the Indians had been serving in north-eastern Sri Lanka. The Tigers accused the soldiers of frequent atrocities and torture and claimed that more than 3,000 Tamils were being held prisoner.

Other sources[1] report that many civilians are beaten by Indian forces. Each time there is an attack on an Indian base or outpost, surrounding areas are cordoned off and large numbers of civilians are arrested; many are then cruelly beaten. The public's anxiety over the abuses committed by Indian soldiers and EPRLF hitmen is compounded by the fact that neither force is accountable to anyone. The police force in the North-Eastern Province has long since disintegrated and courts have not functioned since 1986.

Forty IPKF soldiers were killed by Tamils in a 72-hour period prior to 29 July, Premadasa's deadline for the withdrawal. The withdrawal did not take place. The IPKF's strength late in 1989 was 72,000, although only 52,000, including 1,500 of the Central Reserve Police Force, were permanently stationed on the island. The others were based in southern India.

The War in the South

It was the intervention of the Indian army which brought *Janata Vimukti Peramuna* (JVP) to prominence and notoriety. The JVP had been founded by Rohane Wijeweera, a medical school drop-out. Wijeweera's hostility to India dates from the 1960s when India and China went to war over disputed borders. He was strongly influenced by Mao Tse-tung's propaganda campaign, accusing India of imperialist designs on the entire Asian sub-continent. Breaking away from the Sri Lanka Communist Party, which he considered weak, Wijeweera founded the JVP, which attracted other fiercely chauvinistic Sinhalese leaders.

When IPKF was deployed in Sri Lanka they had an ideal issue and an opportunity for perfect timing. As the Indians went to war against the Tamil Tigers in the north, the JVP opened fire on the Colombo government in the south, accusing it of selling out to New Delhi. It indicted the government for undermining national sovereignty by inviting in foreign troops. This was ironic considering that the JVP hates the Tamils. As the economy went into sharp decline, unemployment increased. Exploiting economic discontent and Sinhalese national pride, the JVP quickly emerged as a powerful voice for the Sinhalese peasantry.

From its stronghold in Akuressa, the JVP spurned invitations by the government and by the parliamentary opposition to join the democratic process and embarked on a campaign of savagery.[2] Families of JVP victims—which amounted to about 20 a day—were forbidden by the killers to acknowledge the deaths with any of the traditional signs of mourning.

The JVP became the target not only of the security forces but also of the death squads that operate with the government's unacknowledged support. The JVP had grown in size so quickly by the end of 1988 that practically the entire 33,000 strong Sri Lankan army, including 9,000 of the 12,000 men normally stationed in the north, was redeployed to the south and the central-west to help contain the virulent guerrillas. The price of 'disloyalty' to the JVP is high. In the small village of Thihagoda the bodies of a woman and her adult son, deemed government sympathisers by the JVP, were found in their homes, their heads smashed in by hammer blows.

The JVP makes life miserable in every possible way. When it calls strikes, it means them to be total. For instance, when it ordered a bus strike, its killers shot several bus drivers to enforce the command.

In August, the JVP started killing the families of security men in their campaign to bring down the government. A chemist was murdered in Colombo for selling a popular acne cream and so 'defying' the boycott the terrorists had declared on Indian goods. In Borrella, the owner of a new Bombay-made tricycle was shot dead as he plied for hire.

Another horrific case was authenticated by foreign witnesses. A driver from one of the few tourist bus companies still operating in Sri Lanka emerged from a hotel in Habarana to find his bus covered with anti-government slogans that had been spray-painted during the night. Attached to the windscreen was a note warning him that he would be killed if he washed the bus clean. The note was signed by the JVP.

Frightened for his life, the driver hurried his group of West German tourists into the bus and hurriedly left the area. At a roadblock he was stopped by a Sri Lankan army patrol who demanded an explanation for the offensive slogans. They dismissed the driver's frantic response and, as the shocked tourists watched, they broke both the driver's arms.[3]

Despite its viciousness, the JVP somehow wins friends. In little more than two years, the once obscure Maoist clique had fanned, by 1989, a virulent epidemic of popular Sinhalese nationalist revolt that threatened the Premadasa regime and Sri Lanka's democratic tradition.

Armed by the government with extra emergency powers, the security forces and vigilantes have imposed their own brutal form of justice. More than 1,000 JVP supporters were killed in just a few weeks of January.

In response to the JVP threat, the Indian army moved an infantry division, two independent brigades and four squadrons of Jaguar, Mirage and MiG-23 Flogger fighters to bases in southern India.

Whatever the Indian-Sri Lankan political developments,[4] JVP violence will continue. This and the growth of the government's vigilante groups and the actions of the Special Task Force gives Sri Lanka dreadful similarities with Latin America and its death squads.

JVP Loses its Leaders

In November 1989 the security forces achieved several decisive breakthroughs. In particular, Rohane Wijeweera himself was captured and killed. In a state of exultation over this 'triumph', the Foreign Minister, Ranjan Wijeratne, said, 'The match is over and we have won.' In a raid on the JVP's radio station, the security forces captured Upatissa Gamanayaka, the military commander of the organisation. He and another JVP leader were killed 'while trying to escape'. President Premadasa ordered a police inquiry into the deaths but told parliament that had the JVP leaders responded to his peace initiatives 'matters could have taken a different turn'.

With six of its seven politburo leaders dead or captured, the JVP ceased its violent acts virtually overnight. The decapitation of the JVP was expected to defuse the southern guerrilla campaign. However, new violence was already building up in eastern Sri Lanka. After the withdrawal of the Indian troops from this zone in October, a three-way battle broke out among Sri Lankan security forces, an illegal army raised by the pro-India local Tamil administration and the rebellious LTTE. The first fighting resulted in 96 deaths. In addition, in December 1989, pro-government vigilantes killed hundreds of Sinhalese radicals suspected of sympathising with the JVP.

References

1. These sources are reliable, being international relief workers. A few have given me the horrific details of atrocities carried out by both Indian soldiers and Tamil guerrillas.
2. *Time Magazine*, 19 December 1988, quoted Vallipuran Pararajasingham, a doctor of Vavuniya: 'I am afraid to smile at anyone in the street. If I smile at a man who happens to be an EPRLF member or supporter I am marked by the LTTE. If I smile at a man who has LTTE connections I am marked by the Indian army and the EPRLF.' *Time* calls the conflict in Sri Lanka 'a surge of savagery that chokes off all reason'.
3. The tourists reported the incident to their embassy in Colombo. Most embassies warn their nationals to stay away from Sri Lanka.
4. For reasons of domestic prestige, Rajiv Gandhi could not agree to immediate or even early withdrawal. The earliest date would be after the Indian elections in December 1989.

War Annual No. 3 carried a comprehensive account of the Indian Army's Operation Pawan. In addition, there is a description of Sri Lankan army organisation.

Sudan Civil War

REBEL TRIUMPHS—KHARTOUM COUP

Background Summary

The first war between the Muslim Arabs of northern Sudan and the Christian negroes and animist tribes of the south occurred between 1955 and 1972. A negotiated peace ended the war but oppression from the state security forces forced the southerners to form a guerrilla defence army. Also, they needed to protect themselves from Islamic pressure, which was intended to subdue the Christians and turn them into a *dhimmi* people—second-class citizens under the harsh Islamic *sharia* law.

The guerrilla army, know as *Anyanya*—'venom of the viper'— grew into a more conventional military force, the Sudan People's Liberation Army (SPLA). West-ern-educated Colonel John Garang became its leader in 1982. Abdullah Chol formed *Anyanya II* in opposition to the SPLA. While SPLA wanted secession from Sudan, *Anyanya II* was ready to collaborate with the Khartoum government of President Gaafer Nimeiri.

Nimeiri was overthrown in a military coup in April 1985 but government activity against the SPLA continued. Abdullah Chol was killed while fighting the SPLA and *Anyanya II* collapsed. In April 1986, Sadiq al-Mahdi became Prime Minister and Garang hoped for peace but al-Mahdi backed the army and accused Garang of being a lackey of the neighbouring Marxist Ethiopia. Garang has no Marxist sympathies but at the time he was receiving most of his weapons from Ethiopia.

Between 1982 and 1987 neither side had a strategy which could end the war. The government could hardly lose it, since Muslims make up two-thirds of the population of 22.5 million. Unable to bring the SPLA to battle, the Sudan armed forces massacred people from the Dinka and Nuer tribes, considered to be allies of SPLA. Garang captured two localities in northern Sudan, Kurmak and Gizen, and caused panic in Khartoum. Libya sent troops to help the government recapture the lost areas but Garang withdrew before they arrived.

Summary of the War in 1988

The war moved further northwards towards the Arab territory, as did more than one million desperate southern refugees. Islamic fundamentalists and Pale-stinian terrorists spread rumours that the SPLA rebels, the Christian Church, foreign missionaries and relief agencies were colluding against the Muslim majority. Five Britons were killed by Palestinians in Khartoum. Relief agencies reported many human rights violations, including torture, by government troops.

SPLA units captured Kapoeta, 800 miles south of Khartoum, on 25 January

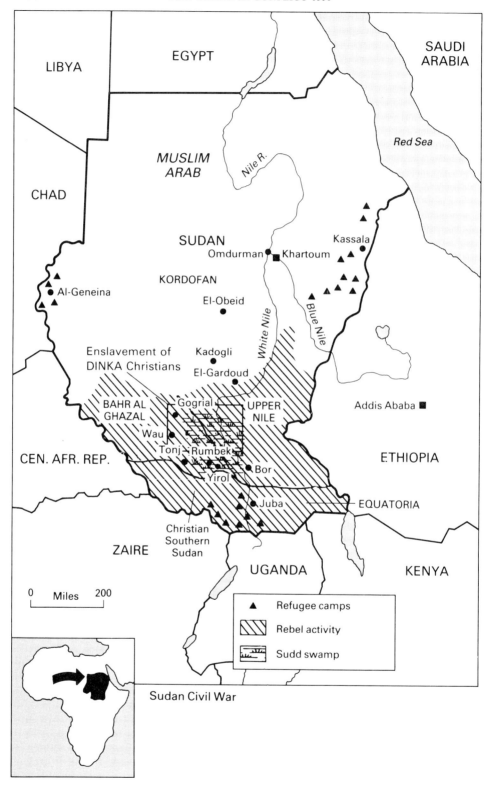

LIBYA

EGYPT

SAUDI ARABIA

Red Sea

MUSLIM ARAB

Nile R.

CHAD

SUDAN

Kassala

Omdurman · ■ Khartoum

KORDOFAN

▲ Al-Geneina

El-Obeid ·

White Nile

Blue Nile

Enslavement of DINKA Christians

Kadogli ·
El-Gardoud ·

Addis Ababa ■

BAHR AL GHAZAL

Gogrial

UPPER NILE

Wau ·

Tonj · Rumbek

CEN. AFR. REP.

Yirol

Bor ·

ETHIOPIA

· Juba — EQUATORIA

Christian Southern Sudan

ZAIRE

UGANDA

KENYA

0   Miles   200

| ▲ | Refugee camps |
| Rebel activity |
| Sudd swamp |

Sudan Civil War

1988. Contrary to their usual tactics, the rebels then held the place until the army had gone to the great effort and expense of preparing a strong relief army. Then Garang ordered a withdrawal.

In December, King Fahd of Saudi Arabia sent his personal troubleshooter, Ali Bin Mussalman, to Khartoum in an attempt to avert the imminent breakup of Sudan. He met Hassan al Turabi of the National Islamic Front and ordered this fundamentalist to end his activities against a peace settlement. However, Turabi continued to hold meetings with Sudanese officers, stressing that 'any peace agreement means dishonour to the Sudanese army'. The solution, Turabi argued, was to give the army more military means to end the war on its conditions.

The War in 1989

In several major engagements against the SPLA, the armed forces suffered sharp setbacks. Despairing of the military's record in Equatoria, the government replaced several garrisons of northern Arabs with Christian troops in the Sudanese army. This had always seemed dangerous but al-Mahdi and his advisers now believed that these troops, under a southern commander, might possess a greater knowledge of the regional terrain. Also, southern commanders within the national army, with their home territory at stake, might perform better than those from the north.

This revised policy first took effect in Juba with the removal of Major General Fadul Ali and his replacement by Major General Allison Magaya, an Equatorian. Major General Magaya is a Zande, the only tribe in Equatoria not known to have joined the SPLA in any significant numbers.

Colonel Kamilo, of the Latuka tribe from the Torit district, was given command of the garrison at Torit, the largest garrison in Equatoria after Juba. The third largest garrison in western Equatoria, Mirdi, also acquired an Equatorian as its commander. He is Brigadier Dominic Kassiano, a Zande, who commanded the *Anyanya I* forces in the region during the first civil war, 1955–72.

These and other replacements indicated a new government strategy of pitting southerner against southerner. In Torit, the commanders of the army and the enemy SPLA are from the same tribe, the Latuka.

While not responsible for the government's revisionist actions towards the military in Equatoria, Joseph Lagu, vice-president of Sudan 1981–85 and former president of southern Sudan (1978–80), gave Khartoum his full support. Lagu encouraged the government to go even further and unify the army in the whole of southern Sudan and appoint him as its commander. He also proposed that the civilian governors of three regions be replaced by retired military officers.[1]

Lagu commands much support in southern Sudan and has consistently pushed for recruitment of more southerners into key army positions. He named several officers who were with him in *Anyanya*. The senior Arab officers, however, argued against Lagu, because of worry over what would become of the *Anyanya* militias. Almost three-quarters of the *Anyanya II* militia, mostly of the Nuer tribe, have defected to the SPLA. The Mundari tribe, who were once the army's closest ally in Equatoria, are now the army's most deadly enemy after the SPLA itself.

In the meantime, Sadiq al-Mahdi was proving himself to be a big disappointment as prime minister. The West hoped he would lead a stable government and stay in the moderate Arab camp. Instead he moved ever closer to Libya and he visited Iran in search of arms. This angered the Saudis. In his three years at the head of the first democratic government in Sudan for 16 years he was unable to bring himself to give up the harsh Islamic law, the *sharia*, the mere threat of which perpetuated the civil war. Also, he failed, during 1988, to provide food for starving famine victims.

The Egyptians were also disappointed in al-Mahdi. Late in 1988 they gave him a 'final warning' that they would not tolerate the presence of Libyan army units on Sudanese territory near Egypt's borders. When Khartoum denied any knowledge of them, the Egyptian General Intelligence Service sent al-Mahdi tapes of intercepted calls from his own office and from the Libyan base in Tripoli. Aerial photographs were supplied as further proof.[2] Just as serious for Egypt was the presence in Libya and Iran for training of militia from al-Mahdi's own party. The final straw was al-Mahdi's refusal to support the provisional peace plan drawn up in November 1988 by the Democratic Unionist Party, one of his coalition partners, and the SPLA. Egypt was the driving force behind this peace plan.

In February, 150 Sudanese officers urged al-Mahdi to introduce political and economic reforms and to spend more money on defence. The Prime Minister failed to meet any of the demands and irate junior officers accused senior officers of compromising with the government. Junior officers were also angered by the arrest of 14 of their number in connection with a coup plot uncovered by the government on 13 June. The plot was the work of supporters of the deposed president, Nimeiri, who lives in Cairo.[3]

On 30 June a coup led by a little-known Egyptian-trained paratroop brigadier, Oman Hassan al-Bashir, threw out the al-Mahdi government. Al-Bashir promoted himself lieutenant-general and installed a 15-man junta composed mainly of middle-echelon officers—six brigadiers, five colonels, two lieutenant-colonels and a major. All these officers were trained at the Nasser Academy in Cairo and have strong links with Egypt.

The new President denied that he had received Egyptian help in planning the coup and seizing power but Egypt was certainly involved, right up to President Mubarak himself.[4] The day following the coup, Egyptian air force planes arrived in Khartoum with cargoes of medicine, children's food, vehicle spare parts and army uniforms. Within hours Egypt became the first country to recognise Sudan's new 'Command Council of the National Salvation Revolution'. Having quickly consolidated his grip in Khartoum, al-Bashir sent a delegation to Cairo for talks with Mubarak while the chief of Egyptian intelligence visited Khartoum. Only a month later al-Bashir himself flew to Cairo, to be warmly greeted by Mubarak.

One of al-Bashir's first acts as leader was to dismiss 28 generals; they constituted virtually the entire high command of Sudan's armed forces. While al-Bashir is a devout Muslim, he is believed to be a political moderate. His junta faces an enormous task in rescuing the country from near bankruptcy. Sudan has foreign debts of $12 billion and inflation was running at 90 per cent in 1989.

The Oxford-educated al-Mahdi promised to hold a referendum on whether the *sharia* should be introduced and to seek an 'honourable end' to the war. He said the war was costing the government $1 million a day and that it had resulted in the death of about one million people since 1983.

President al-Bashir is said to respect John Garang but this is not likely to bring an early end to the war. Garang's military position is stronger than ever before. His army, now 50,000-strong, took and held 16 garrison towns in 1989, proving that SPLA is no longer a guerrilla force but a conventional army. It held the whole of southern Sudan east of the White Nile and south of the river Sobat.

Garang has developed strong ties with Kenya which supplies him with major logistical, material and moral support. He has a base in Nairobi which is becoming more important to him than that in Addis Abbaba. The Ethiopian government and army, increasingly under pressure from the Eritrean and Tigrayan resistance forces, have become unreliable allies for the SPLA. Colonel Mengistu's regime is also politically unstable, so Garang has shown much forethought in strengthening his links with Kenya. In mid-1989 he visited Washington, where he was well received.

President al-Bashir does not have as much political acumen as Garang and his decision to hold a referendum on the *sharia* law, while appearing to be liberal, was a gross error of judgement. Since Sudan is overwhelmingly Muslim and since it will be difficult to administer a referendum in the war-torn south, the result is a foregone conclusion. This step has not impressed Garang and SPLA leaders.

The Amnesty Report

In a report published on 12 December 1989, Amnesty International claimed that Sudanese government forces and their allies had executed tens of thousands of unarmed civilians and tortured rebel prisoners. The report, one of the most disturbing ever produced by Amnesty, stated that the lands of the Dinka people in northern Bahr el Ghazal province had been devastated during the army's six-year oppression of the Dinkas.

'The new government [that of Oman al-Bashir] is not known to have taken any concrete action to remedy human rights violations committed in the past or to prevent abuses in the future,' the report said. It referred to particular atrocities, such as the massacre of 1,000 Dinkas in Ad Daien in March 1987. In addition, 40 women and children were pushed into a hut and burnt to death.

Amnesty also accuses the SPLA of killing prisoners and civilians opposed to its policies and actions. The United Nations puts Sudan's death toll between 1983 and 1989 at 500,000.

References

1. Joseph Lagu in conversation with the author. If southern Sudan were to secede, Mr. Lagu would probably become its president.
2. Details from confidential Egyptian sources.
3. Speaking in Cairo to a Kuwaiti journalist, Nimeiri said that the al-Bashir coup had disrupted his own plans to bring down the al-Mahdi regime. 'I was on the verge of leaving Egypt to lead a war of liberation', he said. It is unlikely that the Egyptians would have permitted him to leave. Al-Bashir has said that nobody would stop Nimeiri from entering Sudan but that 'his right to live in the country would be preceded by a trial to clear him of all the crimes he is accused of having committed'.
4. Egyptian connections with the coup were common knowledge among Western diplomats in Cairo. The Saudi ambassador had also been notified in advance.

War Annual No. 3 carried several separate reports relating to the war in Sudan. They include:
     A description of Sudan's armed forces, their numbers, arms and equipment.
     The resurgent slave trade.
     The influence of the fundamentalists National Islamic Front.
     The attempt to present the war as 'an external problem'.

War Trends

AFTER PERESTROIKA?
Gambling on Gorbachev

Many people in the West have come to believe, that because of President Gorbachev's *glasnost* and *perestroika*, the Cold War has run its course and that the Soviet Union and Warsaw Pact are genuine about a move towards a less offensive-oriented military policy. This belief has become a trend which might well be termed 'Gambling on Gorbie'.

Those in the West who advocate reduction of armed forces, weapons, and defence budgets and a generally relaxed defence posture are basing their assumptions about the decreased dangers on four assumptions:

● President Gorbachev, unlike his predecessors, is wholly sincere about *peaceful co-existence*.
● President Gorbachev will remain in power long enough for reforms within the Soviet Union and other Warsaw Pact countries to become irreversible.
● The Soviet military hierarchy and the Communist Party inner circle have the same peaceful and pragmatic intentions as Gorbachev.
● The Soviet leaders will somehow manage to control the widespread and bitter ethnic, religious and political unrest within their own borders without resorting to force, which might cause a chain reaction in Europe and Asia. The near-war being waged by Azerbaijani Muslims against Armenian Christians is particularly dangerous.

Peace gambled is peace lost. Therefore the West, and free world generally, cannot relax its defence. A lower defence posture takes a short time to implement but to reinstate the original defences takes years. The perceived trend towards peace in Europe is very welcome, the trend towards believing that it will last is dangerous.

General Carl E. Vuono, Chief of Staff of the US Army, apparently has much the same attitude. 'The promise of *perestroika* and the glow of *glasnost* should not lull the Bush administration into a false sense of security', he said. 'The Soviet Union is now, and will remain, a primary threat to our security far into the next century; that is the cold, hard reality'.[1]

Yet there are some appealing reasons to believe that the peace trend is valuable. Superpower representatives, at very high levels, have talked candidly with one another and visited one another's countries during 1989. In addition, in certain fields the superpowers actually co-operated.

In policies towards South Africa and on the Middle East, for example, the

185

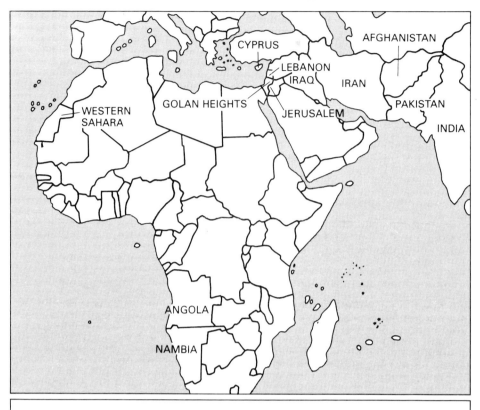

UN Peacekeeping Forces

Golan Heights
Supervise cease-fire
1,327 troops
$34.7 million in 1988

Jerusalem
Supervise truces
298 troops
$20.3 million in 1988

Southern Lebanon
Patrol buffer zone
5,850 troops
$139.4 million in 1988

Iran-Iraq border
Monitor cease-fire
350 observers, 400 troops
$37.5 million in their first
three months

Cyprus
Patrol buffer zone
2,122 troops
$25.2 million in 1988

Afghanistan
Monitor Soviet pullout
50 observers
$7 million in 1988

India-Pakistan
Supervise cease-fire
39 troops
$3.7 million in 1988

Angola
Verify Cuban pullout
70 observers
Estimate: $20.4 million
for 31 months

Namibia
*Supervise election/transition
to independence*
7,500 peacekeeping troops
1,000 civilians
Proposed: $700 million

Western Sahara
(proposed)

UN Peacekeeping Forces

Soviet Defence Minister, General Dmitri Yazov, visited British military bases and was shown and told more than security would have permitted in 1987. In return, senior Western generals visited Soviet army bases, where they saw not quite so much.

Some of Yazov's public comments are interesting and are worth study. He repeated that the Soviet Union had already stated its readiness to give up the status of a nuclear power. 'We set forth the programme for a gradual elimination of nuclear weapons by the year 2000 and for building of a nuclear weapon-free and non-violent world. The implementation of that programme would enable the Soviet Union, and all other states, to have armed forces and armaments of such strength by the year 2000 that would be capable of fulfilling only defensive tasks'.

In another statement, Yazov said, 'Further cuts in the Soviet armed forces are quite realistic'. However, they depended to 'a decisive degree on mutual progress towards the common goal of disarmament'.[2]

It is not possible, however, for a nuclear-weapon state to become a non-nuclear-weapon state—the condition is irreversible. Throughout history, the only reason a weapon has gone out of use is that a better one has replaced it. The use of poison gas was suspended during the Second World War only because the warring nations did not need it. Those that have since needed it have used it.

Despite Soviet claims about reduction of forces it is a fact that during 1989 the number of Soviet main battle tanks (MBTs) increased from 53,300 to 60,000. The International Institute for Strategic Studies (IISS) estimated that the Soviet's 'total active ground forces' had increased from 2,744,000 to 2,855,000. The number of divisions grew from 127 to 153. In addition, information provided by the Warsaw Pact Command itself revealed that it had deployed 300 SS-21 short-range missiles.[3]

The statistics in themselves are not sinister. Many of the MBTs could have been ordered before the beginning of warmer relations between the NATO and Warsaw Pact countries and are probably in storage. Armed forces' manpower could have been increased as a way of coping with unemployment. Honesty about having a larger number of nuclear missiles than the West had suspected may be seen as an indication that the Soviet military has no intention of using them.

More significantly, there is a trend within the Soviet system that arranges reductions in such a way that they leave the Soviets with a quantitative or qualitative advantage—or both—over NATO. For instance, the reductions give the Soviet Union a more balanced combined-arms force than it had before. One of the aims was to design a force in which dismounted infantry would operate with tanks and concentrated artillery support. The qualitative advantage can be seen in other ways. A single example: any reduction in T-55 and T-62 tanks is being made up by the deployment of the new advanced T-80 tanks.

Any trend towards peaceful co-existence between the superpowers and their respective allies does not justify a trend towards complacency—'the years of tension are over'—or towards a downgrading of defence capability—'we no longer need so many personnel and weapons'.

Yet, during 1988–89, Canada radically cut its defence budget, Italy cut back its conscription intake, Belgium withdrew some of its units from West Germany and France began a long-range programme of reductions in defence spending. The

US Congress was eager to reduce spending in the Strategic Defence Initiative (Star Wars) and Secretary of State James Baker, a realist, threatened to ask the President to use his veto.

The trend towards peace in Europe may be lasting; it is too early to tell. The trend towards trusting in it is gathering momentum. Whatever is happening in relation to the superpowers, Europe, NATO and the Warsaw Pact, the trend in the rest of the world is decidedly towards further conflict.

The cease-fire between Iran and Iraq held; but only just. During 1989, United Nations observers logged several hundred complaints about violations of the cease-fire. Both sides see it as a welcome breathing-space and no peace treaty has been agreed.

In Afghanistan, the withdrawal of Soviet troops did nothing more than allow the 'real war' to develop. This is the war between the Kabul regime and the Mujahideen. In Angola and Cambodia, talks about peace were never likely to produce peace, since no party to the conflict is sincere about bringing war to an end other than on its own terms.

In the Middle East, it was clear that the Soviet Union and the United States could not easily be dragged into fighting each other and perhaps trigger a world war. Regional trends, however, are towards war. Bellicose Syria is more likely than ever to attack Israel. The thinking in Damascus is that the Palestinian *intifada* will weaken Israel sufficiently to give Syria a good chance of success with a fierce and massive lightning strike. The Syrians seriously consider the use of chemical weapons. The Israeli government is well aware of this and may issue masks and other protective clothing to the public.

In Central and Latin America the dirty wars, with the exception of that in Nicaragua, have become more vicious. In this region war is a way of life. In a perverted way, it supports the economy, since both sides to any dispute receive great support from outside.

In the Indian sub-continent, the trend is towards more intensified war or the commencement of war. Comments made by Pakistan's Chief of Army Staff, General Mirza Aslam Beg, make this all too clear. Speaking before Pakistan's massive *Exercise Zarb-e-Momin*, in December 1989, Beg explained Pakistan Army doctrine. 'Should there be a war, the Pakistan Army plans to take the war into India, launching a sizeable offensive on Indian territory. In the past we were pursuing a defensive policy. Now there is a big change and we are adopting a policy of offensive defence. I have a large reserve in my hand and this reserve must be used. We do not face a two-front situation and a military threat from Afghanistan does not exist'.[4]

To some extent, the Indians have themselves to blame for Pakistan's new aggressiveness. India's *Exercise Brasstacks* brought the two nations perilously close to war in January 1987. Since then the Pakistan forces have rapidly modernised and now possess some missiles capable of a 300km range and others of 600km.

General Beg said, 'The nuclear option and the missiles act as a deterrence. They contribute to the total fighting ability of the army'. His repeated admission that Pakistan views the country's programme for a nuclear capability as 'a meaningful deterrent' has alarmed the Indian leaders.

While the West has had its eyes fixed on *glasnost* and *perestroika*—as well as arms reduction talks—the East has had a different perspective. Japan, for instance, cannot reconcile Soviet statements about reduction in Soviet military strength with what it sees happening close by in the eastern Soviet Union.[5]

The Soviet Far East Military District has enormous forces at its disposal. It deploys 43 divisions—a total of 390,000 men—east of Baikal. Nine of these divisions are between Vladivostock and Khabarovak; another 12 are west of Khabarovak along the border with China. Two are on Sakhalin Island, one in the Kuril Islands and two on the Kamchatka Peninsula. All these formations are in a position to threaten Japan.

The Japanese Defence Agency claims that the Soviet Far East Air Command has 2,430 aircraft while the Soviet Pacific Fleet has 100 major surface fighting ships and 140 submarines. In all, there are 840 ships, far more than possessed by the other Soviet fleets.

Soviet manoeuvres in the region are aggressive. The air force carries out mock attacks against Japanese early warning radar sites on Hokkaido Island, on the coastal side of the Sea of Okhotsk. Naval squadrons frequently patrol close to the edge of Japanese waters. According to the Japanese Defence Agency, Tu-26 (Backfire) bombers and Tu-95 (Bear-H) strategic bombers armed with As-15 Kent cruise missiles pose a threat to sea lanes.

In its 1989 *White Paper*, the Agency published a general caution. 'Soviet military power in the Far East has been continuously increasing and still poses a serious threat, not only to Japan but to other Far Eastern countries'.

The Agency obviously has no confidence in President Gorbachev's May 1989 statement that 120,000 personnel, 12 divisions, 11 air force regiments and 16 warships would be withdrawn from the Far East area. The Japanese consider Gorbachev's promise 'vague and ambiguous'.

The West should look at it in a different way. If these great forces are withdrawn, where are they being posted? It is hardly likely that they are languishing in barracks in central Siberia.

In the free world the basic trend, it seems to me, is towards delusion—that what we would like to see happen, is happening. The truth is less comfortable.

The Desperate Soviet Dilemma

Between June and December 1989 Communism as an ideology and a form of government in Eastern Europe totally collapsed. One by one, Hungary, Poland, Bulgaria, East Germany, Czechoslovakia and Romania abandoned a discredited social and economic system and in only one, Romania, was there any armed conflict. These six months of independence will surely be seen by posterity as one of the most remarkable periods of human history.

In only one case, that of Poland, did a former Soviet satellite consider that it was necessary to consult the Kremlin before choosing democracy and independence. The others chose unilateral independence and in no case did the Soviet Union attempt to crush them militarily. It could have done so and there were voices within the Soviet Politburo and the Army which urged military intervention, especially in the case of East Germany. However, Gorbachev's will prevailed.

To a considerable extent, the Warsaw Pact amalgamation became irrelevant, if only because the Soviet's satellite countries were no longer satellites. Each acquired an orbit of its own. It had become virtually impossible for the Soviet leaders to say to their Eastern European allies, 'We're going to war against the West', and expect them to leap to arms. They had other matters to think about. Even Comecon, the union of the Communist nations as an economic union, was greatly weakened since all these nations were planning closer economic and trading relationships with the West.

In January 1990, Sergei Ouganov, a member of the Soviet delegation to a Comecon meeting in Bulgaria, made a significant statement to a news conference. 'The Council for Mutual Economic Assistance was a mechanism for co-operation which accomplished much for four decades but then ran into negative tendencies,' he said. 'It has become old and obsolete and should be replaced by a new structure which harmonises the economic inequalities.' A Czech delegate proposed that Comecon should be dissolved. Comecon is unlikely to fade away but it is not the binding force it was before 1989.

Across Eastern Europe in 1990, the national Communist Party branches began desperate attempts to rebuild after the collapse. A standard ploy was to rename themselves 'Socialist' or 'Social Democrat', a rather transparent attempt to survive after decades of loudly proclaiming the virtues of the one-party state system.

The events in Eastern Europe began a trend within the borders of the Soviet Union which has already produced violent disturbances and could lead to civil war. Gorbachev's revisionary thinking and reactions to it upset the balance of control which had kept the 15 Soviet Socialist Republics tightly knit since 1945. The demands for autonomy or independence emanating from at least half of the Soviet republics are not the consequence of Gorbachev's liberalisation but of the years of remorseless Communist repression which preceded Gorbachev. This applies equally to the economic ruin of the Soviet Union.

The forces which came to life are nationalism and religion; sometimes the two in conjunction. Their stirring showed that Communism had merely papered over the religious fervor and nationalist sentiment which have always existed in the Soviet republics.

The Baltic states of Lithuania, Latvia and Estonia caused Gorbachev and his ministers a serious problem. Steps by the Communist Party of Lithuania to attain autonomy from the Soviet Communist Party shocked Moscow. Gorbachev had been willing to see the once subservient nations of Eastern Europe go their own way and he even turned their defection into a triumph for *perestroika*. But could restructuring include the piecemeal dismantling of the Soviet Union itself? For the Lithuanian party chief, Algirdas Brazauskas and his colleagues their declaration of independence was a bid for political survival in a republic dominated by nationalism.

In many ways, the Baltic states have shown that nationalist independence is not negotiable. For instance, in September 1989 hundreds of thousands of Lithuanians, Latvians and Estonians linked hands in a chain of nationalist determination that wound across the three states. The imagery thus created disturbed the diehard Communist conservatives in Moscow.

Disturbances elsewhere were more violent. In Georgia and the Ukraine peaceful freedom marches were violently quelled, thus giving the independence movement greater militancy and determination than before.

One of the most dangerous situations afflicts the republic of Azerbaijan, a

Muslim state adjoining Iran. Soviet Azeris demand that their territory be reunited with Azeri territory in Iran. Teheran and Moscow appear eager to maintain good relations but concord is hard to sustain in the face of Azeri violence. In January 1990, Azeris rioted in their tens of thousands along the Iran–Soviet border, flattening 80 miles of border fences and burning down watchtowers. The Soviet border troops were unable to control the rioters and stopped short of opening up with machine-guns. After the violence, little remained of an international border. The Azeris, like their kinfolk in Iran, are Shia Muslims, the fanatical sect of Islam loyal to Ayatollah Khomeini in his lifetime and now to his successor.

The Azeris are among 60 million Muslims in the southern Soviet Union. Most are not Communists and for years they have been strictly controlled. The building of mosques and printing of the *Koran* has been limited and few Muslims were permitted to make the pilgrimage to Mecca. Collectively, the Soviet Muslims pose a serious problem for the Party in its attempts to keep the Soviet Union unfragmented.

The ethnic Romanians in the Soviet republic of Moldavia are another problem. During Ceaucescu's regime they had no incentive to link with the Romanian Moldavians but with reformation sweeping Romania there is a strong move among Soviet Moldavians to be part of Romania.

In Bulgaria, nationalism showed itself in a fierce and inflammatory form as the Bulgarian people demonstrated their hatred for the 1.5 million ethnic Turks within their borders. Their resentment has its roots in centuries of Ottoman/ Islamic rule which ended in 1878. By forcing the resident Turks to change their names to Bulgarian ones and by prohibiting the practice of the Islamic religion, the Bulgarian government appeased their own people. In January 1990 the government abolished these restrictions in keeping with the spirit of greater tolerance which was sweeping Eastern Europe. Immediately large-scale anti-government and anti-Turkish riots occurred in many Bulgarian towns. The government of Turkey reacting angrily to the Bulgarians' hatred of its ethnic minority. The events in Bulgaria underlined yet again the way in which ardent nationalism is creating a climate in which war may occur.

By the end of 1989 President Gorbachev was no longer able to lead from the front as he encouraged reform and tolerance. He had been overtaken by a tidal wave of events and was being washed along by it. His salvation and that of the ideology he represents could be to adopt the French tactic of *fuite en avant*, or 'flight forward'. This would mean abolition of the Party's central role, the steady privatisation of land, property and business and a change from Moscow-dominated colonialism to a loose confederation of truly autonomous republics.

Overall, the trend within the Soviet union in 1990 is towards demonstration, succeeded by riot, followed by uprising and finally—should uprising be met by armed opposition—by war. It would be a great irony if peaceful independence in Eastern Europe were to be followed by a series of civil wars in the Soviet Union.

References

1. General Vuono is also a member of the Joint Chiefs-of-Staff. He is fond of his alliterative phrases about *glasnost* and *perestroika* and uses them in various speeches and interviews. He was quoted at some length in *Jane's Defence Weekly*, 14 October 1989.
2. General Yazov was widely interviewed during his visit to Britain. These comments were made to

Novosti Press Agency, which interviewed him for *Jane's Defence Weekly*, 30 October 1989. According to a confidential Moscow source, Yazov believes that '*glasnost* and *perestroika* belong, like the words, only within the Soviet Union'.

3. According to *The Military Balance*, 1989, published by the International Institute for Strategic Studies.

4. General Beg calls frequent press conferences. His comments are widely reported in Pakistan and India.

5. The Japanese Government, in association with the chiefs-of-staff, made its fears clear in the 15th *Defence White Paper*. This is published not only in Japanese but several other languages, for distribution to military attaches and certain diplomats in Tokyo.

Background Reading

The books here listed have been published since *War Annual 3*, in which other titles were recommended.

Ethiopia–Eritrea

The Long Struggle of Eritrea for Independence and Constructive Peace edited by Basil Davidson and Lionel Cliffe.
Eritrea—Images of War and Peace by Glenys Kinnock; Chatto & Windus, London.

Holy War

The Politics of Islamic Revivalism: Diversion and Unity edited by Shireen T. Hunter; Indiana University Press.
Islam and Revolution in the Middle East by Henry Munson; Yale University Press.
Terrorism in the 1980s by Edgar O'Ballance; Arms and Armour Press, London.

Iran–Iraq War

The Iranian Military in Revolution and War by Sepehr Zabih; Routledge, London.
US Military Strategy in the Gulf by Amitac Acharya; Routledge, London.
Hostages to Fortune—the Future of Western Interests in the Arabian Gulf by Michael Cunningham; Brassey's Defence Publishers, London.
The Iran–Iraq War: A Bibliography by J. Anthony Gardner; Mansell Publishing, London.
The Gulf War: The Origins and Implications of the Iran–Iraq Conflict by Majid Khadduri; Oxford University Press.

Lebanon

Beirut Outtakes by Larry Pintak; Lexington Books.
A Land Held Hostage: Lebanon and the West by Roger Scruton; Claridge Press, London.

Middle East

Middle East: A Directory of Resources edited by Thomas P. Fenton and Mary J. Heffron; Orbis Books, New York.
Assad of Syria: The Struggle for the Middle East by Patrick Seale, I.B. Tauris.
The Soviet Union and Syria: The Assad Years, Royal Institute of International Affairs, London.

Morocco

War and Refugees: The Western Sahara Conflict edited by Richard Lawless and Laila
   Monahan; Pinter Publishers, New York.

South Africa

African Nemesis: War and Revolution in Southern Africa by Paul Moorcraft; Brassey's,
   London.
Armscor: South Africa's Arms Merchant by James P. McWilliams; Brassey's, London.

Sudan

Class and Power in Sudan: The Dynamics of Sudanese Politics 1898–1985 by Tim
   Niblock; State University of New York Press.

General

Asian Security 1989–90 compiled by the Research Institute for Peace and Security,
   Tokyo; Brassey's, London.
The Military Balance 1989–1990, International Institute for Strategic Studies;
   Brassey's, London.
RUSI and Brassey's Defence Yearbook 1990; Brassey's, London.